A HIGHER LOYALTY

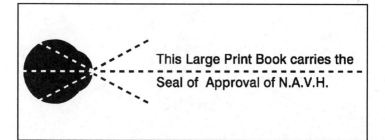

This Large Print Book carries the
Seal of Approval of N.A.V.H.

A HIGHER LOYALTY

TRUTH, LIES, AND LEADERSHIP

JAMES COMEY

THORNDIKE PRESS

A part of Gale, a Cengage Company

Farmington Hills, Mich • San Francisco • New York • Waterville, Maine
Meriden, Conn • Mason, Ohio • Chicago

Copyright © 2018 by James Comey.
Thorndike Press, a part of Gale, a Cengage Company.

ALL RIGHTS RESERVED
Thorndike Press® Large Print Core.
The text of this Large Print edition is unabridged.
Other aspects of the book may vary from the original edition.
Set in 16 pt. Plantin.

**LIBRARY OF CONGRESS CIP DATA ON FILE.
CATALOGUING IN PUBLICATION FOR THIS BOOK
IS AVAILABLE FROM THE LIBRARY OF CONGRESS.**

ISBN-13: 978-1-4328-5583-3 (hardcover)

Published in 2018 by arrangement with Macmillan Publishing Group,
LLC/Flatiron Books

Printed in the United States of America
1 2 3 4 5 6 7 22 21 20 19 18

To my former colleagues,
the career people of the
Department of Justice and the FBI,
whose lasting commitment to truth
keeps our country great

CONTENTS

AUTHOR'S NOTE

Who am I to tell others what ethical leadership is? Anyone claiming to write a book about ethical leadership can come across as presumptuous, even sanctimonious. All the more so if that author happens to be someone who was quite memorably and publicly fired from his last job.

I understand the impulse to think that any book written about one's life experience can be an exercise in vanity, which is why I long resisted the idea of writing a book of my own. But I changed my mind for an important reason. We are experiencing a dangerous time in our country, with a political environment where basic facts are disputed, fundamental truth is questioned, lying is normalized, and unethical behavior is ignored, excused, or rewarded. This is not just happening in our nation's capital, and not just in the United States. It is a troubling trend that has touched institutions across

America and around the world — board-rooms of major companies, newsrooms, university campuses, the entertainment industry, and professional and Olympic sports. For some of the crooks, liars, and abusers, there has been a reckoning. For others, there remain excuses, justifications, and a stubborn willingness by those around them to look the other way or even enable the bad behavior.

So if there ever was a time when an examination of ethical leadership would be useful, it is now. Although I am no expert, I have studied, read, and thought about ethical leadership since I was a college student and struggled for decades with how to practice it. No perfect leader is available to offer those lessons, so it falls to the rest of us who care about such things to drive the conversation and challenge ourselves and our leaders to do better.

Ethical leaders do not run from criticism, especially self-criticism, and they don't hide from uncomfortable questions. They welcome them. All people have flaws and I have many. Some of mine, as you'll discover in this book, are that I can be stubborn, prideful, overconfident, and driven by ego. I've struggled with those my whole life. There are plenty of moments I look back on and wish I had done things differently, and a few that I am downright embarrassed by. Most of us have those moments. The important thing is that we learn from them and hopefully do better.

I don't love criticism, but I know I can be wrong, even when I am certain I am right. Listening to others who disagree with me and are willing to criticize me is essential to piercing the seduction of certainty. Doubt, I've learned, is wisdom. And the older I get, the less I know for certain. Those leaders who never think they are wrong, who never question their judgments or perspectives, are a danger to the organizations and people they lead. In some cases, they are a danger to the nation and the world.

I have learned that ethical leaders lead by seeing beyond the short-term, beyond the urgent, and take every action with a view toward lasting values. They might find their values in a religious tradition or a moral worldview or even an appreciation of history. But those values — like truth, integrity, and respect for others, to name just a few — serve as external reference points for ethical leaders to make decisions, especially hard decisions in which there is no easy or good option. Those values are more important than what may pass for prevailing wisdom or the groupthink of a tribe. Those values are more important than the impulses of the bosses above them and the passions of the employees below them. They are more important than the organization's profitability and bottom line. Ethical leaders choose a higher loyalty to those core values over their own personal gain.

Ethical leadership is also about understanding the truth about humans and our need for meaning. It is about building workplaces where standards are high and fear is low. Those are the kinds of cultures where people will feel comfortable speaking the truth to others as they seek excellence in themselves and the people around them.

Without a fundamental commitment to the truth — especially in our public institutions and those who lead them — we are lost. As a legal principle, if people don't tell the truth, our justice system cannot function and a society based on the rule of law begins to dissolve. As a leadership principle, if leaders don't tell the truth, or won't hear the truth from others, they cannot make good decisions, they cannot themselves improve, and they cannot inspire trust among those who follow them.

The good news is that integrity and truth-telling can be modeled in powerful ways, shaping cultures of honesty, openness, and transparency. Ethical leaders can mold a culture by their words and, more important, by their actions, because they are always being watched. Unfortunately, the inverse is also true. Dishonest leaders have the same ability to shape a culture, by showing their people dishonesty, corruption, and deception. A commitment to integrity and a higher loyalty to truth are what separate the ethical leader from those who just happen to occupy leadership roles. We cannot ignore the difference.

I spent a lot of time thinking about the title of this book. In one sense, it came out of a bizarre dinner meeting at the White House, where a new president of the United States demanded my loyalty — to him, personally — over my duties as FBI director to the American people. But in another, deeper sense, the title is the culmination of four decades in law, as a federal prosecutor, business lawyer, and working closely with three U.S. presidents. In all those jobs, I learned from those around me and tried to pass on to those I worked with that there is a higher loyalty in all of our lives — not to a person, not to a party, not to a group. The higher loyalty is to lasting values, most important the truth. I hope this book is useful in stimulating all of us to think about the values that sustain us, and to search for leadership that embodies those values.

INTRODUCTION

Man's capacity for justice makes
democracy possible, but man's inclination
to injustice makes democracy necessary.
— REINHOLD NIEBUHR

There are ten blocks between FBI headquarters and Capitol Hill, and each of them
is fixed in my memory from countless
shuttle missions up and down Pennsylvania
Avenue. Riding past the National Archives,
where tourists were lined up to see America's documents, the Newseum — with the
words of the First Amendment carved into
its stone front — and the T-shirt vendors
and food trucks had become something of a
ritual.

It was February 2017, and I was in the
back row of a fully armored black FBI
Suburban. The middle row of seats had
been removed, so I sat in one of the two
seats in the back. I had gotten used to

watching the world pass by through the small dark bulletproof side windows. I was on the way to yet another classified congressional briefing on the 2016 Russian election interference.

Appearing in front of members of Congress was difficult on a good day, and usually disheartening. Nearly everyone appeared to take a side and seemed to listen only to find the nuggets that fit their desired spin. They would argue with each other through you: "Mr. Director, if someone said X, wouldn't that person be an idiot?" And the reply would come through you as well: "Mr. Director, if someone said that someone who said X was an idiot, wouldn't that person be the real idiot?"

When the subject involved the most contentious election in memory, the discussion in the immediate aftermath was even more vicious, with few willing, or able, to put aside their political interests to focus on the truth. Republicans wanted to be assured that the Russians hadn't elected Donald Trump. Democrats, still reeling from the election results weeks before, wanted the opposite. There was little common ground. It was like having Thanksgiving dinner with a family eating together by court order.

The FBI, with me as its director, was

16

caught in the middle of the partisan bile. This was not really new. We had been sucked into the election starting in July 2015, when our seasoned professionals at the FBI began a criminal investigation of Hillary Clinton's handling of classified information on her personal email system. It was a time when even using the terms "criminal" and "investigation" was a source of needless controversy. A year later, in July 2016, we began an investigation into whether there was a massive Russian effort to influence the presidential vote by hurting Clinton and helping elect Donald Trump.

This was an unfortunate, if unavoidable, situation for the Bureau. Though it is part of the Executive Branch, the FBI is meant to stand apart from politics in American life. Its mission is to find the truth. To do that, the FBI can't be on anyone's side except the country's. Of course, members of the Bureau may have their own private political views, like anybody else, but when its people rise in a courtroom or in Congress to report what they have found, they can't be seen as Republicans or Democrats or part of anyone's tribe. Forty years ago, Congress created a ten-year term for the FBI director to reinforce that independence. But in a capital city, and a country, torn by partisan conflict, the FBI's separateness was both alien and confusing, and constantly tested. This placed an enormous strain on career professionals in the agency, especially as their motives were routinely being questioned.

I glanced over at Greg Brower, the FBI's new head of congressional affairs, who was riding to the Hill with me. Greg was a fifty-three-year-old Nevadan with salt-and-pepper hair. We had hired him from a law firm. Prior to that, he had been the chief federal prosecutor in Nevada and also an elected state legislator. He knew the business of law enforcement and also the challenging and very different business of politics. His job was to represent the FBI in the shark tank of Congress.

But Brower hadn't signed up for this kind of turmoil, which only grew after the shocking result of the 2016 election. Greg hadn't been part of the Bureau for long, so I was worried this craziness and stress might be getting to him. I half wondered whether he might fling open the door of the Suburban and head for the hills. At a younger age, with fewer turns at the witness table in Congress, I might have considered exactly the same thing. As I looked at him, I assumed he was thinking what I was thinking:

How did I end up here?

I could see that worry on Brower's face, so I broke the silence.

"HOW GREAT IS THIS?" I said in a booming voice that no doubt caught the attention of the agents in the front seats.

Brower looked at me.

"We're in the SHIT," I said.

Now he seemed confused. Did the FBI director just say "shit"?

Yup, I had.

"We're waist deep in the shit," I added with an exaggerated smile, holding my arms out to show just how deep it was. "Where else would you want to be?" Mangling the St. Crispin's Day speech from Shakespeare, I added, "People abed in England tonight will wish they were here."

He laughed and visibly lightened. I lightened, too. Although I'm sure the thought of leaping from the speeding car still crossed Greg's mind, the tension was broken. We took a breath together. For a moment, we were two people on a road trip. Everything was going to be okay.

Then the moment passed, and we pulled up to the U.S. Capitol to talk about Putin and Trump and collusion allegations and secret dossiers and who knew what else. It was just another high-pressure moment in

what was one of the craziest, most conse-
quential, and even educational periods of
my — and, some might say, the country's
— life.

And more than once I found myself thinking that same question: How on earth did I
end up here?

CHAPTER 1
THE LIFE

To not think of dying,
is to not think of living.
— JANN ARDEN

The life begins with a lie.

In 1992, I was an Assistant U.S. Attorney in New York City, and those were the words I heard from a senior member of one of the most notorious crime families in the United States.

Salvatore "Sammy the Bull" Gravano was the highest-ranking American mobster ever to become a federal witness. He'd flipped to avoid a life sentence in jail, and also because he had heard government tapes in which his boss, John Gotti, said bad things about him behind his back. Now in our custody, Gravano introduced me to the rules of Mafia life.

Membership in La Cosa Nostra — "this thing of ours" — became official only after an oath taken in a secret ceremony in front of the boss, underboss, and consigliere of the family. After the ceremony, the criminal would be known as a "made man." The first question of the secret initiation was "Do you know why you are here?" The chosen one was required to answer "No," despite the fact that, as Gravano explained, only an idiot wouldn't know why the leaders of the family were gathered with him in the basement of some nightclub.

For nearly two decades, the leaders of the American Mafia agreed there would be no new members. In 1957, they "closed the books" — a term reflecting that the process involved the actual sharing of paper among the Mafia families containing the aliases and real names of their members — because of serious concerns about quality control and penetration by informants. But in 1976 they agreed that each family could make ten new members and then the books would be closed again, with new members only admitted to replace those who died. For each family these ten were the most hardened all-star gangsters who had been frozen out for years. Gravano came into the Mafia as part of that "super class."

Inducting ten new members after so long a shutdown obviously put burdens on the criminal enterprise. In a typical induction ceremony, an initiate is expected to hold in his cupped hands a flaming picture of a Catholic saint, stained with blood dripped from his trigger finger, and recite, "My soul should burn like this saint if I ever betray Cosa Nostra." Gravano recalled that when they reached the dramatic conclusion of his ceremony, he was forced to recite those words while holding a flaming bloodstained tissue instead. The Gambino family hadn't bothered to get enough saint pictures to burn.

Gravano's induction ceremony not only began with lies, it also ended with them. The boss reviewed for him the rules of American Cosa Nostra: no killing with explosives; no killing law enforcement; no killing other made men without official permission; no sleeping with another made man's wife; and no dealing in narcotics. As a general rule, the Mafia did a good job following the first two rules. The American government would crush anyone who harmed innocents with explosions or killed law enforcement. But the promises not to kill made guys, bed their wives, or deal dope were lies. Gravano and his fellow Mafia members routinely did all three. As my fellow prosecutor Patrick Fitzgerald explained it, they were like the rules against fighting in hockey — on the books as a no-no, but still a regular feature of the game.

The closely related Sicilian Mafia had a different rule, one that highlighted the centrality of dishonesty to the entire enterprise of organized crime on both sides of the Atlantic. Newly inducted members were told that they were forbidden to lie to another "made member" — called a "man of honor" in Sicily — unless, and this was a big unless, it was necessary to lure him to his death. I once questioned another government witness, Sicilian Mafia killer Francesco Marino Mannoia, about this rule.

"Franco," I said, "that means you can trust me unless we are about to kill you."

"Yes," he replied, confused by my question. "Men of honor may only lie about the most important things."

The Life of Lies. The silent circle of assent. The boss in complete control. Loyalty oaths. An us-versus-them worldview. Lying about things, large and small, in service to some warped code of loyalty. These rules and standards were hallmarks of the Mafia, but throughout my career I'd be surprised how often I'd find them applied outside of it.

My early career as a prosecutor, especially

my role in confronting the Mafia, reinforced my belief that I'd made the right career choice. The law hadn't been an obvious route for me. Ultimately I chose a career in law enforcement because I believed it was the best way I could help other people, especially those suffering at the hands of the powerful, the crime bosses, the bullies. I didn't know it at the time, but it's possible that a life-altering experience I had when I was sixteen years old, with a gun literally pointed to my head, made that choice inevitable.

The gunman didn't know I was home that night. He had been watching through a basement window and saw my parents say good-bye to the figure lying on the floor of the family room, lit only by the television's light. He probably thought that figure was my sister, Trish. But it actually was my younger brother, Pete (Trish had returned to college after fall break and our youngest brother, Chris, was out at a Boy Scouts meeting). Minutes after my parents drove away, he kicked in the front door of our modest ranch-style house and headed straight downstairs.

October 28, 1977, the day that changed my life, was a Friday. For most of the New

York area, the prior few months were known as the Summer of Sam, when the city and its suburbs were gripped by a serial killer preying on couples sitting in cars. But for northern New Jersey, it was the summer — and fall — of the Ramsey Rapist. The attacker was named for the dozen attacks that had begun in a town called Ramsey; our town, sleepy Allendale, was just to the south.

Hearing heavy steps on the creaking basement stairs and a low growl from our dog, Pete jumped up and moved out of view. But the gunman knew he was there. He pointed a handgun and ordered my brother to come out from his hiding place. He asked if anyone else was home. Pete lied and said no.

At the time, I was a high school senior and a nerd with few close friends. As if to prove it, I was home that night, finishing a piece for the school's literary magazine. It was to be a brilliant social satire of the cool kids, the bullies, and the suffocating peer pressure of high school. The piece was late, and short on brilliance, but I had nothing else to do on a Friday night. So I sat at the desk in my little bedroom, writing.

In the basement with Pete, the gunman demanded to be taken up to the master bedroom. Shortly I heard two sets of footsteps just outside my door, headed for my parents' room. Then I heard more sounds, as the closet and dresser drawers opened and closed. Out of annoyance and curiosity, I stood and opened the sliding wood door to the bathroom that connected my room to my parents'. Their room was brightly lit, and through the bathroom I could see Pete lying on the side of the bed, his head turned toward me, but with his eyes tightly closed.

I stepped into the room, looked to my right, and froze. A stocky, middle-aged white guy wearing a knit cap was holding a gun and looking in my parents' closet. Time slowed down in a way I have never again experienced. I lost my sight for an instant; it returned in a strange haze and my entire body pulsed, as if my heart had grown too big for my chest. Spotting me, the gunman moved quickly to Pete and put his knee in the middle of his back, using his left hand to push the gun barrel against my fifteen-year-old brother's head. He turned to me.

"You move, kid, and I'll blow his head off."

I didn't move.

The gunman had angry words for Pete. "I thought you told me nobody else was home."

The gunman then stepped off Pete and

ordered me to lie on the bed next to my brother. Standing at my feet, he demanded to know where he might find money. I later learned Pete had money in his jeans pocket as we lay there, and never gave it up. I gave it all up. I told him every place I could possibly think of — piggy banks, wallets, dollar coins received from grandparents for special events, everything. Armed with my leads, the gunman left us lying on the bed and went searching.

A short time later, he returned and simply stood above us, pointing his gun in our direction. I don't know how long he pointed it without a sound, but it was long enough that the moment changed me. I was certain I was about to die. Hopelessness, panic, and fear smothered me. I began to pray silently, knowing that my life was about to end. In the next instant, a strange wave of cold washed over me, and my fear disappeared. I began reasoning, thinking that if he shot Pete first, I would roll off the bed and try to grab the gunman's legs. And then I began to speak — to lie, more precisely. The lies came pouring out. I explained how estranged we were from our parents — hated them, actually — didn't care what he took from them, and wouldn't tell anyone he had been there. I lied again and again and again.

The gunman told me to shut up and ordered both of us to our feet. He then began pushing us down the narrow hallway from my parents' room, pausing to search rooms and closets he passed. I was now convinced, temporarily at least, that I was going to live and began trying to get a clear look at his face so I could tell the police about him. He jammed me in the back several times with the gun barrel, telling me to turn my head away from him.

I again began talking, telling him over and over that he should just put us someplace and we would stay there so he could get away. I began racking my brain, trying to think of such a place in the house — a place where we could be locked. Against all reason, I suggested the basement bathroom, telling him we couldn't open the small window because my father had sealed it for the winter. That was only partly true: my dad had put clear plastic on the window frame to reduce the draft, but the window opened simply by raising the bottom half.

He took us to the basement bathroom, motioned us inside, and said, "Tell your mommy and daddy you've been good little boys." He wedged something against the bathroom door to keep us from escaping.

We heard the door to the garage open and

close as the gunman left. I started to shudder as the adrenaline wore off. Shaking, I looked at the little window and suddenly the gunman's face filled it. He was checking the window from the outside. The sight made me gasp for air. After his face disappeared, I told Pete that we were going to stay there until Mom and Dad came home. Pete had other ideas. He said, "You know who that is. He is going to hurt other people. We've got to get help." In my shaky state, I don't think it fully dawned on me what Pete was saying, or how the evening might have played out if our nineteen-year-old sister, Trish, actually had been home.

Instead I resisted. I was afraid. Pete argued with me briefly and then announced that he was leaving. He pulled the plastic from the window, turned the half-moon latch, and raised the window open. He swung himself out feetfirst and into the backyard.

Though it was probably only a second or two, in my memory I stood for a long time contemplating the open window and the dark night. Should I stay or should I follow? I swung my feet through the window. The moment they hit the cold dirt of my mother's garden, I heard the gunman shouting. I dropped to my hands and knees and crawled furiously into thick bushes at the back of the house. The gunman already had grabbed Pete and now was shouting toward me, "Come out of there, kid, or your brother is getting hurt." I emerged, and the gunman berated me for lying to him. Fresh out of another clever lie, I replied, "We'll go right back in," and I moved toward the open window.

"Too late," he said. "Against the fence."

For the second time that night I thought I was going to die. That was, until I heard our neighbor's huge Siberian husky, Sundance, bound into our backyard with his owner, Steve Murray, the high school German teacher and football coach, bounding in after him.

The next seconds are a blur in my memory. I remember running from the gunman into my house with Pete and Coach Murray close behind and then slamming the door behind me. We locked the door, leaving the gunman outside to terrorize Coach's wife and mother, who had followed him toward the commotion at our house — a move that makes me cringe with guilt even decades later.

We then raced up the stairs, turning out all the lights and arming ourselves. I held a large butcher knife. We didn't have 911 in those days, so we dialed the operator and I asked to be connected to the police. I spoke to a dispatcher, who kept telling me to calm down. I explained that I couldn't calm down, that a man with a gun was at our house and he was coming back in and we needed help now. We waited by the front door in the dark and debated going after the gunman. A police car pulled up in front of my house. We blinked the front lights and the car came to a stop. We ripped open the front door and ran straight at the officer, me barefoot and holding a large butcher knife. The officer quickly stepped from his car and his hand went to his weapon. I shouted, "No, no!" and pointed toward the Murrays' house. "There he goes. He has a gun!" The gunman burst out from the Murrays' front door and took off running toward the nearby woods.

As police cars from many jurisdictions converged on our little street, I jumped on my Schwinn ten-speed, barefoot, and pedaled the quarter mile to the church hall where my parents were taking ballroom dancing lessons. I jumped off the bike, letting it crash, ripped open the church hall door, and yelled "Dad!" at the top of my lungs. Everyone stopped and the crowd moved toward me, my mother and father in the lead. My mother started crying the moment she saw my face.

The police didn't find the Ramsey Rapist that night. A suspect was arrested days later, but the case was never made and he was released. But that night the long string of Ramsey Rapist robberies and sexual assaults stopped.

My encounter with the Ramsey Rapist brought me years of pain. I thought about him every night for at least five years — not most nights, *every* night — and I slept with a knife at hand for far longer. I couldn't see it at the time, but the terrifying experience was, in its own way, also an incredible gift. Believing — knowing, in my mind — that I was going to die, and then surviving, made life seem like a precious, delicate miracle. As a high school senior, I started watching sunsets, looking at buds on trees, and noticing the beauty of our world. That feeling lasts to this day, though sometimes it expresses itself in ways that might seem corny to people who fortunately never had the experience of measuring their time on this earth in seconds.

The Ramsey Rapist taught me at an early age that many of the things we think are valuable have no value. Whenever I speak to young people, I suggest they do something that might seem a little odd: Close your eyes, I say. Sit there, and imagine you are at the end of your life. From that vantage point, the smoke of striving for recognition and wealth is cleared. Houses, cars, awards on the wall? Who cares? You are about to die. Who do you want to have been? I tell them that I hope some of them decide to have been people who used their abilities to help those who needed it — the weak, the struggling, the frightened, the bullied. Standing for something. Making a difference. That is true wealth.

The Ramsey Rapist didn't drive me to law enforcement in any conscious way, at least not immediately. I still thought I wanted to be a doctor, and became a premed student with a chemistry major at the College of William & Mary. But one day I was headed to a chem lab and noticed the word DEATH on a bulletin board. I stopped. It was an advertisement for a class in the religion department, which shared the building with the chemistry department. I took the course, and everything changed. The class allowed me to explore a subject of intense interest to me and see how religions of the world dealt with death. I added religion as a new second major.

The religion department introduced me to the philosopher and theologian Reinhold Niebuhr, whose work resonated with me deeply. Niebuhr saw the evil in the world, understood that human limitations make it impossible for any of us to really love another as ourselves, but still painted a compelling picture of our obligation to try to seek justice in a flawed world. He never heard country music artist Billy Currington sing, "God is great, beer is good, and people are crazy," but he would have appreciated the lyric and, although it wouldn't make the song a hit, he probably would have added, "And you still must try to achieve a measure of justice in our imperfect world." And justice, Niebuhr believed, could be best sought through the instruments of government power. Slowly it dawned on me that I wasn't going to be a doctor after all. Lawyers participate much more directly in the search for justice. That route, I thought, might be the best way to make a difference.

CHAPTER 2
THIS THING OF OURS

Keep your friends close,
but your enemies closer.
— AL PACINO (AS MICHAEL CORLEONE),
THE GODFATHER, PART II

There are ninety-four federal districts in the United States, each presided over by a United States Attorney nominated by the president and confirmed by the Senate. The offices vary greatly in size and reach. The office in Manhattan, known as the Southern District of New York, is both one of the largest and the most well regarded. It is famous for its energy and its expansive sense of its own ability to bring cases. The office has long been accused of considering only one question relevant to its claims of jurisdiction: "Did it happen on the earth?"

I joined the United States Attorney's office in Manhattan in 1987. It was my dream job. I would work for a man who was already becoming legendary: Rudy Giuliani.

When I graduated from the University of Chicago Law School in 1985, I still didn't know exactly what kind of lawyer I wanted to be. After my second year, I had applied to be a federal law clerk, a one- or two-year apprenticeship working as an aide to a federal trial judge. In my final year of law school, I finally got one — with a new federal judge in Manhattan.

The judge, John M. Walker Jr., would encourage us to sit in the courtroom and watch if there was an interesting case going on. In the spring of 1986, the government was trying to use a new federal law to detain a defendant without bail on the grounds that he was a danger to the community. This wasn't just any defendant, but Anthony "Fat Tony" Salerno, the boss of the Genovese crime family, one of the five New York Italian Mafia gangs.

Fat Tony was straight out of a Mob movie. He was overweight, bald, walked with a cane, and kept an unlit cigar in his mouth, even in court. He had a gravelly voice and would use it to call out in court to supplement something his lawyer had said. "Dat's an outrage, ya honah," he erupted from his seat. His codefendant Vincent "Fish" Cafaro, with his narrow face and dark eyes, actually looked like a fish to my twenty-five-year-old eyes. To prove Salerno was a danger to the community and bail should be withheld, the federal prosecutors offered tapes of conversations made by an FBI bug planted under a table at Fat Tony's social club, the Palma Boys, located in an Italian enclave in East Harlem. Salerno could be heard talking about ordering beatings and killings, and being quite clear about his role: "Who am I? I'm the fucking boss."

The case showed that in a Mafia family the boss was not to be questioned. His words about life and death meant someone was going to die. And the worst sin was betraying the family, becoming a "rat." The Mafia was all about loyalty, and you left it when you left this earth, whether by natural causes or otherwise. Only rats left the Mafia alive.

I sat there, mesmerized, as the two federal prosecutors, both Assistant United States Attorneys, made the case against Fat Tony. They had tapes and witness testimony about Fat Tony and Fish ordering "hits," breaking legs, intimidating unions, and running a Mob family. The defense argued it was all just "tough talk," but the prosecutors presented powerful evidence undermining that preposterous claim. The two prosecutors were only a few years older than I was. They stood straight, spoke clearly and candidly. They didn't overstate, they didn't posture. They seemed to have no other motivation than tackling injustice and telling the truth. I was struck by lightning. "This is what I want to do with my life," I thought. I would join a law firm in New York and get the extra year of experience I needed before I could apply to be a federal prosecutor. And it would be a year I would never forget, because of one person.

I was a twenty-five-year-old lawyer in New York at a law firm that did me the great favor of shipping me off to Madison, Wisconsin, for most of that year to work on an incredibly complicated, and boring, insurance case. It was a gift, though, because Richard L. Cates was the so-called "local counsel" on the case, which was being litigated in state court in Madison. Cates, then sixty-one, was hired to offer local knowledge to the big shot, big-city lawyers who were going to handle the case. I saw in Dick kindness and toughness, confidence and humility. It would take me decades to realize that those pairs were the bedrock of great leadership. I also saw in this man of extraordinary judgment a fierce commitment to balance.

Dick died in 2011, after a life that began in a New York orphanage and was spent seeking joy in his work and his relationships. He married the love of his life, had five kids, went in and out of public service, including two stints in the Marine Corps during wartime, and never lost his drive, in the words of his son, "to protect the weak from being crushed by the strong." He moved his family to a farm outside Madison so his children didn't get soft. He rode his bike miles to work. He played with his kids endlessly, and then with their many children.

Despite all the darkness he had seen, Dick found life and people endlessly interesting, and would laugh about both. He would take a deposition with nothing in front of him, not even a piece of paper, beginning the session by giving the witness a big smile and saying, "Tell me your story." His mind and memory let him track the story and ask follow-up questions for hours.

I don't think Dick Cates taught me a single explicit lesson in the year we worked together. At least I don't remember any. But for a year, as a brand-new lawyer and soon-to-be husband, I sat at his side and watched him. I watched him laugh at pretension and at pressure. I watched him make commonsense decisions when big-city lawyers were tied up in knots of overthinking and arrogance. I watched him light up at the mere mention of his wife and children and grandchildren. I watched him move heaven and earth to be at their events, their dinners, their projects. I watched him not care that he earned a fraction of what the New York and Los Angeles lawyers on the case were paid. He was a happy man.

This is the person I want to be, I thought. My effort at life-plagiarism has been imperfect, but the lessons were priceless. That is what it means to lead and keep a life. "I'm so glad I went to a big law firm" is not something you hear often, but I am.

Assistant United States Attorney is a nonpolitical career lawyer position, in which the lawyer represents the United States in criminal or civil cases in the district where he works. In 1987, I was assigned to the criminal division. My job was to assist federal agents — FBI, DEA, ATF, Secret Service, or United States Postal Inspectors — in investigating federal crimes and, where appropriate, bringing charges and prosecuting the cases in court. Over the next six years, I investigated and tried all kinds of cases, ranging from mail theft, drug dealing, and bank robbery to complex frauds, arms exporting, racketeering, and murder. My first case involved the attempted murder of federal ATF agents by a drug gang during the execution of a search warrant. The dealers had fired down on the agents from a fire escape as the feds tried to penetrate a fortified drug location.

In an effort to convince a reluctant witness to cooperate against the gang, the lead agent on the case drove me to an apartment building in northern Manhattan — turf controlled by drug gangs. He said that if she trusted the prosecutor who would speak to her in court, it might convince her to testify. We climbed six flights of stairs to her apartment and the agent knocked on the door. The witness opened the door and admitted us to the small apartment. She led us through the front room, where a man in his twenties sat on a stool with his back to a wall. He didn't move or speak, but stared at us intensely. In a back room we spoke privately and quietly with the woman. I made my best case for her to cooperate, but she wouldn't commit. As we walked out, the man on the stool remained motionless, again just staring. As the agent and I left the building and crossed the sidewalk to the agent's car, I said that the guy on the stool looked pretty scary and guessed that he likely had a gun in the back of his waistband.

"Good thing that guy knew we were armed, so he didn't do anything," I said. Assistant U.S. Attorneys did not carry firearms. That was the agent's job.

The agent whipped his head around. "You had a gun? 'Cause I forgot mine under the seat." He reached into the car and retrieved his weapon.

It would be a long time before I would tell my wife about that little field trip.

There was something of an unwritten code about working in the office of Rudy Giuliani, as I suppose there is in most organizations. In his case, the message was that Rudy was the star at the top and the successes of the office flowed in his direction. You violated this code at your peril. Giuliani had extraordinary confidence, and as a young prosecutor I found his brash style exciting, which was part of what drew me to his office. I loved it that my boss was on magazine covers standing on the courthouse steps with his hands on his hips, as if he ruled the world. It fired me up.

Prosecutors almost never saw the great man in person, so I was especially pumped

43

when he stopped by my office early in my career, shortly after I had been assigned to an investigation that touched a prominent New York figure who dressed in shiny tracksuits and sported a Nobel-sized medallion around his neck. The state of New York was investigating Al Sharpton for alleged embezzlement from his charity, and I was assigned to see if there was a federal angle to the case. I had never even seen Rudy on my floor, and now he was at my very door. He wanted me to know he was personally following the investigation and knew I would do a good job. My heart thumped with anxiety and excitement as he gave me this pep talk standing in the doorway. He was counting on me. He turned to leave, then stopped. "Oh, and I want the fucking medal," he said, then walked away. But we never made a federal case. The state authorities charged Sharpton, and he was acquitted after a trial. The medal stayed with its owner.

It took me a while to realize that Giuliani's confidence was not leavened with a whole lot of humility. The cost of that imbalance was that there was very little oxygen left for others. An early clue was my first press conference. I had worked with the FBI to bust a criminal ring that was stealing SUVs from Manhattan parking garages and loading them on shipping containers in the Bronx. The containers were then hustled onto ships bound for Africa or the Caribbean, where the cars were resold. The investigation, led by Special Agent Mary Ellen Beekman, who had been a Roman Catholic nun before joining the Bureau, had penetrated the operation and was secretly photographing the loading. Mary Ellen's specialty was car-theft rings and convincing hardened criminals to become government informants. And although she didn't approve of the foul language so common in law enforcement, she was an extraordinary interrogator; she had retained from her prior career the ability to use guilt in powerful ways to make thugs melt. The thieves in this case were so efficient that cars were on their way out of the country before being reported stolen. It was a cool case, and the FBI and Giuliani decided to do a press conference.

My supervisor told me I was to stand behind the podium while Giuliani, the NYPD commissioner, and the head of the FBI's New York office spoke to the press. I was not, under any circumstances, to speak or move. He then repeated a line I had heard before: "The most dangerous place in

New York is between Rudy and a micro-phone." I stood frozen in the back, looking like an extra from a basketball movie who had wandered onto the wrong set.

Though Giuliani's confidence was excit-ing, it fed an imperial style that severely nar-rowed the circle of people with whom he interacted, something I didn't realize was dangerous until much later: a leader needs the truth, but an emperor does not consis-tently hear it from his underlings. Rudy's demeanor left a trail of resentment among the dozens of federal judges in Manhattan, many of whom had worked in that U.S. At-torney's office. They thought he made the office about one person, himself, and used publicity about his cases as a way to foster his political ambitions rather than doing justice. It was a resentment that was still palpable when I became the chief federal prosecutor in Manhattan — and sat in Giu-liani's chair — a dozen years later.

One of Giuliani's top priorities was orga-nized crime, a focus that actually started well before he took office. His prosecutors brought cases against individual Mob bosses like Salerno and also charged the leaders of the five Cosa Nostra families who sat on "the Commission," which divided up crimi-nal money among the families and refereed disputes. Most important, Rudy's office brought civil cases to allow the government to take control of large trade unions — the Teamsters, electricians, carpenters, and dockworkers among them — to starve the Mafia of its major source of cash and influence, which came from using unions to extort money from legitimate businesses. That successful effort to destroy La Cosa Nostra continued long after Rudy stepped down as United States Attorney to run for political office.

The most powerful of the five Mafia families was the Gambino family. Like the other families, it traced its roots to Sicilian immigrants to the United States who had found wealth and power terrorizing first their fellow immigrants and then entire neighborhoods and cities. In an early effort to battle the Mafia, in 1946, the American government deported a famous mobster, Charles "Lucky" Luciano, who was sent back to Sicily, where he promptly energized and reorganized the Mafia on that island, solidifying a transatlantic link between criminal organizations that would facilitate a thriving heroin trade for decades. At the heart of that drug trade in the 1970s and 1980s was a man named John Gambino, a fluent Sicilian speaker who served as the "channel" or connection between the Sicilian Mafia families and the American Gambino family, of which he was a senior leader.

I was lucky to be part of a case against "the channel" and the Gambino family as one of two prosecutors in the case of *United States v. John Gambino.* The case had been started by two other prosecutors, who had to step aside for personal reasons. By that point, I had risen to be a supervisor in the office, and I recruited another prosecutor, Patrick Fitzgerald, a close friend since our days in law school, to work on the case. A graduate of Harvard Law, Pat was the son of Irish immigrants and had grown up in a small apartment in Brooklyn. His father worked as a doorman, and Pat would sometimes substitute for him when home from school. He had a quick wit and no pretense at all, which was why he had no problem crashing on our couch — and borrowing our beer — at a New Jersey beach house some friends and I rented during summer break from law school.

Fitzgerald joined the United States Attorney's office in 1988, a year after I did, and I was assigned to supervise him during his first federal criminal jury trial. He was a legendary slob with an uncanny memory. In his trial cart — a modified shopping cart used to move documents and exhibits back and forth to court — I saw a messy stack of key documents for the case. "You gotta put these in folders," I coached. He nodded. I returned later to find that he had put each document in an unlabeled file folder and returned them to the stack. Somehow, he still knew where each document was.

By the time the Gambino case came around, we were both veteran prosecutors and on the phone discussing possible partners for him because the Gambino case required two prosecutors. I wasn't a candidate because my family was planning to move out of the New York area. My wife, Patrice, was more accustomed to the cornfields of her native Iowa and the leafy suburbs of northern Virginia, and had endured New York City for years. Early in our marriage, when the opportunity to work for Rudy Giuliani had come up, I had reneged on a deal that we would raise our family in Virginia. So Patrice and I had lived in the New Jersey suburbs for six years, first in a shoebox apartment over a bike shop, then in a modest two-family house rental. With our two growing daughters, half of a house had become too cramped.

As I stood in the kitchen talking to Fitzgerald, Patrice was listening to my end of the conversation. Suddenly she interrupted, asking me to hang up because she needed to speak with me. I told Pat I would call him back.

"That sounds like the case of a lifetime," she said.

"It is," I replied.

"I'll stay for that. I'll stay for you to do that case with one of your best friends. Call him back and tell him you found his partner." We postponed our move for a year.

Pat and I spent months learning the case and the Mafia. We started by talking to the one man in the United States who knew La Cosa Nostra best. Luckily for us, his office was down the hall from ours. Kenneth McCabe was a former NYPD detective who joined the United States Attorney's office in Manhattan as an investigator early in the war on the Mafia. A gentle giant of a man, standing six foot four and weighing more than 250 pounds, with a deep voice and thick New York accent, Kenny knew every Mafia member by sight, name, and nickname. And he knew all that because for over twenty years with the NYPD and then the U.S. Attorney's office he had conducted endless surveillance of weddings, wakes, and funerals, and done hundreds of interviews with Mafia members and turncoats.

For reasons that were never clear to me, the FBI Mafia squads in New York had long been reluctant to "cover" Mafia funerals and weddings. My guess is that agents didn't want to come in from the suburbs to cover events of marginal value that were always on weekends or at night. McCabe saw it differently and believed that was where you could learn the most, just by watching. So he watched and photographed, in all weather, weekends and nights, for years.

The Mafia also knew Kenny McCabe and, in a strange way, respected him as a noble adversary. Kenny understood the peculiar need of Mafia members to believe they were people of honor, so he treated them with what they saw as respect, by never serving a subpoena at their homes and never embarrassing them with an arrest in front of their wives or children. As a result, members considering betraying La Cosa Nostra would frequently contact McCabe first.

Kenny McCabe taught us La Cosa Nostra 101, then traveled with us and the FBI case agents to meet the Mafia turncoats hidden around the country, who were to be the bedrock of our case. One of those turncoats was Sammy the Bull Gravano, the former underboss — number two — of the Gambino crime family.

I met Gravano for the first time when Pat, Kenny, and I traveled to a special federal prison for witnesses in a remote part of the United States in 1992. I remember being slightly anxious waiting for the Gambino family underboss to walk into the room. How would it go? How would he react to these two young prosecutors? What would it be like to meet with a man who had committed, by his own admission, nineteen murders?

The diminutive Gravano stepped into the room in prison garb and rubber-soled shoes with no laces. His quick eyes swept the space and settled on the mountainous McCabe. He didn't need an introduction. "It's an honor," he said to Kenny, extending his hand. Gravano then turned and spoke to me and Fitzgerald. If we were with McCabe, we were okay.

Gravano was a critical witness. The U.S. government took a man who'd climbed to the top of the Mafia by lying and forced him to tell the truth to destroy La Cosa Nostra on both sides of the Atlantic. His life of lies and murder became essential to the search for truth and justice. When he finished cooperating, he was released to life in the Witness Security Program. (Not surprisingly, he ended up back in prison for new crimes committed in his new identity.)

Gravano taught me a great deal about the Mafia's culture and how, as I noted earlier, "The Life begins with a lie." So, too, did Sicilian Mafia killer Francesco Marino Mannoia.

Like Gravano, Franco Mannoia was confused about the U.S. justice system. He wondered why, for example, Fitzgerald and I insisted upon knowing all acts of violence in which he had engaged before we would present him as a witness in an American court. Of course, we were obligated by American law to disclose information that might call into question the credibility of our witnesses. Although confused, he was also required by his immunity agreement with the Italian government to cooperate with the Americans, so he reviewed in great detail all twenty-five murders in which he had personally participated.

Many Mafia murders in Sicily in the 1980s involved luring the doomed man of honor to a remote location and then strangling him to death. We sat for hours listening to Mannoia matter-of-factly recount the elaborate ruses and brutal final minutes of his work. He believed strangulation, which required the assistance of four other strong men, to be an honorable way to kill, in contrast to the cowardly use of a gun at a distance.

Mannoia explained to us the complicated rule that Mafia members were forbidden to reveal themselves directly as members of La Cosa Nostra. As in the American Mafia, the identity was to be secret, and one member could only be introduced to another member by a third member known to both. This rule against revelation once played a strange role in a double murder in which Mannoia had participated.

He said that he and other members of his Mafia family had been assigned to investigate some unauthorized crimes that had taken place on his family's turf. They dutifully rounded up the usual suspects, zeroing in on two men. They took the two to a remote location and interrogated each separately. Even after using classic techniques like the prisoner's dilemma — assuring each suspect that the other was going to implicate him — the Mafia members did not obtain confessions. The two interrogation teams conferred and, by Mannoia's account, concluded that these two criminals were actually innocent of the misdeeds in question. We asked what happened next.

"We strangled them," came his matter-of-fact reply.

"Why would you do that?!" exclaimed Pat Fitzgerald. They had been innocent.

"Because by our questioning we had revealed ourselves to be Cosa Nostra. We could not let them live with that knowledge."

"So what was the point of the questioning in the first place?" I interjected.

Mannoia furrowed the placid brow that framed his sad eyes and replied, "I do not understand. It was our obligation."

Mannoia was the first Mafia killer we called to the witness stand against John Gambino. We followed him by presenting another Sicilian Mafia killer, Gaspare Mutolo, who also had become a cooperating witness. Our Italian colleagues had been hiding him in an empty convent in the Italian countryside, and prior to his testimony, Fitzgerald and I, along with FBI agents, flew to Rome to interview him. As we ate homemade pasta prepared for us by this professional killer, Mutolo laid out his life as a Cosa Nostra man of honor.

I wish I could say I felt something different when I was in the presence of a mass murderer, handing me a cup of espresso in an empty convent. In the movies, some foreboding music might play in the background or the light might dim. But there was none of that. Evil has an ordinary face. It laughs, it cries, it deflects, it rationalizes, it makes great pasta. These killers were people who had crossed an indelible line in human experience by intentionally taking another life. They all constructed their own narrative to explain and justify their killing. None of them saw themselves as bad people. And to a person, they all said the same thing: The first time was really, really hard. After that, not so much.

Mutolo had killed so many people that he couldn't remember them all. After naming nearly thirty, he added that we should assume there were seven or eight more. At one point, he recalled killing a man named Galatalo. Then he recalled hitting another man named Galatalo with a meat cleaver, but the man had not died. On the witness stand, he remembered that he had actually killed yet *another* man named Galatalo, making it two Galatalos killed and one Galatalo merely hit in the chest with a meat cleaver.

During the day, I was in court as Mutolo testified, spilling the secrets of the Mafia's reign of death and crime, while my evenings were spent meeting with Sammy the Bull Gravano in a safe house controlled by the United States Marshals Service. Gravano had previously testified in Brooklyn federal court against family boss John Gotti, where defense lawyers made much of his involvement in nineteen homicides. Sammy the Bull didn't know it, but part of our strategy was to present the Mob killers in such a way that the jury would actually be bored with the details of Mob murders by the time Gravano, our star witness, hit the stand. Our hope was that this would make Gravano more palatable to the jury.

Gravano, though, saw this as a bit of professional embarrassment. One evening I walked into a safe-house conference room. Gravano threw a New York tabloid onto the table before me with a look of disgust. He had been reading an article about the grim body count of our Sicilian killer witnesses, which was far higher than his own. Pointing at the paper, Gravano barked, "Jesus, Jimmy, you're makin' me look like a fuckin' schoolgirl."

Thanks to the work of dozens of investigators and prosecutors, La Cosa Nostra's grip on unions was broken, its leaders jailed, and its dominance on both sides of the Atlantic shattered. John Gambino's trial jury actually hung 11–1 on all the most serious charges, in suspicious circumstances, but he pled guilty before his retrial, was sentenced to fifteen years in federal prison, and has since died. There are still people in New York who call themselves Italian Mafia, but it is a motley collection of low-level criminals that would embarrass Lucky Luciano. It more closely resembles *The Sopranos,* without the therapist.

CHAPTER 3
THE BULLY

Courage is fire, and bullying is smoke.
— BENJAMIN DISRAELI

Mafia members may dress and talk in distinctive ways, but they are part of a fairly common species — the bully. All bullies are largely the same. They threaten the weak to feed some insecurity that rages inside them. I know. I've seen it up close.

When people see me, their first reaction is always to make note of my height. At six foot eight, I'm hard to miss. But when I was a kid, I was anything but imposing. In fact, when my parents moved us from Yonkers, New York, to Allendale, New Jersey, I was in the fifth grade and quickly went from being a popular kid to being a popular target for bullies.

From birth I had lived in a modest house, packed together with other modest houses, in Yonkers. Nearly all of my relatives were from Yonkers, a blue-collar city on the northern edge of the Bronx, one of the five boroughs of New York City. My great-grandparents were part of a wave of Irish immigration to the area in the late 1800s. My mother and father grew up blocks from each other on "the hill," an Irish enclave in the northwest part of the city. My grand-father dropped out of school in the sixth grade to go to work to support his family after his father was killed in an industrial accident. He later became a police officer and rose to lead the Yonkers Police Department.

Our home was immediately behind Public School 16, the school where I happily spent my early childhood years. My mother had attended P.S. 16. One of my grandmother's best friends was the principal. And by the time we moved, I was one of the most popular kids in my fifth-grade class.

Yonkers and School 16 were the center of my world. I could see the big red-brick school through the tall chain-link fence separating my backyard from the school playground. My older sister, two younger brothers, and I would walk to school every day, circling the block because the fence was too tall to climb. I knew everybody, and as far as I knew, everybody thought I was a pretty cool fifth grader. I fit in. I felt like I belonged somewhere. That was a great feeling. But it ended when my dad brought us news that changed my life.

My father, Brien Comey, worked for a big oil company. He started out selling cans of motor oil to gas station operators and moved up to finding locations for new stations. For decades afterward, he could drive around the New York metropolitan area and show you the corners he spotted, "his" gas stations. In the 1960s, both the car business and the gas business were booming.

When my dad took a new job with a company in northern New Jersey in 1971, it meant we had to move — to a place that, until then, had existed in my mind only as tall cliffs called the Palisades. Yonkers sits on the eastern bank of the mile-wide Hudson River. In the spaces between houses on my street, I could see the Palisades forming a dark stone wall on the western bank. I don't think I ever believed the world ended at that formidable wall, because we had driven to Indiana once, but it might as well have. We were moving to the other side of the wall, where a new world awaited the coolest kid in the fifth grade at School 16.

I was not the coolest kid at my new school, Brookside Elementary, in Allendale,

New Jersey, something I figured out pretty quickly. My parents were always trying to save money, so my mother cut her boys' hair with her own electric clippers and dressed us in clothes she purchased at a Sears outlet. My pants were too short, and I wore white socks and heavy-soled black shoes to support the fallen arches in my huge feet. I didn't know it, but it turns out I had a New York accent different from the kids in Allendale. I stuck out like a sore thumb.

The soreness quickly became more than metaphorical. One of my first days on the fifth-grade playground, I was surrounded by a group of boys who taunted me and my looks. I don't remember what I said to them, but I probably said something, because I was a confident kid with a big mouth, even though I was not tough enough to back up what I said. They knocked me to the ground.

The bullies regularly invited their victims to fistfights staged after school in a nearby park. I was called out numerous times but never showed up, walking well out of my way to avoid the park. I remember one time attempting to reason with one of the bullies when he said he wanted to fight me. "If you don't like me, and I don't like you, and we then punch each other in the head with our fists, what will that change?" I asked. The reasoning approach only made him angrier. Maybe if I had let one of them pummel me they would have moved to another target, but I didn't have the courage to try that.

Much of the next three years was spent avoiding the bullies. I absorbed their verbal taunts frequently, but I was keen to avoid physical confrontation. I just wasn't tough or strong. So I kept to myself, played mostly with my two brothers, and walked odd, elliptical routes around town.

Allendale shared its high school with another town, so ninth grade offered the opportunity to meet bullies from a whole different municipality. Again, they found me quickly. I'm not entirely sure why. I wasn't big — and wouldn't be until after high school — but I was smart and verbal, which may have drawn their attention. Although I was trying out for football, I was also in the choir. Maybe because they were seen as artsy, or simply different, the choirboys seemed to be prime targets for abuse.

Unlike the tough boys at my high school, I still carried baby fat and was from the first day a prime target for taunts about my body. Being body-slammed into a locker hurt, but I could handle it; more dangerous were the "wedgies." If memory serves, a wedgie involved ripping another boy's underwear out of his pants by grabbing the rear waistband of his underwear and yanking upward. The offense typically involved two assailants, and I endured several in the ninth grade.

When the abuse began, I did nothing. I told no one. So it continued. Bullies would grab, pinch, and twist the skin on my chest or arm passing me in the hallway. Or if they couldn't get close enough to pinch, they would throw a hard punch to the shoulder. I learned to see them coming and get out of the way.

So once again, I tried to avoid confrontation. This was harder to do in the locker room, dressing for gym or during the three weeks of my football career. I tried out for the football team, but after weeks of being battered (to the point where I severely bruised my coccyx — a part of my body that at that point was unknown to me) my mother finally had had enough. Without my knowledge, she walked across the street to Coach Murray and tendered my resignation. I was both humiliated and, secretly, relieved. My mother saw a truth I didn't see, and she put it higher than worrying about my disappointment. I wasn't tough enough yet to play football. Still, although my mother's unilateral action may have saved my life, it didn't stop the abuse from the other kids. I began to dress for gym in an empty locker room.

Those were hard times. But, thankfully, I had a couple of close friends, and adults I could look up to, people who reminded me that I mattered. Which is an easy thing to forget when you are a target for abuse. There were my parents, for starters. My parents were tough, but kind. They were report-card-on-the-refrigerator people, with the shakiest report card always seeming to be on top so your siblings could see it. They pushed us, but also constantly supported us. My mother, Joan, would snap the shades open in my bedroom nearly every morning with the same catchphrase — "Time to rise and shine and show the world what you're made of." When I became deputy attorney general decades later, my parents gave me a snow globe with the scales of justice inside and RISE & SHINE inscribed on the base. It still sits on my desk.

During high school, I would come home from school and sit with my mom to talk about my day; when she was dying from cancer in 2012 we spoke of those hours. Starting when I was a little boy, she told me much was expected of me. Before she died, my mother showed me a note I had written to her after getting sent to my room at the age of seven or eight. "I am sorry," the note read. "I will be a great man someday." She had saved it in her dresser for almost fifty years.

I also had some wonderful teachers, with whom I became close, especially English teacher Andy Dunn, the adviser to the school newspaper, where I was an aspiring journalist. Somehow, although I had a couple of good friends, I connected better with the teachers at my high school than the students.

And there was a man named Harry Howell.

During my junior and senior years of high school, I worked for Harry at a large grocery store near Allendale. I didn't make much money stocking shelves, retrieving carts, and working the cash register, maybe four dollars an hour, but I loved my job. That was in large part due to the kind of leader he was.

Harry was a trim white guy of average height, with tightly cropped hair, who wore a white short-sleeved shirt most days with his nameplate pinned to the chest pocket. He wore a black belt and black, brightly shined wing-tip shoes, no matter what color his pants. As I see him in my memory, he bears a striking resemblance to a forty-five-year-old Robert Duvall.

Looking back, even after working for presidents and other prominent leaders in and outside government, I still think Harry Howell was one of the finest bosses I have ever had. This was in part because he loved his job and was proud of his work. Harry knew the grocery business, having worked his way up to store manager. He insisted his store be the cleanest, best-run in the entire corporate chain.

The stock clerks, most of us teenagers, were a group of amateur comedians. We laughed during our work, much of which was done after the store closed, played practical jokes, and worked like maniacs to make whatever aisle we were responsible for look perfect. All of that was Harry's doing. Somehow, he created an environment that was both demanding and incredibly fun. He suppressed a smile at our silliness — just letting the corner of his mouth turn up slightly so we could see his amusement — and told us bluntly when our work wasn't good enough. We loved him. But we also feared him, in a healthy way. Because he made us feel important, because he so obviously cared about what he was doing and about us, we desperately wanted to please him. Harry Howell made me love the look and feel of a grocery store aisle that has been expertly "blocked" — or "faced," as some stores called it — with each can or package pulled forward to the shelf edge so the aisle looks clean and undisturbed to the customers, as if they are the first humans to find it.

In pre-bar-code days, we used handheld ink stamps to put prices on items sold in the store. This was a slow process that required great attention to setting the correct price on the stamping device. A pricing error would be tattooed in ink, forever.

During my stint at the store, the company invested in new "technology" — hard plastic label "guns" to put price stickers on items. We only had two or three of these prototype label guns because, we were told, they were very expensive. They were to be treated with extreme care.

One evening, I was busy with my specialty, stocking the paper aisle — paper towels, toilet paper, tissues, napkins. I was about one-third of the way up the aisle from the front of the store, cutting boxes open with my razor and using the fancy label gun to hit each item before filling the shelf. I was a blur of stocking excellence. Then I heard the voice of one of my fellow stockers, standing at the end of my aisle. With urgency, he called, "Comey, lemme borrow the gun. I just need it for a second," and he extended both hands in front of his body to catch the gun. Without thinking, I tossed it.

The moment the gun left my hand, he turned quickly and disappeared. I can still see the expensive prototype label gun arcing through the air; in my mind, it is rotating backward, end-over-end, as it slowly flies the twenty or thirty feet to the spot where my coworker no longer stood. In my memory, I am crying "noooooo" in slow motion, but I doubt I had time to do that before that expensive gun landed at the feet of Harry Howell, who had conveniently stepped into my aisle. The gun smashed into pieces. My coworker had seen him coming and timed it perfectly.

There are many leaders, and I've known a few in my life, who would have lost it, hurling expletives and accusations at a stupid kid. As Harry looked down at the plastic parts now spread around his wing-tip shoes, he said only, "Clean it up," and walked away. I don't remember him asking for an explanation or mentioning it again. My sixteen-year-old self concluded that Harry immediately realized I had been scammed; in his stoic, suppressed-smile way, he understood that I'd been the victim of a slightly mean prank and pitied me.

Maybe the guns really weren't expensive, or maybe Harry made my coworker pay for the one that I tossed. But Harry's grant of mercy left a lasting impression and made me love him more. I worked even harder, making the paper aisle a Bounty-filled paradise. And I tested him again.

One evening, I was assigned to stock the dairy case, which was a level of complexity far beyond paper. This was the big leagues. I pulled open the huge door to the dairy cooler in the far rear of the building to retrieve gallons of milk. They stood in tall stacks, four gallons to a plastic crate. In the days before plastic milk bottles, these were made of paper and looked like gigantic versions of the box of milk you bought with your school lunch. I grabbed a hand truck and began loading it with crates. Overconfident rookie that I was, I made it a big stack of six crates — holding twenty-four gallons of milk. My mother would have called it a "lazy man's load." I tilted the two-wheeled hand truck back, noting the impressive weight, and made my way out of the cooler, pushing my right shoulder into the back of the hand truck, left hand on top of the stack. I banged through the swinging backroom doors and rolled along the dairy display cases. The weight was making me go faster and faster, so I took quick steps to keep the stack from falling back on me. At the milk display case, I stopped abruptly and pushed the hand truck hard upright, heedless of the basic laws of physics. The universe and the milk, of course, were not heedless.

When I stopped short and heaved the hand truck upright, the crates kept going, momentum conserved, and fell like a towering tree in the very direction I had been pushing them before I stopped short. The tree of plastic crates hit the floor, hard. Instantly, the tops of those paper gallons burst open in unison, dumping more milk in one place than I had ever seen before. A twenty-four-gallon lake of milk began spreading along the dairy case and down the cereal, canned goods, and international foods aisles. It was a catastrophe beyond words.

I ran to the back, grabbed a mop and bucket, and began frantically soaking up Lake Milk and squeezing the mop with the mechanism on top of the bucket. It had all been so quiet. Paper milk gallons don't shatter. They just open. If I hurry, I thought, I might get this cleaned up before anyone sees the mess.

I was minutes into mopping when Harry appeared. He stood on the far side of Lake Milk, hands on hips, careful not to get any on his wing tips. After an eternity of admiring the lake, he asked, "Have you learned something?"

"Yes, sir," I replied.

"Good," he answered. "Clean it all up." And he walked away.

I was too young to see it clearly, but, at sixteen, I was getting a look at great leadership. I knew I wanted to be more like Harry than the kids who tormented me on the playground. And maybe Harry was open enough to see that about me. Maybe he even instinctively knew what school was like for me, that I was a kid just trying to fit in somewhere and be something.

Being an outsider, being picked on, was very painful, but in hindsight it made me a better judge of people. In my life I would spend a lot of time assessing threats, judging tone of voice, and figuring out the shifting dynamic in a hallway or locker room crowd. Surviving a bully requires constant learning and adaptation. Which is why bullies are so powerful, because it's so much easier to be a follower, to go with the crowd, to just blend in.

Those years of bullying added up, minor indignity after indignity, making clear the consequences of power. Harry Howell had power, and he wielded it with compassion and understanding. That wasn't always easy for him, because he had to deal with a lot of immature kids. Others had power, like the bullies at school, and they found it far easier to wield it against those who were defenseless and to just go along with the group rather than stand up to it.

I learned this lesson, too, in one of the great early mistakes of my life.

In 1978, I attended the College of William & Mary. I was one of many insecure, homesick, frightened kids living away from home for the first time, although we would admit none of that to one another, or even to ourselves. Because of overcrowding, I was among seventeen freshman boys living in a physically separate annex to one of the large dormitories, without a resident advisor or any kind of on-site supervision. I shudder looking back through the lens of adulthood; my college had unintentionally created a Lord of the Flies dormitory annex.

There was a boy in that annex who was

mildly annoying. He was a bit arrogant and uptight, and had a hometown girlfriend he talked about constantly. He had potted plants in his immaculately neat dorm room. He went his own way most of the time. But somehow the group of boys decided that this mildly annoying boy was not to be tolerated. So the group messed with his belongings, trashed his room, recorded voices over portions of his favorite cassette tapes, and performed other idiocies I can't remember. I was part of that group. Some things I did, some things I helped do, some things I laughed about after they were done. I caused someone else pain.

Four decades later, I'm still ashamed of myself. How on earth could I be part of bullying another boy? But I was. After all, everyone was doing it. Maybe I was afraid that if I didn't go along with this, I'd be the new target. Or maybe it was because I'd spent so many years on the outside of the group that I wanted in. I was one of the guys. Finally, I belonged.

I was raised by parents who constantly emphasized the importance of resisting the group. A thousand times, in many contexts, my mother said, "If everyone is lined up to jump off the George Washington Bridge, are you just going to get in line?" I gave a speech at my high school graduation about the evils of peer pressure. I carried in my wallet from the age of sixteen a quotation by Ralph Waldo Emerson: "It is easy in the world to live after the world's opinion; it is easy in solitude to live after our own; but the great man is he who in the midst of the crowd keeps with perfect sweetness the independence of solitude." (I just typed that without looking it up.)

Despite all that training, all that reflection, and in the face of whatever guilt or hesitation I felt, I surrendered to the loud laughter and the camaraderie of the group and maybe to a feeling of relief that I wasn't the target. I harassed and bullied another boy, who wasn't very different from me. I was a timid hypocrite and a fool.

I was a living example of something I knew then and have come to know even better decades later. We all have a tendency to surrender our moral authority to "the group," to still our own voices and assume that the group will handle whatever difficult issue we face. We imagine that the group is making thoughtful decisions, and if the crowd is moving in a certain direction, we follow, as if the group is some moral entity larger than ourselves. In the face of the herd, our tendency is to go quiet and let the

75

group's brain and soul handle things. Of course, the group has no brain or soul separate from each of ours. But by imagining that the group has these centers, we abdicate responsibility, which allows all groups to be hijacked by the loudest voice, the person who knows how brainless groups really are and uses that to his advantage.

Had my family stayed in Yonkers, where I was a cool kid, where I was part of a group, I don't know what kind of person I would be now. Being an outsider, being picked on, was very painful, but it made me a better person. It instilled in me a lifelong hatred for bullies and sympathy for their victims. Some of the most satisfying work I did as a prosecutor, in fact, was putting bullies of all kinds in jail, freeing good people from their tyranny. After my experience in college, I was never going to surrender to the group again simply because it was easy. And I was going to make sure my life had some meaning, because I'd already seen how fleeting life could be.

CHAPTER 4
MEANING

I have always believed, and I still believe,
that whatever good or bad fortune
may come our way we can always
give it meaning and transform it into
something of value.
— HERMANN HESSE

I have worked with great men over the years, but two of my most important teachers about life and leadership were women.

In 1993, after my work on the Gambino trial ended, I kept my promise to Patrice and we moved our family to Richmond, a place where we had few connections but where we could raise a family more cheaply and comfortably.

After working briefly at a law firm, I returned to work as an Assistant United States Attorney, this time in the Virginia state capital. The law firm was fine, the pay good, and the people smart, but I missed public service, even with its mismatched furniture and low pay. I couldn't tell my law firm colleagues this, but I ached to be useful again, to do some good for my community and to represent the victims who really needed me.

My new boss was Helen Fahey. She was the United States Attorney, the supervisor of all federal prosecutors in the eastern half of the state. Fahey's rise to the top was unusual and inspiring. She had stayed home with her young children as they grew, then worked in various roles for a Defense Department agency, starting as a typist. All the while, for seventeen years, she pursued her education, as she told a newspaper, "one job, one month, one class at a time." She never actually completed a college degree, but was admitted to law school anyway given her high test scores and work history.

I was thirty-five years old when I started working for Helen in 1996. I was the supervisor in the Richmond office, one of four Fahey oversaw, and I had dreams of energizing it to make bigger contributions in all kinds of areas, especially against violent crime and public corruption. Having been an Assistant United States Attorney in Manhattan and a partner at a big Richmond law firm, I thought I was "hot stuff," as my mother used to say — not meaning it as a compliment. Maybe unconsciously picking up on traits exhibited by Rudy Giuliani, I was everywhere in the city and became the face of federal law enforcement in Richmond, representing the office with local law enforcement, the community, and the media. A free weekly Richmond newspaper put a picture of me on its cover, calling me "One of the Good Guys" and identifying me incorrectly as the "U.S. Attorney," instead of an assistant. I had posed for the picture in my office in Richmond. Worse, I hadn't told my boss anything about it. A stunt like that back in Rudy Giuliani's office would have ended very badly. My first reaction to seeing the newspaper with me splashed across the cover was that I would be a dead man unless I seized every copy in the city. Then I remembered who I worked for. Fahey was secure enough to want me to succeed. She laughed at me a bit, which was appropriate and deserved, but she laughed *with* me more often.

Helen Fahey was comfortable in her own skin in a way few leaders are. I think some derided her behind her back as weak — "she let Comey take over Richmond" — but she knew exactly what she was doing. She was letting me grow, gently smacking me behind the ears every so often to make sure I stayed on track, and getting good results in the process. And she also didn't care much what misinformed people said about her, a lesson I would find very valuable as I grew older. She put the interests of the team and the important job we had to do higher than her own feelings or worries about reputation.

Our effort to prosecute gun crimes and reduce Richmond's homicide rate was bitterly resisted by some of the federal judges in Richmond, who saw those kinds of cases as unbefitting a "federal" courtroom. I didn't care and my team in Richmond didn't care. We were trying to save lives, so we plowed ahead, infuriating one senior judge. He responded by issuing an order holding Helen Fahey, our U.S. Attorney, in contempt for some minor administrative error: failing to put in a request to have the U.S. Marshals bring a prisoner to a scheduled court date. Fahey had nothing to do with the little pieces of paper we filled out to schedule prisoner movements. She typically came to Richmond once a month, and there was no conceivable basis for involving her personally. But the judge did it to rattle us and her.

He didn't know Helen Fahey.

The day of her contempt hearing, the

courtroom, courthouse hallways, and street outside were packed with dozens of police officers and federal agents, including police horses and motorcycles on the street. Fahey walked calmly to the "defendant's" table in the courtroom and waited. The judge came out and was so rattled himself by the show of law enforcement community support that he began ranting about what a problem I was, ignoring Fahey entirely and directing his venom to the audience, where I sat. He then dismissed the case against her. She thought it was hilarious, and told us we were doing the right thing and to press on.

I owe my entire career in leadership to Helen Fahey's confidence, not just in me, but in herself. She glowed in the achievements of her people — who loved her back — and we blossomed in her glow. She had the confidence to be humble.

But the person who taught me the most about leadership is my wife, Patrice.

All of us have encounters with death in our lives. It's inevitable. I've had my share, even after the Ramsey Rapist receded into my nightmares. There was, for example, the time I visited Patrice, who at this time was just my girlfriend, while she was in the Peace Corps in a remote village in Sierra

Leone, West Africa, and I nearly died from contracting malaria. If she had not driven me in the middle of the night on the back of her motorcycle and literally dragged me into a remote hospital, I would not have made it. But sometimes it isn't when we face death ourselves, but rather when death takes away those we love the most, that we really learn about just how short our time on earth is and why what we do with that time matters.

In the summer of 1995, Patrice and I lived in a five-bedroom colonial on a dead-end street in a planned neighborhood in Richmond. It was the kind of place where the local fire company would bring the truck to your house on a child's birthday, where the neighbors all knew each other, where the kids spent endless hours out in the quiet street drawing chalk roads to play bike games. Our two little girls thrived in the new house, and were joined by a little brother in 1994. And then came Collin.

Collin Edward Comey was born on August 4, 1995. He was born healthy, seven pounds, six ounces, and like all Comey babies, he was long. Patrice nursed him at the hospital and our three kids visited and held him. It was a wonderful day, one experienced by many parents with a new-born. But as that day wore on, Patrice sensed a change in him. He became strikingly irritable, so she kept asking the hospital staff if something was wrong. They assured her he was fine and all was normal. One nurse patronized this mother of four, telling her, "You've just never had a colicky baby."

He was not fine. We didn't know it yet, but Collin's little body was fighting a deadly infection. About one-quarter of all women carry bacteria called Group B streptococcus. The bacteria are harmless to the mothers, but can kill their babies. They can be reliably detected toward the end of pregnancy and easily treated with penicillin during delivery. But in 1995, that testing and treatment protocol was not yet a regular feature of American medical practice. Though some hospitals and some doctors tested for the bacteria, the medical association representing obstetricians had not yet endorsed the practice and state boards of medicine had not made it a standard of care.

By the next morning, Collin had a high fever and a raging infection in his blood, called sepsis. Under extraordinary care in a neonatal intensive care unit, he battled for nine days. He was soon on a ventilator, the machine inflating his little chest again and again. Patrice hardly slept, and often drifted off while sitting up in a chair by his side. She explained that he had heard her and touched her for nine months and he needed that voice and that touch more than ever. So she sat with him, hour after hour, day after day, holding his little fingers and singing nursery rhymes to him.

The doctors then showed us the devastating brain scans. The infection had destroyed huge sections of his brain. Only the ventilator is keeping him alive right now, they told us. Your son is gone. But they wouldn't tell us what to do; they wanted us to tell them whether to remove Collin from the ventilator. How could we do that? He was there, alive, right in front of us, and we were being asked to give up and let him die.

I went home to check on the other kids. My parents were staying at our house. As I typically am when under stress, I was calm, even a little cold. But as I explained to my mom and dad what was happening and the decision we faced, I burst into tears. I don't think either of them knew what to do.

Back at the hospital, Patrice and I made the decision. In the midst of indescribable grief, she somehow saw what else needed to be done. Our other son was not yet two and couldn't understand what was happening, but our older girls could. For their sake, Patrice decided that they deserved, they needed, to face the truth. Once they knew the truth, and could accept it, they would have a chance to see Collin one last time. The girls had held our baby in his first minutes of life, Patrice reasoned. They should hold him at the end. His death shouldn't be hidden from them or it would loom too large as they grew. I never would have had the wisdom to see this. Expose a five- and seven-year-old to their dying baby brother? Who would do that? A wise woman would, and she gave a gift to our daughters. They got a chance to say good-bye.

To prepare our daughters for this, we took them out for a picnic and, through many tears, explained what was happening and why. My mom then brought the girls into a private room shortly after the machines were turned off. Patrice was holding Collin, and handed him to each of his sisters. The girls took turns rocking him and speaking to him, saying good-bye, and then handed him back. After the girls left, I held the little guy for a while and then Patrice held him. His mother sang to him until he stopped breathing, and then long after. It is difficult for me even now to describe that scene, as a brokenhearted mother rocked her baby to the end of his short life.

We were very angry. Had Collin been born with another doctor or in another hospital that required testing, he would very likely be alive, because Patrice would have been tested late in pregnancy and treated as she delivered him. But because he was born with a doctor who didn't support testing and in a hospital that didn't require all doctors to order it, he was dead. That didn't make any sense. Patrice dug into the science and developed a relationship with a researcher at the Centers for Disease Control and good people at the Group B Strep Association, made up of others who had lost babies. Infants were dying needlessly all over the country as the medical profession slowly pivoted and changed its practices.

"I can't bring our son back," Patrice said, "but I can't bear the thought of another mother feeling the pain I feel. I've got to do something." She framed it in religious terms, based on one of her favorite lines from the New Testament. In his letter to the Romans, Paul writes, "We know that God causes all things to work together for good, for those who love God, for those who are called according to his purpose."

She couldn't explain why a loving God

would allow Collin to die, and she rejected glib explanations about "God's will." She would reply, often to me after the well-meaning person had moved out of earshot, "What kind of loving God wants to kill my baby? I don't believe that." But she did believe she had to make something good come from her loss. That good, she announced, would be saving other mothers' babies by forcing all doctors to test. So she went to it, channeling her grief into a nationwide campaign.

Patrice wrote publicly about our son and traveled the country supporting efforts to change the standard of care. She poured effort into speaking to the Virginia legislature, and succeeded in getting statutory language passed embracing universal testing and treatment for Group B strep. She didn't do anything alone, but her voice, along with the voices of many other good people, changed our country. All mothers are tested now, and their babies live. Something good followed unimaginable bad. Other mothers will never know what might have been, which is as it should be.

Patrice's quest — to try to make things right for others — undoubtedly influenced my own views on the purpose of the law and the justice system to which I've devoted most of my adult life. In the years that followed Collin's death, I have seen a lot of bad things happen to good people, and I have been asked to help explain it and give those losses some sense of meaning. In 2002, when I went back to serve as the United States Attorney in Manhattan, I stood in the freshly excavated pit at Ground Zero, a place where thousands died, including hundreds of whom no trace was found. I had invited the country's ninety-two chief federal prosecutors to that spot. I explained that those lost innocents were all around us, even though we couldn't see them. This was a place of suffocating loss. It was holy ground.

Channeling Patrice, I told them that I didn't know why bad things happen to good people. I recalled that, for those of us from a Judeo-Christian tradition, the Book of Job rebukes us for even asking the question. The voice from the whirlwind replied, in essence, "How dare you?" The truth is, I can't explain God's role in human history. To do that would require an understanding far beyond the loss of my son, and sweep in the suffering and loss of countless innocent sons and daughters. I just don't know, and I have little patience for those who claim to know. What I do know is what Patrice taught me:

There is meaning and purpose in not surrendering in the face of loss, but instead working to bind up wounds, ease pain, and spare others what you have seen. Our obligation, our duty, is to ensure that something good comes from suffering, that we find some kind of gift in good-bye. Not to somehow, perversely, make the loss "worth it." Nothing will ever justify some losses, but we can survive, even thrive, if we channel grief into purpose and never allow evil to hold the field. In that mission lie the beauty and genius of our justice system.

Patrice and I were planning to stay in Richmond forever. We had good public schools, and a nice and relatively inexpensive house in a safe neighborhood. After Collin's death, we had a healthy baby girl in 1996 and added another in 2000. We would raise the five kids in Richmond. I would do work I loved. We were set. Then the country was attacked on 9/11, and my phone rang.

I was home from work one day in October 2001, watching the two youngest girls. Patrice was at church for the foundational meeting of a women's group she was starting. She spoke inspiringly to the women about growing old together. But she couldn't hear our phone ring from there. I heard it at home and answered. The man said he was calling from the White House because the president would like to know if I would be willing to return to Manhattan as the United States Attorney, the chief federal prosecutor. I assumed it was one of my hilarious friends, so I began to say, "Yeah, why don't you kiss my a—" when the man cut me off, saying this was not a joke. President George W. Bush needed to appoint a new United States Attorney, there was something of a political logjam in New York over the pick, and they had decided I was the right person: I had worked in that office, I had done terrorism cases, and I would be acceptable to Democrats and Republicans. Would I do it?

It is difficult at this distance to capture the feeling of the fall of 2001, a time of unity and purpose and anxiety in the country. Of course I will do it, I replied, "but my wife's not home right now. I will call you back if she has a problem." I hung up the phone, abandoned my caregiving responsibilities, and went out to stand in the driveway to wait for Patrice, my heart pounding.

After what seemed like hours, she came driving up in our red Ford minivan. She got out, took one look at my face, and asked, "What's wrong?"

"Nothing's wrong," I answered, standing in the driveway without my little girls. "A guy called from the White House and asked me to be the U.S. Attorney in New York."

Her eyes started to well up. "You can't say no."

"I didn't say no. But I told him I would call back if you had a problem."

She began crying, her open hands covering her face. "I'm going back to New York. Oh my God, I'm going back to New York."

We were going back to New York, where the World Trade Center site still smoked. I would lead 250 prosecutors with hundreds of cases, ranging from terrorism to violent crime to corporate fraud, including what would be one of the most high-profile cases of my career.

Patrice opened the minivan's sliding door and the large ceramic plate that had held the bagels she took to church slid out. In a moment that was hard not to take as a prophetic metaphor, it shattered on the driveway.

CHAPTER 5
THE EASY LIE

He who permits himself to tell a lie once,
finds it much easier to do it a second
and third time, till at length it becomes
habitual; he tells lies without attending to
it, and truths without the world's believing
him. This falsehood of the tongue leads
to that of the heart, and in time depraves
all its good dispositions.
— THOMAS JEFFERSON

When Martha Stewart was released from prison in March 2005, the press was making much of the fact that her net worth grew during her time in custody. As if the goal of prosecutors had been to destroy her, rather than punish her for lying during an investigation and send a message that people, no matter who they are, can't obstruct justice.

I was in Las Vegas giving a speech and knew the media would try to get an ambush reaction from me on camera, because I was the United States Attorney who had indicted her and received an enormous amount of media attention and criticism as a result. As expected, a cameraperson and a local reporter with a microphone approached. The reporter stuck the microphone in my face and said, breathlessly, "Mr. Comey, Martha Stewart is getting out of prison today worth two hundred million dollars more than when she went in. How does that make you feel?" (For some reason, he pronounced "feel" to sound like "feeeeel.")

I paused, looked into the camera, and delivered a line I had practiced in my head a dozen times, willing myself not to smile. "Well," I said, slowly, "we at the Department of Justice are all about the successful reentry of our inmates into society. Ms. Stewart may have done better than most of our convicts, but that's certainly no cause for concern." Stone-faced, I nodded and walked off. The reporter had no idea I was fooling around, but the cameraperson — they tend to be the more down-to-earth members of a media team — laughed so hard that the camera bumped up and down. The shot was too shaky to use.

Martha Stewart didn't commit the crime of the century. At first, I found it an annoyance compared to those we were dealing with on a daily basis, cases that had a bigger impact on people's lives. But something caused me to change my mind. This case was ultimately about something higher, something more important than a rich person trying to sell some stock before it crashed. And in a number of ways I couldn't imagine then, it had a significant impact on me for the rest of my career in law enforcement — offering lessons I'd make use of long after.

Everyone lies at some point in their life. The important questions are where, about what, and how often?

One of the inevitable questions someone at my height is asked, especially by strangers in elevators, is whether I played basketball in college. The answer is that I didn't. But it was a long story as to why, involving growing late, knee surgery, and various time demands. I figured nobody wanted to hear all that and, even if they did, it took too long for an elevator ride. So for a few years after college I took the easy way out and just nodded or said "yup" to any stranger who asked me that question. I did the same thing with friends I played basketball with once I entered law school. I don't know why

I did that. Maybe I was insecure. Maybe it was just easier. Or maybe I liked people to think I was a college jock. This was a seemingly small and inconsequential lie told by a stupid kid, but it was a lie nonetheless. And it ate at me. So after law school I wrote to the friends I'd lied to and told them the truth. They all seemed to understand. One of them replied — as only a true friend could — "We knew you didn't play in college and we didn't care. You are a great friend and a great player. Of course, you suck for other reasons."

I guess what concerned me most about the small lie was the danger of it becoming a habit. I've seen many times over the years how liars get so good at lying, they lose the ability to distinguish between what's true and what's not. They surround themselves with other liars. The circle becomes closer and smaller, with those unwilling to surrender their moral compasses pushed out and those willing to tolerate deceit brought closer to the center of power. Perks and access are given to those willing to lie and tolerate lies. This creates a culture, which becomes an entire way of life. The easy, casual lies — those are a very dangerous thing. They open up the path to the bigger lies, in more important places, where the consequences aren't so harmless.

Every year a small number of people are prosecuted for insider trading. A few people wearing nice suits and handcuffs get paraded in front of cameras and walk into courthouses, but their cases generally go without much notice outside the financial press. But in January 2002, that was about to change, when a case about one little-known biotech company with one well-known shareholder came across my desk as the United States Attorney in Manhattan.

In late 2001, Sam Waksal, owner of a company called ImClone, sold his many shares of the company in a panic after learning that regulators were going to deny a license for ImClone's new wonder drug. The problem for Mr. Waksal was that the general public didn't know anything about the denial of the license. Under the law, a CEO can't just sell his stock when he learns something big that ordinary stockholders don't know. That's insider trading. Waksal's behavior was like lighting himself on fire in front of law enforcement authorities. That he was guilty and should be charged was obvious; the remaining question for investigators was whether anyone else who sold ImClone shares after Christmas 2001 did so based on material, nonpublic information.

Because the transactions happened in Manhattan, which was my jurisdiction, I assembled an all-star team of Assistant U.S. Attorneys to help run the investigation. My deputy was David Kelley, a career prosecutor and close friend. The chief of the Criminal Division, supervising all criminal prosecutors in the office, was another longtime friend and former prosecutor, Karen Seymour. I had convinced her to leave her partnership at a Wall Street law firm to help me lead the office. Together, the three of us chewed over all hard decisions, like the old friends we were — laughing, teasing, arguing. I valued them because they would always tell me the truth, including when I was full of it.

The danger in every organization, especially one built around hierarchy, is that you create an environment that cuts off dissenting views and discourages honest feedback. That can quickly lead to a culture of delusion and deception. And in a leader, the tendency of too much confidence to swamp humility can lead to a dangerous self-indulgence at the expense of others. That was a major factor in the downfall of the Mafia in New York. And, ironically, it was a significant weakness at the U.S. Attorney's office that broke the Mafia under Giuliani. I worked very hard to keep this in mind now that I had Rudy Giuliani's old job.

It was now my responsibility to build my own culture within the U.S. Attorney's office, one that would get the best out of our team and drawing, in different ways, on the lessons of Giuliani and Fahey. I tried to attend to this task from the very first day. I hired about fifty new prosecutors during my time as U.S. Attorney and sat with each of them as they took the oath of office. I invited them to bring their families. I told them that something remarkable was going to happen when they stood up and said they represented the United States of America — total strangers were going to believe what they said next. I explained to them that, although I didn't want to burst their bubbles, this would not happen because of them. It would happen because of those who had gone before them and, through hundreds of promises made and kept, and hundreds of truths told and errors instantly corrected, built something for them. I called it a reservoir. I told them it was a reservoir of trust and credibility built for you and filled for you by people you never knew, by those who are long gone. A reservoir that makes possible so much of the good that is done by the institution you serve. A remarkable gift. I would explain to these bright young lawyers that, like all great gifts, this one comes with a responsibility, a solemn obligation to guard and protect that reservoir and pass it on to those who follow as full as you received it, or maybe even fuller. I would explain that the problem with reservoirs is that they take a very long time to fill but they can be drained by one hole in the dam. The actions of one person can destroy what it took hundreds of people years to build.

On the Waksal case, government investigators, including agents and analysts at the FBI, ran through the basics: they got a list of everyone who had sold ImClone stock at the same time as Waksal. One of those names was Martha Stewart. She had dumped her shares the same day Waksal did and before the public learned about the FDA denial on the new drug, avoiding a loss of about fifty thousand dollars. The loss was a rounding error for a wealthy person worth hundreds of millions of dollars like Stewart, but investigators would have been negligent if they didn't at least interview her and ask her why she sold when she did.

Stewart was a friend of Waksal's, and investigators expected her to tell them that when she learned Sam was selling stock, she had sold hers, too. Surely she would tell them that she didn't know there was anything wrong with that sale, and that she was very sorry if there was. There would have been a stern warning, maybe a modest financial penalty, and everyone would go on with their lives.

Except that wasn't what Martha Stewart did.

Instead, she told the investigators that she had a standing agreement with her broker that he should sell her ImClone shares immediately if its stock price dropped below a certain price, or "floor." Stewart said she had known nothing in advance about Waksal selling his stock. Maybe his sale had caused the price to drop, triggering her sell order, but this was all a big coincidence. Nothing to see here.

Federal investigators usually aren't big believers in coincidences. Stewart's answer prompted them to look further. Among many oddities, they discovered that Stewart and Waksal had the same broker. They also learned the broker had called Stewart the morning of Waksal's sale. Stewart was unavailable at the time, flying by private jet to a Mexican resort, so the broker left a message with Stewart's secretary saying that he needed to speak to her about Sam Waksal, urgently.

After the investigation began, the feds obtained handwritten notes from the broker. Those notes did reflect that there was a previously agreed-upon floor for selling the ImClone stock, just as Stewart had said. But the notes were written in two distinct inks. Everything was written in one brand of ink, except for the part that bolstered Stewart's claims.

Investigators then learned other troubling details. They interviewed Stewart's secretary and learned that, after the federal investigation into the ImClone sale began, Stewart asked her secretary to open the telephone message from her broker on her computer. Then Stewart asked her secretary to stand up, after which Stewart took her seat at the computer. She highlighted the part that said her broker was calling about Sam Waksal, then typed over it to remove the reference to Waksal. Stewart then paused. Apparently thinking better of obstructing justice in such a clumsy way and in full view of a potential witness to a major crime, Stewart stood abruptly and instructed her secretary to restore the words she had just deleted.

I disliked the Martha Stewart case from the beginning. It was a distraction, a shiny object, when we had so much more important work to do. The tech bubble of the late 1990s had burst, and dramatic swings in the market had exposed an extraordinary amount of corporate fraud. To paraphrase the memorable words of Warren Buffett, when the market crashed, the tide had gone out quickly and exposed a lot of naked bathers. There on the beach were the fraudsters of Enron, WorldCom, Adelphia, and so many more — those who had bankrupted companies, destroyed countless jobs, and defrauded billions from investors. We were working like mad at the U.S. Attorney's office in New York to make these big cases. And they were very hard to make, because they all turned on the content of people's minds. In a drug-dealing prosecution, of which I had done many, the mission for the government was simply to connect the defendants to the transaction. If federal agents burst into a hotel room and find a kilo of heroin piled in the middle of a table, everybody sitting at that table is going to jail. It isn't open to any of them to say it had never occurred to them that this activity was illegal, or that their accountants and lawyers had reviewed the heroin and concluded it was lawful and appropriate under governing rules and regulations. Nope. Everybody is going to jail.

In a corporate fraud case, the challenge was reversed. At the end of the day, the government would understand the transactions completely. We would know who was sitting at the table and exactly what the deal was. But everybody at the table would say they had absolutely no idea this complicated, mortgage-backed, reverse-repo, foreign-exchange-swap transaction was illegal. They would invariably say they were deeply, deeply sorry people had lost their life savings, but committing a crime was the furthest thing from their minds.

It fell to investigators and prosecutors to prove the content of a person's mind beyond a reasonable doubt to a jury of twelve, who must unanimously agree that the government met its burden. Really hard. Not impossible, thanks to the twentieth century's great gift to law enforcement — electronic communications — but still hard. Sometimes email offered "kilo on the table" kind of evidence. In one case I dealt with, a financial executive emailed another, saying, "I just hope the SEC doesn't find out what we are doing here." His fellow executive replied, "Forget the SEC, when the FBI comes, I'm going out the window." Good stuff.

But more often, the government was stymied in its effort to prove criminal intent, even in the face of huge financial losses. People shouting that the CEO "must have known" or "should have known" was not good enough. Where is the proof beyond a reasonable doubt that he knew he was committing a crime? Senior executives are shocked, shocked that lower-level employees may have been breaking the law.

In the middle of all these massive cases that we were working so hard to make, why did I want to have anything to do with Martha Stewart? It was a marginal case about a lie by a rich person who sold some stock because her friend did. We had some evidence that might add up to insider trading, if we took an aggressive view of the law, and we had a willful obstruction of justice, but it was far from an open-and-shut case, particularly if it involved a jury and a sympathetic character in America's most beloved TV hostess. Everyone had learned something from her. I once had personally pushed basil leaves under the skin of a Thanksgiving turkey, at Martha Stewart's suggestion. Why go to the trouble? Who cared?

But the case was no longer marginal when one afternoon the lead investigating Assistant U.S. Attorney barged into my big office with its view of the Manhattan end of the Brooklyn Bridge and NYPD headquarters. All day long, I could watch people flow to and from Brooklyn and to and from the police. With a broad smile and both arms extended above his head as if signaling a touchdown, he told me he'd gotten the goods.

The final piece to the case had come, unexpectedly, from Martha Stewart's best friend, Mariana Pasternak. Just days after the allegedly coincidental stock sale, the two were sitting on a hotel balcony in Cabo San Lucas, Mexico, enjoying a New Year's vacation drink. As they chatted, gazing out at the jewel-like Pacific, Pasternak told investigators, Stewart said she was worried about Sam Waksal. Stewart explained that she had sold all her stock in ImClone because she learned through her broker that Waksal had. She added, "Isn't it nice to have brokers who tell you such things?"

In other words, Martha Stewart had told us a whopper, and now we could prove it well beyond any reasonable doubt. Ugh. The lie she had told was so unnecessary. She could have offered to repay the fifty thousand dollars she had saved, chump change to her, expressed remorse, and vowed never to trade on insider information again. Instead she engaged in an elaborate deception and then involved others to try to cover her tracks.

In addition to a celebrity fan base who cheered her on, Stewart had aggressive lawyers. One of their main arguments was that it was laughable to think that a person worth hundreds of millions of dollars would get personally involved — while jetting to Mexico — to sell stock simply to avoid a fifty-thousand-dollar loss. Her time was too valuable for such trifles, they said. Faced with this argument, I asked her lawyers a question: If Ms. Stewart were at her country estate and walked to the end of her winding driveway one Sunday morning to retrieve her *New York Times* — steaming cup of coffee in hand — and saw a five-dollar bill lying on the ground next to her paper, would she pick it up or would she not bother with such a trifle? They didn't answer. Of course she would pick it up. Of course she would make a single phone call to her broker to save herself fifty thousand dollars. Most of us would, especially if we weren't familiar with laws on insider trading.

I asked Karen Seymour, the Criminal

Division chief, to see if she could arrange a plea deal. Karen didn't love that idea because she now had a strong case and worried we would signal weakness by looking for a deal, but she gave it a shot. Stewart's lawyers at first said she would go for a guilty plea, then said she would not. My guess is they were either testing our resolve or had failed to persuade their client into pleading in a case she couldn't win. If we wanted Stewart to pay for her crime, we were going to have to indict her and try this case against a well-known and widely admired public figure. Though the case seemed like a no-brainer, I still hesitated. I knew defenders of Stewart in the media would say just what her lawyers intimated to me when they fought against the charges — that I was bringing this case to get famous. That I was celebrity hunting — tipping the scales of justice to make an example out of someone who had been in the public eye. That I was just another Rudy Giuliani, out to make a name on the backs of others. I spent long hours staring out at the Brooklyn Bridge, hesitating to bring on the criticism and the circus I knew would come. Then, while I worried about myself and my image, I remembered a young black minister.

He was an associate pastor and youth

minister at the historic Fourth Baptist Church in Richmond, Virginia, when I was the supervising federal prosecutor in that city in the late 1990s. The senior pastor at his church was the charismatic mayor of Richmond, Leonidas B. Young. Unfortunately, Mayor Young was a bit too charismatic for his own good. Although married with children, he was simultaneously carrying on an ambitious number of affairs with other women. To maintain those relationships in the face of some sexual performance issues, Young had undergone an expensive mechanical penile implant, which then catastrophically failed, leading to additional procedures and costs. With his medical bills and purchases of gifts, trips, and hotels for multiple paramours, Young was struggling financially. Sadly, he decided to use his city government position to raise cash, and turned to his associate pastor to help him do it.

At the time, Richmond was considering privatizing city cemeteries. Executives of one company interested in bidding on the cemeteries met with Young. The mayor told them their chances of winning the bid would be materially enhanced if they hired certain people, such as his junior minister at Fourth Baptist, as "consultants." The company then wrote checks for thousands of dollars to that junior minister, among others. Bank records showed the minister cashed the checks and then funneled the money to the mayor.

My fellow prosecutor Bob Trono and I met with the young minister. There was something about him that made me want to help him. I looked him directly in the eye and said I believed he was a good person, that he had done something as a favor to his mentor and senior pastor at his church, Mayor Leonidas Young. From what we could tell, the young minister hadn't kept any of the money he had helped Mayor Young embezzle. Admit this, I told him, and you will be okay. Lie, and I will have to prosecute you for it. Mayor Young will turn on you, someday, I told him. He began to sweat, but he insisted the cemetery company had hired him for his expertise and that he had not given any money to Young.

I felt deep sadness as the meeting ended, because I could see the future and what it held for a young pastor from Richmond who had a promising career ahead of him. Leonidas Young was indicted, pled guilty to racketeering, and was sentenced to federal prison. As part of an effort to reduce the length of that sentence, he named the associate pastor as one of his money launderers. The young minister was indicted and convicted of lying during the investigation. At the trial, prosecuted by Bob Trono, Leonidas Young testified against him. The young pastor was sentenced to fifteen months in federal prison for lying. I have left his name out of my book because I hope he has made a good and happy life after prison.

As I stared out of my Manhattan office window and remembered that young minister, I was suddenly ashamed of myself. He was not famous. I was probably the only person outside Richmond who even knew his name. And here I was, the United States Attorney in Manhattan, hesitating to prosecute Martha Stewart because it would bring criticism. I was actually considering letting her go *because* she was rich and famous. What a miscarriage of justice. What a coward I was.

I asked Dave Kelley to find out how many people had been indicted in the United States the previous year for lying to federal investigators. How many "regular people" lied and then paid dearly for it? The answer was two thousand. Kelley told me I needed to stop wringing my hands; this was the right thing to do and I should get on with it. He was right. I told my staff to indict Martha Stewart and decided Karen Seymour should lead the case at trial.

Charging Martha Stewart was my first experience with getting a lot of hate and heat for a decision that had been carefully and thoughtfully made. People just could not, for the life of them, understand how I could make a mountain out of a molehill in an effort to ruin Martha Stewart. I was obviously out of control, making decisions that no reasonable person could support. The onslaught was bracing, but I was comfortable we had made the right decision, and in the right way. It would also prove to be good practice for a future I couldn't have imagined back then. Stewart was convicted and sentenced to five months at the federal prison in Alderson, West Virginia.

The Stewart experience reminded me that the justice system is an honor system. We really can't always tell when people are lying or hiding documents, so when we *are* able to prove it, we simply must do so as a message to everyone. People must fear the consequences of lying in the justice system or the system can't work.

There was once a time when most people worried about going to hell if they violated an oath taken in the name of God. That divine deterrence has slipped away from our modern cultures. In its place, people must fear going to jail. They must fear their lives being turned upside down. They must fear their pictures splashed on newspapers and websites. People must fear having their name forever associated with a criminal act if we are to have a nation with the rule of law. Martha Stewart lied, blatantly, in the justice system. To protect the institution of justice, and reinforce a culture of truth-telling, she had to be prosecuted. I am very confident that, should the circumstance arise, Martha Stewart would not lie to federal investigators again. Unfortunately, many others who crossed my path would continue to commit the same foolish act.

As United States Attorney in Manhattan, I reported to the deputy attorney general at the Department of Justice in Washington. The deputy attorney general — often called the DAG — was the number-two official, the chief operating officer of the department. Everyone in the organization, with the exception of the attorney general's small personal staff, reported to the DAG, who reported to the attorney general. It was a crazy organizational chart, one you could only find in the government. But I figured it likely made for an interesting job.

In the summer of 2003, Larry Thompson, who was then serving in the post, came to see me in Manhattan. He was burned out and told me he would be leaving in the fall. He intended to recommend to the George W. Bush White House that I replace him as deputy attorney general. Was I interested?

The answer was yes. I loved being United States Attorney, but New York, as before, was not a great situation for me or my family. For cost-of-living reasons, we lived fifty miles north of my office. The rough commute made it very hard for me to see Patrice and the kids as much as I would have liked. It meant plenty of missed recitals, games, and parent-teacher conferences. I once left my office at 4 P.M. for a 6 P.M. Little League game, and because of the hellish commute missed nearly the entire game. That kind of thing made me ache. It was not who I wanted to be. If we could move the kids to Washington, I knew I would have a job that would keep me plenty busy, but I also knew I could avoid three or four hours commuting every day. Of course, there was danger in moving closer to the political heart of the country. One New York journalist captured the views of many of my colleagues when he wrote a piece titled "Mr. Comey Goes to Washington," saying there was no doubt I would retain my sense of humor when I moved to Washington; the harder question was whether I would lose my soul. I confess I shared the concern, but the move would be best for my family. And how bad could it be?

So I traveled to Washington to meet with President George W. Bush's White House counsel, Alberto Gonzales. We met in his office on the second floor of the West Wing. This wasn't my first visit to the White House counsel's suite of offices. In 1995, I had worked briefly for the Senate committee investigating Bill and Hillary Clinton's investments in an Arkansas development called Whitewater and a variety of related issues. One of those issues involved the suicide of President Clinton's deputy White House counsel Vince Foster and the subsequent handling of documents left in his office. During my five months on the committee legal staff, I was assigned to visit the second floor of the West Wing to examine the suite of offices in which Foster had worked. One of the questions the committee had was whether First Lady Hillary Clinton or anyone acting on her behalf went to Foster's office after his death and removed documents. I left the investigation long before any conclusions were reached, but I can recall pacing off the distance between Hillary Clinton's office on the second floor and the White House counsel's suite.

I had also been to the West Wing in the spring of 2001. As an Assistant United States Attorney in Richmond, I was handling a terrorism case and expected the indictment in the case to accuse Iran of funding and directing the devastating 1996 attack on a United States Air Force barracks in Saudi Arabia that killed nineteen Americans and wounded hundreds. Such an accusation would have foreign policy implications, and the new Bush administration gathered its senior national security team to hear Attorney General John Ashcroft's explanation as to why the accusation against Iran was well founded. Ashcroft's staff decided I would accompany him to the White House but sit outside the Situation Room meeting, just in case he needed me as a resource for details. I was relaxed and enjoying my first visit to the Situation Room, because I had no speaking role and wasn't even in the meeting. I could just look around and soak it in. The soaking didn't last long. Soon I was underwater.

Minutes after the door to the secure meeting room closed, it opened again and there stood the secretary of state, Colin Powell.

"Who's the prosecutor? You the prosecutor?" he barked, fixing his gaze on me.

"Yes, sir," I stammered.

"Get in here," he ordered. Apparently, the start of the meeting had not gone well.

General Powell ushered me into the small conference room and directed me to a seat at the table, directly across from him and the secretary of defense, Donald Rumsfeld. The national security adviser, Condoleezza Rice, sat at the head of the table. I sat between the slightly flushed-looking attorney general and FBI Director Louis Freeh. For the next twenty minutes, the two strong-willed cabinet secretaries grilled me about my case and my evidence as I sweated through my suit. When they ran out of questions, they asked me to leave. I walked out, numb, while the meeting continued. Several weeks later, I got the approval to include the accusation that Iran was behind the Khobar Towers attack.

Now here I was, back again. The main floor of the West Wing is home to grand, high-ceilinged offices, including, of course, the Oval Office. It always seemed to me that the architects got the space for those high ceilings by taking it from the levels above and below, especially the basement. Down there, where I would spend so much of my later career in national security meetings, the doorframes were about six feet, seven inches high. To navigate, I would discreetly bob my head down as if nodding to an unseen companion as I walked. I had no idea how finely calibrated my ducking was until I got new soles and heels on a pair of dress shoes during the George W. Bush administration. Apparently, this refurbished footwear made me about a half-inch taller than usual. Rushing so as not to be late to a Situation Room meeting with the president, I did the usual bob and smacked my head so hard that I rocked backward, stunned. A Secret Service agent asked me if I was okay. I said yes, and continued walking, stars in my eyes. As I sat at the table with the president and his national security team, I began to feel liquid on my scalp and realized I was bleeding. So I did the obvious thing: I kept tilting my head in different directions to keep the running blood inside my hairline. Heaven only knows what President Bush thought was wrong with me, but he never saw my blood.

The top floor, where Gonzales had his office, was only slightly less claustrophobic, with small windows jammed against the low ceiling. I was relieved when we sat. Gonzales, the White House counsel who had worked for Bush when he was governor of Texas, was a warm, friendly, and almost painfully soft-spoken person. Most conversations with him involved awkward pauses. I don't remember him asking me much at my "interview" to be deputy attorney general. He said the White House was looking for someone "strong enough to stand up to John Ashcroft." He wanted to know whether I thought I could do that.

That struck me as an odd question to ask about the president's handpicked attorney general. But, as I was quickly learning, Washington was a city where everyone seemed to question other people's loyalties and motivations, most often when they weren't in the room. Ashcroft was a conservative who had considered running for president in 2000, the year that saw George W. Bush elected. Although I couldn't see it from my job in Manhattan, there was tension between the White House and Ashcroft over the perception that the attorney general was preparing his own political future and that his interests didn't align entirely with President Bush's. I didn't know whether any of that was true, but assured the White House counsel that I would not be cowed by anyone and that I would always try to do the right thing. That answer seemed to satisfy him, at least then. Gonzales and the political higher-ups in the Bush White House approved me for the position; I met briefly with Ashcroft, who already knew me well; and in December 2003, I moved into an office at Department of Justice headquarters and began moving the family to the Washington suburbs.

The job of deputy attorney general came with a staff of about twenty lawyers to help with the heavy workload and the various demands of a hundred others who reported directly to me. Although I had been in federal law enforcement for fifteen years, the DAG position was my first chance to work on a near-daily basis with cabinet members. My immediate boss, of course, was John Ashcroft, who, despite Gonzales's implication, I found to be warm, decent, and committed to his job over his own ambitions. We were cordial with each other but never close, something I attributed to the eighteen-year gap in our ages and our very different styles. Although he laughed easily and enjoyed team sports — I had once played a rough game of basketball against him and failed, despite great effort, to knock him down — Ashcroft was formal in many respects. A deeply religious man, he didn't dance or drink or curse, and he disdained some of the more colorful turns of phrase I liked to use.

One day he held me back after a meeting in his office to gently chastise me for the language I used in a meeting that had just ended. He explained that he viewed the office in which he sat as something he held in trust for the American people. I said I very much agreed. He went on, "Given that, I would ask that you be attentive to your language."

I gave him a blank look, because I couldn't recall using any epithets in the meeting that had just ended. I didn't curse much, but I did on occasion, for emphasis and effect.

"What did I say?" I asked, mystified.

He looked visibly uncomfortable at the prospect of repeating what I had said. It must have been an F-bomb, I reasoned. How could I not remember that?

"It rhymes with 'word,' " Ashcroft finally said.

I racked my brain for four-letter words that fit his description. Then I remembered. At some point during our discussion about a case, I used the word "turd," as in the phrase "turd in the punch bowl." Trying not to smile, I apologized and said I would be more careful in the future.

My position also occasionally afforded me the privilege of visiting the Oval Office. My first visit was in late 2003 when I substituted for Attorney General Ashcroft at President Bush's daily terrorism threat briefing. For years after 9/11, every morning President Bush was in town, he met with the leaders of the counterterrorism agencies — which included the FBI and the Department of Justice. I was nervous about these meetings for a couple of reasons. Obviously, I didn't want to embarrass myself or my department by saying anything stupid. But I was also going to a meeting with the president of the United States in an office that is hallowed ground in the life of my country. And in 2003, two years after the 9/11 attacks, there was no higher-priority agenda item than what we were discussing.

This was my first meeting with the leader of the free world. As I sat there, I couldn't get over how brightly lit the place was. There was a ring of lights in the recessed ceiling that lit the place like the noonday sun. I didn't have to speak in this meeting unless called upon, so I let my eyes sweep over the faces that were familiar from TV —

the president, Vice President Dick Cheney, FBI Director Bob Mueller, National Security Adviser Condoleezza Rice, and Secretary of Homeland Security Tom Ridge.

In that moment, something hit me: It's just us. I always thought that in this place there would be somebody better, but it's just this group of people — including me — trying to figure stuff out. I didn't mean that as an insult to any of the participants, who were talented people. But we were just people, ordinary people in extraordinary roles in challenging times. I'm not sure what I had expected, but I met the top of the pyramid and it was just us, which was both comforting and a bit frightening. Suddenly Bob Dylan was in my head, singing, "What looks large from a distance, close up ain't never that big."

One of the first cases that I stepped into in my new role at the Justice Department was another case about lying in the justice system. In June 2003, a couple of months after the invasion of Iraq, an article by reporter Robert Novak had revealed the name of a covert CIA employee. The revelation had come days after the CIA employee's husband had written a newspaper opinion piece attacking one of the Bush administration's main rationales for the war in Iraq, namely that Saddam Hussein was trying to acquire nuclear material. Speculation was rampant that members of the Bush administration had illegally disclosed the name of this CIA employee to Novak in retaliation for the negative article.

Novak attributed his reporting to two Bush administration sources. As the scandal widened, it soon became apparent that at least three, and as many as six, Bush officials had spoken to reporters about the covert CIA employee. Richard Armitage, the deputy secretary of state, was one official who freely admitted mentioning the CIA employee's name to Novak. In fact, he had called the Justice Department shortly after the investigation began. He explained that he hadn't intended to reveal classified information; he had just been gossiping with Novak and didn't realize what he had done. The identity of Novak's second source was President Bush's chief political advisor, Karl Rove. Rove had had a conversation with Novak, in which Novak mentioned that the author of the critical opinion piece on Iraq was married to a CIA employee. Rove said something like, "Oh, you heard that, too." Although it doesn't seem like great journalistic craft, Novak took this as a confirmation of what he had learned from Armitage.

But there was also evidence that a third official, the vice president's chief of staff, Lewis "Scooter" Libby, spoke to numerous reporters about the CIA employee. By the time I became deputy attorney general, Libby had been interviewed by the FBI and admitted doing so, but said he only knew about the CIA employee from a reporter. Like Armitage, Libby maintained he was just passing gossip, not proactively disseminating the name of a covert agent. Unfortunately for Libby, the reporter Libby named, NBC News Washington bureau chief Tim Russert, had been interviewed by the FBI and said that Libby was lying. Russert hadn't passed along the covert agent's name to Libby. Three years later, a jury would conclude the same thing: Libby lied to the FBI.

This was one of my early experiences in Washington of people deciding motivations based on their partisan allegiance. To Democrats, it was obvious that key members of a Republican administration were subverting justice to undermine and punish their critics. To Republicans, it was just as obvious that this was a witch hunt against people who made an inconsequential mistake. My job would make at least one of these groups, or tribes, very unhappy.

The law prohibiting the disclosure of the identity of a covert intelligence agent required specific and evil intent. Under the relevant statute, it was not enough to show that the people who disclosed the agent's identity were stupid or careless. We had to prove that these men *knew* the CIA employee was undercover and that they also knew that revealing the name was against the law. Based on what we knew to that point, it seemed unlikely that we could prove, at least beyond a reasonable doubt, that Armitage or Rove had acted with the required criminal intent in speaking with Novak and other reporters. Novak backed their story that this had been gossip or a mistake, and there was likely not enough evidence to prove otherwise.

That put the Department of Justice in a tough spot. Though the people investigating the case were professionals, I knew that it would be very difficult, if there was insufficient evidence, for a department led by Republican John Ashcroft to credibly close an investigation against his colleagues in the same administration without recommending charges. We would also never want to bring charges just to avoid an accusation of conflict. Complicating matters was the fact that Karl Rove had managed one of John Ashcroft's political campaigns back in his home state of Missouri before Ashcroft became attorney general. On top of that, Scooter Libby, whose conduct still needed to be sorted out, was a senior White House official with whom Ashcroft and senior Department of Justice officials interacted frequently.

The credibility of the Department of Justice is its bedrock. The American people must see the administration of justice as independent of politics, race, class, religion, or any of the many other things that divide humans into tribes. We had to do everything we could to protect the department's reputation for fairness and impartiality, its reservoir of trust and credibility. Ashcroft understood that, and when I met with him to discuss my recommendation that he recuse himself from the case, he agreed. I immediately appointed Patrick Fitzgerald, then serving as the United States Attorney in Chicago, as special counsel to oversee the investigation. Although Fitzgerald was a political appointee and a close friend of mine, he had a strong reputation for independence and, as the U.S. Attorney in Chicago, was far enough away not to be seen as part of the executive branch leadership. I went one step further: because I was also a senior political appointee of President Bush, I delegated to Fitzgerald all my powers as acting attorney general. I remained his supervisor, but he didn't need to ask me for permission to take any step in the case, which emphasized the independence of the investigation.

In December 2003, I held a press conference to announce the appointment. The Department of Justice routinely makes press announcements of significant developments in its work, including decisions to bring public charges or lawsuits, or the resolution of those cases. In matters of significant public interest, the department has long confirmed investigations and reported the completion of significant investigations without charges. Anytime a special prosecutor is named to look into the activities of a presidential administration it is big news, and, predictably, my decision was not popular at the Bush White House. A week after the announcement, I substituted for the attorney general at a cabinet meeting with the president. By tradition, the secretaries of state and defense sit flanking the president at the Cabinet Room table in the West Wing of the White House. The secretary of the treasury and the attorney general sit across the table, flanking the vice president. That meant that, as the substitute for the attorney general, I was at Vice President Dick Cheney's left shoulder. Me, the man who had just appointed a special prosecutor to investigate his friend and most senior and trusted adviser, Scooter Libby.

As we waited for the president, I figured I should be polite. I turned to Cheney and said, "Mr. Vice President, I'm Jim Comey from Justice."

Without turning to face me, he said, "I know. I've seen you on TV." Cheney then locked his gaze ahead, as if I weren't there. We waited in silence for the president. My view of the Brooklyn Bridge felt very far away.

I had assured Fitzgerald at the outset that this was likely a five- or six-month assignment. There was some work to do, but it would be a piece of cake. He reminded me of that many times over the next four years, as he was savagely attacked by the Republicans and right-leaning media as some kind of maniacal Captain Ahab, pursuing a case that was a loser from the beginning. Fitzgerald had done exactly as I expected once he took over. He investigated to understand just who in government had spoken with the press about the CIA employee and what they were thinking when they did so. After careful examination, he ended in a place that didn't surprise me on Armitage and Rove. But the Libby part — admittedly, a major loose end when I gave him the case — turned out to be complicated.

Libby not only lied about his interaction with Tim Russert, claiming that he'd heard the covert agent's name from him, but eight Bush administration officials testified that they talked to Libby about the covert agent's name. More evidence revealed that Libby had proactively discussed the CIA employee with reporters, at the vice president's request, to "push back" on stories critical of the administration's basis for invading Iraq. Why Libby — an attorney who graduated from Columbia Law School — lied is not clear. Maybe he didn't want to admit that the leak started at the vice president's office, which would have caused political embarrassment, or he didn't want to admit to an angry President Bush that he had been among the leakers.

It took Fitzgerald three years of litigation to get to a place where he charged, tried, and convicted Libby of making false statements in a federal investigation, perjury, and obstruction of justice. Republican loyalists howled that he was persecuting Libby because prosecutors could never prove the underlying crime — the intentional leaking of a covert agent's name with prior knowledge of its illegality. Of course, these were the same Republicans who passionately believed that President Bill Clinton's lies under oath over an affair with an intern simply had to be pursued, because obstruction of justice and perjury strike at the core of our system. Meanwhile, Democrats, who six years earlier attacked the case against Bill Clinton as a silly lie about sex, had discovered in the Libby case that they cared deeply about obstruction of justice crimes — when the obstructers were Republicans.

I would discover in the coming months that the pressures to bend the rules and to make convenient exceptions to laws when they got in the way of the president's agenda were tempting. And it was a temptation fed by the urgency of the topic and the nature of the people around the president, people who couldn't take the long view or understand the importance to the country of doing things the right way, no matter the inconvenience. They would be painful, exhausting lessons in the importance of institutional loyalty over expediency and politics. And more preparation for the future I couldn't yet see.

CHAPTER 6
ON THE TRACKS

If you can keep your head when
all about you Are losing theirs and
blaming it on you . . .
— RUDYARD KIPLING, "IF"

It was after 7:00 P.M. on March 10, 2004. Another long, hard day as acting attorney general of the United States, a post I'd temporarily assumed on behalf of an ailing John Ashcroft that had put me in the center of an ugly battle with the Bush White House. It was about to get even uglier.

My security team was driving me in an armored black Suburban, headed west on Constitution Avenue, past museums, the Washington Monument, and the South Lawn of the White House. Senior government officials are assigned protective details based on threat assessments. As the United States Attorney in Manhattan, I didn't have one, but since 9/11 the deputy attorney general was driven in an armored Suburban and shadowed by armed Deputy U.S. Marshals.

At the end of a long day, I was tired and ready to get home. Then my cell phone rang. On the line was David Ayres, Attorney General John Ashcroft's chief of staff. Ayres was one of those rare people who seem to grow calmer in the middle of a storm. And there was a metaphorical hurricane hitting, so his voice was stone cold. Ayres had just gotten off the phone with Janet Ashcroft, who had been keeping vigil at her husband's bedside at George Washington University Hospital. Attorney General Ashcroft had been hospitalized with acute pancreatitis, so severe that it had immobilized him with pain in the ICU.

Minutes earlier, Ayres reported, the White House operator had attempted to put a call through to the ailing attorney general from President Bush. I knew what this was about. So did Ayers. And so did the savvy Janet Ashcroft, who, like her husband, was a sharp and accomplished attorney.

Janet Ashcroft had refused the call. Her husband was too sick, she said, to talk to the president. Undaunted, President Bush then told her he was sending his counsel, Alberto Gonzales, and his chief of staff,

Andrew Card, to the hospital to discuss a vital matter of national security with her husband. She immediately alerted Ayres, who called me.

After finishing the call, I spoke in an unusually sharp voice to the United States Marshals Service driver. "Ed, I need to get to George Washington Hospital immediately." The urgency in my tone was all he needed to hit the emergency lights and begin driving as if the armored car had dropped onto a NASCAR track. From this moment forward, I was in a race — a literal race against two of the president's most senior officials in one of the wildest, most improbable moments in my entire career.

The deputy attorney general job, especially in the years immediately after 9/11, was incredibly stressful. The more stressful the job, the more intentional I've always been about helping my team members find joy in our work. Laughter is the outward manifestation of joy, so I believe if I'm doing it right, and helping people connect to the meaning and joy in their work, there will be laughter in the workplace. Laughter is also a good indication that people aren't taking themselves too seriously.

When I was deputy attorney general, as

part of that search for joy and fun, I sometimes engaged in a bit of staff tourism. If I
was going to a large White House meeting,
for example, I would look to take a member
of my staff who hadn't been there before.
Usually this was a fun experience for them.
Once it almost went horribly wrong.

One of President Bush's major initiatives
involved finding ways, consistent with the
law, for various departments and agencies
to make grants to faith groups. Most agencies, such as the Department of Justice, had
an office devoted to this faith-based initiative. In 2004, President Bush summoned
the leaders of the departments to give him
a report on their progress. I was attending
for Justice. Shortly before the meeting, I
learned that each "principal" meeting participant — which is what I was — could
bring a "plus one," meaning a staff member
to support me.

I knew our faith-based work well, so I
didn't need a plus one, but it occurred to
me that Bob Trono, one of my most valuable staff members, had never been to a
White House meeting. Bob had been a
federal prosecutor with me in Richmond
and handled the Leonidas Young case,
including the prosecution of the young
minister who lied for Mayor Young. I asked

him to come to Washington and help me oversee the United States Marshals Service and the Federal Bureau of Prisons. These were vital parts of the Department of Justice but rarely got White House attention. I thought it would be fun for him to get a chance to go.

When I suggested the idea, however, Bob wasn't feeling it. He didn't know anything about the faith-based efforts — literally nothing — and didn't feel comfortable going to a briefing with the president of the United States on the subject. I replied that I would do all the talking and didn't need his help. After further protests and reassurances, he reluctantly agreed. "Don't worry," I said. "I got this. I'm not going to screw you."

Two things, besides me, screwed Bob. First, before the faith-based meeting was to start, I was unexpectedly called to a meeting in the Situation Room at the White House that went longer than I expected. Second, President Bush, who was not with me in the Situation Room, continued his disturbing pattern of starting meetings early. This was not quite as disruptive as President Clinton's notorious tardiness, but having a president occasionally start early meant everyone had to show up well ahead. Soon after becoming deputy attorney general, I missed a morning terrorism briefing with the president because, arriving fifteen minutes early, I decided to go to the bathroom just outside the Oval Office (known in my family as "the highest potty in the land") and returned to find the Oval Office door already closed and the meeting under way. I had no idea what the protocol was for entering an Oval Office meeting in progress, and I was new, so I didn't test it. I left.

A nervous Bob found a chair against the wall in the Roosevelt Room, far back from the action. He could see an empty spot at the table where my name was spelled out on both sides of a triangular "tent card." And true to form, George W. Bush walked into the room ahead of schedule and with a look of impatience. Poor Bob.

Bush could be impatient, and it drove me nuts that he started things early, but I was struck by his strong, and occasionally devilish, sense of humor. That year, 2004, he was in the thick of his reelection battle against Democrat John Kerry, who was hammering him for presiding over what Kerry called a "jobless" economic recovery.

In one of our daily morning terrorism meetings with the president, FBI director

Bob Mueller told him that a suspected Al Qaeda operative named Babar, whom we were closely monitoring, had just gotten a second job in New York.

Mueller, not known as a comedian, then paused, turned his head toward me and added, "And then Jim said . . ."

Bush looked at me, and so did Vice President Cheney. I froze. Before our meeting, Mueller and I had discussed Babar's second job and I'd made a private joke to the FBI director that I hadn't expected to repeat to the president, who could occasionally display a temper.

Time slowed down, way down. I didn't reply.

The president prompted me. "What'd you say, Jim?"

I paused and then, horrified, plunged in. "Who says you haven't created any jobs; this guy's got two."

To my great relief, Bush laughed heartily. Cheney did not. On the way out of the Oval Office, I tugged Mueller's arm.

"You're killing me," I said with a smile. "Don't ever do that to me again."

"But it was funny," he replied, with the grimace that passed for his smile. Bob was not a jokester, and his severe demeanor intimidated most people. Word at the Bureau was that he had knee surgery not long after 9/11 and declined anesthesia in favor of biting on a leather belt. But I had seen enough to know he had a dry and slightly dark sense of humor. I was seeing it now.

"And it was also private, Bob. It was a joke between us." He got it, although he still thought it was funny. From this distance, I can see that he was right.

I saw the devilish side of President Bush one cold winter morning, with the city covered by a freshly fallen snow. This frigid morning, Bush was seated in his normal armchair, with his back to the fireplace and close to the grandfather clock. The president was apparently about to head somewhere on Marine One, so, as was the custom, reporters were bundled in their winter coats and huddled outside near the Rose Garden to record his departure.

As I began briefing the president on a terrorism case, I could hear the sound of his approaching helicopter. The sound grew louder. Stone-faced, the president held up his hand. "Hold on a minute, Jim," he said.

He kept his hand aloft to pause me, turned slightly in his chair, and looked out onto the South Lawn, where the press corps was gathered. I turned to follow his gaze and watched as the descent of the helicopter swept up the snow on the ground, creating a whiteout blizzard that coated all of the reporters in snow. Some of them looked like snowmen. Embarrassed snowmen. Without any expression on his face at all, Bush turned back to me, dropping his hand. "Okay, go," he said.

Bush may have had a slight mean streak — he clearly enjoyed watching that scene — but he understood that humor was essential to the high-stress, high-stakes business we were in. We could be talking with deadly seriousness about terrorism one minute and then filling the Oval Office with laughter the next. It was the only way to get through the job — to intentionally inject some fun and joy into it. But in the White House that day, my friend Bob Trono found nothing joyful or humorous about his meeting with the president.

"Who're we waitin' on?" Bush asked, after he entered the Roosevelt Room five minutes before the scheduled start time.

Someone answered that Comey was downstairs in the Situation Room.

"Jim can catch up when he gets here," Bush said. "Let's get going."

Bob could feel the perspiration trickle down his neck. The meeting marched through the departments, as various principals gave the president their briefings. *Labor. Housing and Urban Development. Education. Agriculture.* My seat sat empty. Bob's ears began ringing as he realized he didn't even know enough to give the president a bullshit answer. He had neither bull nor shit. *Veterans Affairs. Health and Human Services.* His head was swimming; he could feel his heart beating through his suit. *Commerce. Small Business Administration.* Beads of sweat on the back of his neck had by now soaked through his collar. Then the door burst open and, like the cavalry, I strode in.

"Hey, Jim, perfect timing," Bush said. "I was just about to turn to Justice."

I sat and gave him my spiel, the president thanked everyone for coming, and the meeting broke up. Bob didn't look happy. "I'm going to kill you," he whispered.

Although I may have had a different idea of "fun" than most, there were some parts of the Justice Department that had become black holes, where joy went to die. Places where morale had gotten so low and the battle scars from bureaucratic wrangling with other departments and the White House so deep, I worried that we were on the verge of losing some of our best, most capable lawyers. One of those places was the Justice Department's Office of Legal Counsel, a kind of Supreme Court within the executive branch. Its gifted lawyers — who I often described as an obscure and isolated order of monks — would be given the hardest legal questions by people in other parts of the executive branch. Their job was to think about them well and render an opinion whether a proposed action was lawful, taking into account what the courts, Congress, and any earlier Office of Legal Counsel opinions had said on the topic. This was hard stuff, because often they had very little to go on in forming the opinion. It was harder still when the subject was classified, limiting their ability to talk about it with colleagues.

The head of the office was Jack Goldsmith. He was a former law professor and a generally sunny, cherub-faced man. But after only four months in his job, his list of problems was starting to dim that angelic glow. He had inherited a set of legal opinions written quickly and under great pressure by his predecessors following the attacks of September 11, 2001. Those lawyers had attested to the lawfulness of aggressive counter-terrorism activities by the Central Intelligence Agency and the National Security Agency. The president and the intelligence community had relied on those opinions for more than two years. The opinions were dead wrong in many places, Goldsmith concluded. And the debate within the Bush administration over them was getting nasty.

Goldsmith's primary concern was a then highly classified NSA program code-named "Stellar Wind." Goldsmith and another brilliant department lawyer named Patrick Philbin had concluded that Stellar Wind, a program of NSA surveillance activities conducted in the United States against suspected terrorists and citizens without the need for judicial warrants, had been authorized by their predecessors on legally dubious grounds. Meanwhile, the entire Bush administration had come to rely on the program as a source of intelligence in the fight against terrorism. What Bush appeared not to know was that the NSA was engaging in activity that went beyond what was authorized, beyond even the legally dubious, and into what Goldsmith and Philbin concluded was clearly unlawful.

I understood the urgency behind these activities. Just two years had passed since the terrorist attacks of 9/11, when three thousand innocent people had been murdered in our country on a single, clear blue morning. That day changed our country and it changed the lives of all of us in government. We swore to do all we could to prevent such loss again. We would change the government, reshape the FBI, break down barriers, get new tools, and connect dots, all so we could avoid a pain so large as to be almost beyond description. I became the United States Attorney in Manhattan when Ground Zero, where thousands died, still smoldered. Late at night, I would stand at the fence and watch firefighters sift through the dirt to find those lost. Nobody needed to tell me how hard we needed to fight terrorism, but I also understood we had to do it the right way. Under the law.

Goldsmith and Philbin had shared their concerns with the White House — where the president's counsel, Alberto Gonzales, and the vice president's counsel, David Addington, were the primary contacts. Of the two, Addington was the dominant force. He was a tall, bearded lawyer with a booming voice that showed just a hint of a southern accent. In philosophy and temperament, he was a reflection of Vice President Cheney. He did not tolerate fools and had an ever-expanding definition of those who fit that category. After infuriating Addington by telling him the legal foundation of the program was falling apart, Goldsmith and Philbin then set about trying to convince Addington that I, the new deputy attorney general, should be told about — or "read into" — the Stellar Wind program so I could actually see what was going on.

Addington resisted this mightily. Since the program was conceived and authorized, he had succeeded in keeping the number of those who knew the details of the program to an absolute minimum — maybe a couple dozen throughout the U.S. government. Four people at the entire Justice Department had previously been read into the program, and that did not include my predecessor as deputy attorney general. On an activity of such profound importance, one that tested the limits of the law, that small circle was unusual if not unprecedented. Addington had even arranged to have the documents on the program held outside the normal process for presidential records. He — the *vice* president's lawyer — kept the orders bearing the president's signatures in a safe in his own office. Eventually, and only after considerable pressure, Addington relented and allow me to be briefed.

In the middle of February 2004, I found myself in a Justice Department secure conference room with the director of the National Security Agency, Air Force General Michael Hayden, getting from him a long-awaited briefing on the highly classified surveillance program. Hayden was an impeccably dressed, amiable man, with wire-rim glasses, a bald head, and a talent for folksy sayings and Pittsburgh Steeler references. As we sat down at the table, the general offered a preamble that I will never forget. "I'm so glad you are getting read into this program," he said, "so that when John Kerry is elected president I won't be alone at the green table."

The reference to congressional testimony, behind a table that is often green, was jarring. What was this man about to tell me that required him to express his joy that I would join him in a congressional grilling once a new president arrived? And why on earth would he say such a thing to the second-ranking official of the United States Department of Justice? I had no time to do more than think these questions, because General Hayden plowed right into his briefing. His way of mixing folksy aphorisms and NSA-speak was both entertaining and reassuring. The problem, I would come to realize, was that his briefings were a river of really great-sounding stuff that didn't make much sense once the briefing was over and you tried to piece together what you had just heard.

After Hayden departed, my Justice Department colleagues, Jack Goldsmith and Patrick Philbin, visibly exhaled. They then explained to me how the surveillance program actually worked and why so much of it was totally screwed up, as a matter of both law and practice. The NSA was doing stuff, they maintained, that had no legal basis because it didn't comply with a law Congress had passed a generation earlier, which governed electronic surveillance inside the United States. The president was violating that statute in ordering the surveillance. The NSA was also doing other stuff that wasn't even in the president's orders, so nobody had authorized it at all. This wasn't General Hayden's fault. He wasn't a lawyer or a technologist and, like Attorney General Ashcroft — who was prohibited from discussing the program even with his personal staff — Hayden was strictly limited in who he could consult about the program. The program was set up as a short-term response to a national emergency, because even Addington knew this was an extraordinary assertion of presidential power, so the president's orders were for short periods, usually about six weeks. The current presidential order expired on March 11. Goldsmith had told the White House that he could not support its reauthorization.

Given what I knew, I had to ensure that my boss had all of the facts. Many times over the past two-plus years, Ashcroft had approved Stellar Wind, and he needed to know that had been a mistake and could not continue. On Thursday, March 4, 2004, I met alone with Attorney General Ashcroft to tell him in detail about the problems with the program and why we could not approve another extension. We ate lunch together at a small table in his office. I brought my own store-bought sandwich in butcher paper. (It was either turkey or tuna. I was so busy in those days that my assistant, Linda Long, held my money and followed instructions to alternate those two sandwiches, forever.) The attorney general had a fancier setup from his chef, which was good because I needed the salt and pepper shakers and pieces of silverware to represent parts of the program. I showed him which pieces we could make reasonable arguments to support and which we simply couldn't and that would need to stop or be changed. Ashcroft listened carefully. At the end of lunch, he said the analysis made sense to him and we should fix the program to be consistent with the law. I told him we had been keeping the White House informed and I would now march out and execute on his authority.

After our lunch, Ashcroft headed to the United States Attorney's office across the Potomac in Alexandria to do a press event. He never made it. He collapsed and was rushed to George Washington University Hospital in the District of Columbia with acute pancreatitis, an extraordinarily painful ailment that can also be fatal. By this time, I had gotten on a commercial flight to Phoenix for a government meeting. I learned of the attorney general's condition as I walked off the plane. My chief of staff, Chuck Rosenberg, called to tell me that with Ashcroft incapacitated, I was now the acting attorney general and needed to be back in Washington. They were sending a government plane to retrieve me.

Back in Washington, I met on Friday with Goldsmith and Philbin. They had communicated the Department of Justice position to the White House. The renewal date was March 11, one week away, and we were not going to support a renewal in the program's current form. That weekend, Goldsmith was summoned to meet with Gonzales and Addington, but no progress was made. Gonzales was, as usual, pleasant. Addington was, as usual, angry. Neither man could explain to Goldsmith why we were wrong. Goldsmith had also informed them that I had assumed the duties of the attorney general.

On Tuesday, March 9, I was summoned to a meeting at the White House in Chief of Staff Andrew Card's office. Card was a pleasant man who was usually quiet in meetings I attended. He saw his role as ensuring that the process supporting the president worked. He was not an adviser, at least not in my experience. Goldsmith and Philbin were with me. The vice president was presiding. He was sitting at the head of the conference table. I was offered a seat to his immediate left. Also at the table were General Hayden, Card, Gonzales, FBI Director Bob Mueller, and senior CIA officials. Goldsmith and Philbin found chairs at the far end, down to my left. David Addington stood, leaning against a windowsill behind the table.

The first part of the meeting was a presentation by NSA personnel using charts to show me how valuable the surveillance program had been in connection with an ongoing Al Qaeda plot in the United Kingdom. The intelligence collected had produced a link chart that showed connections among members of a terrorist cell. That was important stuff. Of course, I knew enough about the matter to have serious doubts about whether the NSA's program was needed to find those links, given the other legal tools we had. Still, I said nothing. Our concerns were not based on the usefulness of the program. That was for others to decide; our job was to certify that the program had a reasonable basis in law.

After the analysts rolled up their charts and left the room, the vice president took over. He and I were sitting close enough to touch knees, with Addington out of focus behind Cheney. The vice president looked at me gravely and said that, as I could plainly see, the program was very important. In fact, he said, "Thousands of people are going to die because of what you are doing."

The air in the room felt thin. It was obvious that the purpose of this meeting was to squeeze me, although nobody said that. To have the vice president of the United States accuse me of recklessly producing another 9/11 — even seeming to suggest that I was doing it intentionally — was stunning.

He didn't want to hear another side. He didn't seem to accept the obvious truth that there was another side. To him, he was right, everyone else was wrong, and a bunch of weak-willed and probably liberal lawyers weren't going to tell him otherwise. My head was swimming, the blood rushing to my cheeks in anger, but I regained my footing.

"That's not helping me," I said. "That makes me feel bad, but it doesn't change the legal analysis. I accept what you say about how important it is. Our job is to say what the law can support, and it can't support the program as it is."

Cheney then expressed a frustration that was entirely reasonable. He pointed out that the Department of Justice's Office of Legal Counsel had written a memo to support the program in 2001 and that the attorney general had repeatedly certified the program's legality in the two and one-half years since. How can you now switch positions on something so important? he asked.

I sympathized with him and told him so, but I added that the 2001 opinion was so bad as to be "facially invalid." I said, "No lawyer could rely upon it."

From the windowsill came Addington's cutting voice: "I'm a lawyer and I did."

I didn't break eye contact with the vice president. "No good lawyer," I added.

It was unusual for me to be nasty like that. But Addington reminded me of someone. He seemed like a bully, not too different in some ways from the kids who picked on me back in school, or even like me when I overturned that poor college freshman's room. I didn't like it. I had lived in a foxhole with Goldsmith and Philbin for the short several months I had been DAG. I had seen the impact of Addington's threats and bullying on these exhausted and fundamentally decent people. In my opinion, his arrogance was the reason we were in this mess, and these two guys were really good people. I had had enough. So I was nasty. It was no surprise that the meeting ended shortly after, without resolution.

Attorney General Ashcroft's chief of staff, David Ayres, had been keeping me informed about our boss's condition. The situation was grim. He was in terrible pain in intensive care, with an illness that could cause organ failure and death in severe cases like his. Doctors had operated on him the very day I was meeting with the vice president.

That Wednesday was strangely quiet on the Stellar Wind front, despite the fact that the current order expired the next day. And then, late that day, Ayres called to pass on Janet Ashcroft's urgent message — Andy

Card and Al Gonzales planned to do an end run around me. They were on their way to the hospital, and I had to figure out what to do.

On the way to George Washington University Hospital, I called my chief of staff, Chuck Rosenberg. I deeply trusted him and his judgment. I told him what was happening and asked him to come to the hospital. Then I added, "Get as many of our people as possible." I'm not sure, but I think this was an instinct from my days as a federal prosecutor in Manhattan. When a prosecutor was struggling in court, a call would go out in those days for "all hands to courtroom X." When that announcement came, we would all get up from our desks and go, having no idea what it was about. One of our colleagues needed our support, so we went.

Whatever the source of my instinct, Chuck Rosenberg gave it life. He ran to members of my staff and soon a dozen lawyers were headed to the hospital, having no idea why they were going, except that I needed them there. After that, I called FBI Director Bob Mueller, who was at a restaurant with his wife and one of their children. I wanted Bob Mueller to be a witness to what was happening. Mueller and I were not particularly close and had never seen each other outside of work, but I knew Bob understood and respected our legal position and cared deeply about the rule of law. His whole life was about doing things the right way. When I told him what was happening, he said he would be there immediately.

My vehicle screeched to a stop in the driveway of the hospital. I jumped out and ran up the stairs to Ashcroft's floor, relieved to learn that I had arrived ahead of Card and Gonzales. Ashcroft's intensive care room was at the end of a hallway that had been cleared of other patients. The hall was dimly lit, occupied only by half a dozen FBI agents in suits, there to protect the attorney general. I nodded to the agents and immediately went into Ashcroft's room. He was lying in the bed, heavily medicated. His skin was gray and he didn't seem to recognize me. I did my best to tell him what was happening and to remind him that this was related to the matter we had discussed at lunch before he got sick. I couldn't tell whether he was absorbing any of what I was saying.

I then went out into the hall and spoke to the lead agent for Ashcroft's FBI protective detail. I knew Card and Gonzales would arrive with a Secret Service detail and, as incredible as it seems now, I feared they might try to forcibly remove me so they could speak with Ashcroft alone. While standing with the FBI special agent, I called Bob Mueller again on his cell phone. He was on his way.

"Bob," I said, "I need you to order your agents not to permit me to be taken from Ashcroft's room under any circumstances."

Mueller asked me to pass the phone to the agent. I stood as the agent listened, crisply answered, "Yes, sir," and passed the phone back.

The agent looked at me with a steely expression. "You will not leave that room, sir. This is our scene."

I went back into Ashcroft's room. By this point, Goldsmith and Philbin had joined me. I sat in an armchair just to the right of Ashcroft's bed, staring at the left side of his head. He lay with eyes closed. Goldsmith and Philbin stood just behind my chair. I didn't know it at the time, but Goldsmith had a pen in his hand, taking detailed notes of what he was seeing and hearing. Janet Ashcroft stood on the far side of the bed, holding her semiconscious husband's right arm. We waited in silence.

Moments later, the hospital room door opened and Gonzales and Card walked in.

Gonzales was holding a manila envelope at his waist. The two men, both among President Bush's closest confidants, stopped on my side of the bed, by Ashcroft's left leg. I could have reached out and touched them. I remember thinking I might have to do that if they tried to get Ashcroft to sign something. But that the idea even crossed my mind seemed crazy. I'm really going to wrestle with these men at the attorney general's bedside?

Gonzales spoke first, "How are you, General?"

"Not well," Ashcroft mumbled to the White House counsel.

Gonzales then began to explain that he and Card were there at the president's direction about a vital national security program, that it was essential that the program continue, that they had briefed the leadership of Congress, who understood the program's value, wanted it continued, and were willing to work with us to fix any legal issues. Then he paused.

And then John Ashcroft did something that amazed me. He pushed himself up on the bed with his elbows. His tired eyes fixed upon the president's men, and he gave Card and Gonzales a rapid-fire blast. He had been misled about the scope of the surveillance program, he said. He vented that he had long been denied the legal support he needed by their narrow "read-in" requirements. Then he said he had serious concerns about the legal basis for parts of the program now that he understood it. Spent, he fell back on his pillow, his breathing labored. "But that doesn't matter now," he said, "because I'm not the attorney general." With a finger extended from his shaking left hand, he pointed at me. "There is the attorney general."

The room was quiet for several beats. Finally, Gonzales spoke two words. "Be well."

Without looking at me, the two men turned toward the door. When their heads were turned, Janet Ashcroft scrunched her face and stuck her tongue out at them.

About five minutes later, after Card and Gonzales had left the building, Bob Mueller entered the room. He leaned down and spoke to Ashcroft in intensely personal terms — terms that would surprise those who knew the stoic Mueller well.

"In every man's life there comes a time when the good Lord tests him," he told Ashcroft. "You passed your test tonight." Ashcroft did not reply. As Mueller wrote in his notes that night, he found the attorney general "feeble, barely articulate, clearly stressed."

The moment had taken a toll on me. My heart was racing. I was feeling slightly dizzy. But when I heard Bob Mueller's tender words, I felt like crying. The law had held.

But neither Gonzales nor Card were finished with me yet. An agent summoned me to the temporary command center the FBI had set up in the next room. Card was on the phone, and the president's chief of staff, still reeling from his experience with Ashcroft, was pissed. He instructed me to come see him at the White House immediately.

I was so offended by the effort to manipulate a sick, possibly dying man to subvert the law that I couldn't hold back any longer. "After the conduct I just witnessed," I told Card, "I will not meet with you without a witness."

He got hotter. "What conduct?" he protested. "We were just there to wish him well."

That lie was poison, but I wasn't going to rise to it. I said again, slowly and calmly, "After the conduct I just witnessed, I will not meet with you without a witness." And then I added, because it had just occurred to me, "and I intend that witness to be the solicitor general of the United States."

"Are you refusing to come to the White House?" Card asked, clearly taken aback.

"No, sir. I will come as soon as I am able to reach the solicitor general to come with me." The call ended. I thought of Ted Olson, the solicitor general, for the same reason I earlier thought of Bob Mueller. As with Bob, Ted and I weren't friends, but I liked and respected him; more important, so did the president and vice president. I needed his stature, his weight with them. I also had no doubt he would see the legal issues as we did, if the vice president would let him in the circle. I reached Olson, who was also out at dinner. He agreed to meet me right away at the Justice Department and to accompany me to the White House.

Just after 11:00 P.M., as a light rain began to fall, the solicitor general and I rode together in the U.S. Marshals armored car to the White House. We walked up the carpeted stairs to Card's West Wing office, just steps from the Oval Office, where Card met us outside his door, asking Ted Olson to wait outside while he spoke with me. Card seemed calmer, so my instincts told me not to fight to have Olson in the room.

Once we were alone, Card began by expressing his hope that people would calm down. He said he had heard "talk about resignations." I learned later that Jack Goldsmith had asked his deputy, who like most others was not read into the program, to prepare a letter of resignation for him. The deputy alerted a friend at the White House, who apparently had informed Card. The chief of staff could see catastrophe coming in the form of disastrous headlines and an election-year political scandal.

"I don't think people should ever threaten to resign to get their way," I replied. Instead, I said, they should work hard to get something right on the merits. If they can't get there, and the issue is important enough, then they should quit.

The door to Card's office opened. Gonzales walked in. He had seen Olson sitting outside and invited him into Card's office as well. The four of us sat and quietly reviewed the state of play. We reached no agreement, and they did not explain what they had been doing at Ashcroft's bedside, but the emotional temperature had dropped. We adjourned.

Years later, I had the chance to hear how my staff experienced that night, when so many of them knew something bad was happening and raced to the hospital, but didn't know what was actually going on. Chuck Rosenberg, my chief of staff, walked the streets around the hospital but couldn't find his car. He had jumped out of it and run to the hospital to be with me. In his haste, he forgot to mark where he had parked. He took a cab home to Virginia at 2:30 A.M. Rosenberg didn't drink alcohol, so his wife was mystified by his inability to find his car. The mystery was only deepened by his explanation that "someday I may be able to tell you." It was years before she would know the story. Fortunately, he found the family car at first light the next day.

Deputy Chief of Staff Dawn Burton's story is my favorite. Around 7:00 P.M., with the boss gone for the night, she had been checking in with other staff members on the fourth-floor hall, trying to recruit a group to go have drinks. After being repeatedly told everyone was too busy, she retreated to her office to continue her own work. A short time later, a colleague burst into her office and said, "Grab your coat and meet us in the garage." "Yes!" she shouted and hurried to the garage. There, she was bustled into the backseat of a car packed with staff for a harrowing but silent drive to George Washington University Hospital. She ended up pacing with colleagues in the hall down from Ashcroft's room, with no idea why they were there. She made a last pitch for drinks as the group filed out of the hospital, but nobody had fun that night.

When I finally arrived home in the early morning hours of Thursday, March 11, the house was dark and quiet. Patrice and the five kids were long asleep. For days, Patrice knew I was struggling with a very hard problem, involving major conflict with the White House. I couldn't talk to her because any communication about classified topics requires that both parties have the appropriate clearance and a work-related need to know the information. She didn't have either. That separation from my family and closest friend added to my stress, as it does to many couples involved in classified work. I was sleeping little and deeply troubled, although she didn't know what it was about. I went into the kitchen to grab a snack. Patrice had printed out an excerpt from my Senate confirmation hearing — less than six months earlier. As she and the kids sat behind me that day, senators had pressed me on how as deputy attorney general I would handle conflict with the White House. The context for their questions was how I would handle politically controversial investigations, but she had taped part of my answer to the refrigerator door:

> I don't care about politics. I don't care about expediency. I don't care about friendship. I care about doing the right thing. And I would never be part of something that I believe to be fundamentally wrong. I mean, obviously we all make policy judgments where people disagree, but I will do the right thing.

I awoke only a few hours later to news that terrorists had attacked commuter trains in Madrid during the night. The day was consumed by those terrible attacks and our effort, in conjunction with the CIA and other intelligence agencies, to find out whether there were serious threats of similar plots in our own country. We met early at FBI headquarters, and then Director Mueller and I drove to the Oval Office threat briefing. We met with the president, the vice president, and their senior team. There was no mention of Stellar Wind.

After the briefing, I stopped Fran Townsend in the hallway. I had known Fran since our days as prosecutors in New York. She was now serving as National Security Adviser Condi Rice's deputy. Rice had not been at the Tuesday meeting with the vice president. Was it possible the national security adviser wasn't read into the Stellar Wind program? If she were read in now, I wondered, might she be a voice of reason?

I told Townsend that I wanted to say a term to her and I needed to know if her boss recognized the term. Fran looked confused, but I pressed on. "Stellar Wind," I said. "I need to know if she knows that term." She said she would find out. Later that day, Townsend called me to say her boss knew that term, was fully up to speed, and had nothing to add. I would get no help from Rice.

Back at Justice, Goldsmith and Philbin confirmed that the White House had gone silent on Stellar Wind. We waited. Late that afternoon, the two came to see me. The president had reauthorized the program despite our warnings. The new order had some significant differences. The line for the attorney general's signature had been removed and replaced with a line for White House Counsel Al Gonzales. Addington also added language to authorize NSA activity that had not been covered by his earlier drafts of the president's orders.

We were done here. I knew this would be my final night in government service. The same for Bob Mueller. Like me, he could not continue to serve in an administration that was going to direct the FBI to participate in activity that had no lawful basis.

I drafted a resignation letter and went home and told Patrice I was quitting the next day. Again, I had to leave out the particulars of why.

Friday, March 12, was a somber morning. I was up and gone before breakfast, so I didn't hear Patrice tell the kids, "Daddy may be getting a new job, but it is all going to be fine." Bob Mueller and I went through the motions at our usual early-morning terrorism threat session at FBI headquarters, then we drove together to the White House for the regular Oval Office threat briefing. We both stood silently looking out the window at the Rose Garden as we waited for the door by the grandfather clock to open so we could join the president's morning briefing. I was trying to memorize a view I would never see again. The door opened.

The meeting felt surreal. We talked about Madrid and Al Qaeda and everything other than the collision that was threatening to topple the administration. Then we got up and headed for the door. Mueller was ahead of me. I was just rounding the end of the couch, steps from the door, when I heard the president's voice.

"Jim," the president said, "can I talk to you for a minute?"

I turned back and President Bush led me across the Oval Office, down a short hall, and into the president's private dining room. We sat at a table with one chair on each of four sides; the president sat with his back to the windows and I took the chair nearest the door.

"You don't look well," the president began, adding, with typical bluntness, "We don't need anybody else dropping." One of my colleagues from another agency had fainted when leaving the West Wing a day or so earlier.

"I haven't been sleeping much," I confessed. "I feel a tremendous burden."

"Let me lift that burden from your shoulders," the president said.

"I wish you could, Mr. President. But you can't. I feel like I'm standing in the middle of railroad tracks. A train is coming that is going to run over me and my career, but I can't get off the tracks."

"Why?"

"Because we simply can't find a reasonable argument to support parts of the Stellar Wind program."

We then discussed the details of the

program and the problematic parts. I finished by saying, "We just can't certify to its legality."

"But I say what the law is for the executive branch," he replied.

"You do, sir. But only I can say what the Justice Department can certify as lawful. And we can't here. We have done our best, but as Martin Luther said, 'Here I stand. I can do no other.' "

"I just wish you hadn't sprung these objections on us at the last minute."

I was shocked. "If that's what you were told, Mr. President, you've been badly misled by your staff. We have been telling them about this for weeks."

He paused, as if digesting that revelation. "Can you just give me until May 6 so I can try to get a legislative fix? This program is really important. If I can't get it, I will shut it down."

"We can't do that, Mr. President. And we've been saying that for weeks."

I paused, took a breath, and then overstepped my role as a lawyer to offer policy advice to the president. "And Mr. President, I feel like I should say something else. The American people are going to freak when they find out what we have been doing."

He seemed irritated for the first time. "Let

me worry about that," he said sharply.

"Yes, sir. But I thought it had to be said."

He paused, and I knew our conversation was coming to an end. As I had told his chief of staff Wednesday night, I didn't believe in threatening resignation to win an argument. I thought the argument should be fought on the merits, and then people could decide whether to quit after the decision. It always felt like cheating to say you would take your ball and go home if you didn't get your way.

Still, I wanted to find a way to help Bush. This man, whom I liked and wanted to see succeed, appeared not to realize the storm that was coming. The entire Justice Department leadership was going to quit, and just as he was running for reelection. An uprising of that sort hadn't even happened during the worst days of Watergate. I had to tell him, to warn him, but I didn't want to break my rule. So I clumsily tried another approach.

"You should know that Bob Mueller is going to resign this morning," I said.

He paused again. "Thank you for telling me that." He extended his hand and showed me back to and across the Oval Office. I walked out past the clock and went immediately downstairs, where Bob Mueller stood waiting for me in the West Wing lower level. I had just started to describe my conversation with the president when a Secret Service agent approached to say that the president wanted to see Mueller upstairs, immediately.

Bob came down about ten minutes later. We went out to his armored Suburban and climbed in the back. He asked his driver to step out. (The driver later told me that he knew something was up because it was the first time in a decade of driving that he had been asked to step out.) He told me he and the president had covered much of the same ground. Bob confirmed to him that he could not stay as director under these circumstances and implored the president to listen to us. The president replied with a directive: "Tell Jim to do what needs to be done to get this to a place where Justice is comfortable."

That was all we needed, an order from the president. That took us around the vice president, Card, and Gonzales, and even around Addington and his safe full of secret orders. We headed back to the Justice Department, where we briefed our senior staff. Our first task was to get more good lawyers read in. Ted Olson was preparing for a Supreme Court argument, so his deputy, Paul Clement, was added to the team, as were more of those brilliant monks from the Office of Legal Counsel. CIA and NSA lawyers joined the team. Addington couldn't stop us from making the circle bigger.

The team worked all weekend to shape a new draft presidential order that narrowed the scope of the NSA's authority. I decided to send a classified memo to the White House summarizing the problems and our recommended fixes. That would make it a presidential record forever and answer in a formal way the president's direction to Mueller; this memo documented what needed to be done for Justice to be comfortable. It was a bit of a jerk move, because it created a permanent and complete record of all the ways they had been out of bounds, but the time to be a bit of a jerk was now. Goldsmith and Philbin hand-delivered the memo to Gonzales at home late Sunday night. It really pissed off some people at the White House.

On Tuesday, Gonzales called me to say a memo would be coming back to us from the White House. He asked me not to overreact and said the White House was committed to working with us. I don't know whether I *over*reacted, but I sure reacted, and very strongly. The memo was a big middle finger, clearly written by Addington. It said we were wrong about everything, and acting inappropriately by usurping presidential authority. It rejected all our proposed changes, saying they were unnecessary legally and factually. It said nothing about our mothers being whores, but it might as well have.

I pulled out my resignation letter and changed the date to March 16. Screw these people. They had just gone back on the president's directive to Bob Mueller and were leaving in place an unlawful order. I told Ashcroft's chief of staff that I was resigning, again. He asked me to wait. He was sure Ashcroft would want to quit with the rest of us, but he was still too ill. Could we give him a few days to get stronger? Of course. I put the letter back in my drawer.

Two days later, without notice, the president signed a new order. It incorporated all the changes we had requested. All the changes that the middle-finger letter said were unnecessary. The order said the president was making these changes for operational reasons. Not because we said he had to or because our interpretation of the law required it. That was childish, but we really didn't care. With that order, the program was now in a place where the Office of Legal Counsel could articulate reasonable arguments to support it, and they did, in a memo Goldsmith and Philbin and the new team members completed in early May.

The Stellar Wind crisis was over.

Now things would get really tough.

CHAPTER 7
CONFIRMATION BIAS

It ain't what you don't know that
gets you in trouble. It's what you
know for sure that just ain't so.
— MARK TWAIN

In April 2004, while Jack Goldsmith and
his team at Justice were still trying to put
the NSA surveillance program on firmer
legal footing, sickening images of prisoner
mistreatment at Abu Ghraib, a U.S. military
detention facility in Iraq, became public.
The pictures showed a small number of
American service members mistreating Iraqi
prisoners in horrific ways. Iraqi detainees
were put in humiliating positions — some
pictures showed prisoners hooded and
disrobed; one of the more memorable had
unclothed human beings stacked on top of
each other in a naked pyramid. There were
images of angry dogs being sicced on hand-
cuffed prisoners, and others of vulnerable

detainees being mocked and laughed at by American soldiers.

Very quickly a single word surfaced in the coverage to describe these acts: torture. Coming six or seven months before a competitive presidential election, the images took a devastating toll on the Bush administration. In nationally televised testimony before Congress, the secretary of defense offered public apologies to the detainees and their families and promised a thorough investigation into wrongdoing. The secretary of state compared the Abu Ghraib abuses to the My Lai massacre in Vietnam, an event that helped turn public opinion against the war. And there were more revelations still to come.

With the entire civilized world condemning the images of "torture" by the United States government, the CIA, understandably, became very nervous about a clandestine program of its own, under which the agency had beaten, starved, humiliated, and nearly drowned captives in 2002 and 2003. These were people the CIA believed had information about terrorist plots against the United States, and who were being held at so-called black sites outside of U.S. territory. At the start, in the summer of 2002, the CIA turned to the Department of

Justice to determine the limits of what it could do, legally, while interrogating these suspected terrorists in their custody.

In June 2004, two months after the Abu Ghraib photos surfaced, Jack Goldsmith came to me to explain his findings on the interrogation program. He had spotted serious problems six months earlier and told the intelligence agencies they could not rely on the earlier legal work, but now, with Stellar Wind fixed, he had completed his analysis and knew the Justice Department's opinions could not stand. As with the Stellar Wind program, he found that the earlier legal work supporting the interrogation program was deeply flawed. And as in Stellar Wind, he believed the agency was going beyond even what the flawed opinions allowed. This was another mess — one that, following Abu Ghraib, found itself all over the media after someone leaked a classified draft of Department of Justice guidance on torture. And it led to another battle within the Bush administration between a secret policy agenda and the rule of law.

In 1994, Congress had decided, as a legal matter, to define "torture" differently from how most of us understand the term. In ratifying the United Nations Convention

Against Torture, Congress defined "torture" for American law as the intentional infliction of severe mental or physical pain or suffering. There is a whole lot that most of us would call torture that falls short of "severe pain" or "severe suffering." Most of us would think that confining someone in a dark, coffinlike box or chaining them naked to the ceiling for days without sleep is torture. But the way Congress chose to define it, by requiring that the pain and suffering be "severe," a judge or lawyer could conclude those actions do not meet the legal definition of torture.

In 2002, after the 9/11 attacks, the CIA wanted to use coercive physical tactics to get captured Al Qaeda leaders to turn on other terrorist leaders, reveal plots, and, hopefully, save innocent lives. Agency officials asked the Justice Department's Office of Legal Counsel whether the interrogation tactics they had in mind — such as cramped confinement, sleep deprivation, and simulated drowning called "waterboarding" — would violate the law against torture. To be clear, they didn't ask Justice Department lawyers, "Is this a good idea?" They only asked them to outline what the boundaries of the law were.

As with the Stellar Wind program, the

Justice Department was asked to make these decisions during a time of crisis, when leaders feared more 9/11-style attacks were coming. The Justice Department lawyers were assured by CIA officials and others in the Bush administration that physically abusive interrogations of captured Al Qaeda leaders were not only effective but essential to saving countless innocent lives. Under that kind of pressure, and working almost entirely alone, a Justice Department lawyer — the same one who did the flawed Stellar Wind legal work — prepared a legal opinion interpreting the torture statute very broadly. He also issued a separate opinion saying the tactics the CIA had in mind for its first captured subject, Abu Zubaydah, did not constitute "torture" under the law. The CIA was cleared to use the full menu of tactics on Zubaydah, from slapping him and keeping him awake to making him think he was dying during waterboarding. By late 2003, when Jack Goldsmith became head of the Office of Legal Counsel and I became deputy attorney general, the CIA had already relied on that legal advice to aggressively interrogate suspects at various black sites outside the United States.

I wasn't looking forward to another ugly, draining fight against the same powerful faction in the White House. The fight over the surveillance program had been a stressful time, not just for me but also for my family. I thought I was going to lose my job. Patrice and I had a floating, interest-only mortgage on our home, and we were not in a good place financially as parents of five kids fast approaching college age. As the United States Attorney in Manhattan and as the number-two person in the Department of Justice — and later as FBI director — I made about what a first-year lawyer at a New York law firm was paid. Of course, plenty of people raise kids on that salary; we just hadn't planned well. But I agreed with Goldsmith that the legal opinion about torture was just wrong. So I went to Attorney General Ashcroft and, in a private meeting, told him why I believed it made sense to take the dramatic step of withdrawing the Justice Department's earlier opinion on the legality of these actions. He agreed.

We both recognized that it would leave CIA personnel exposed, in a sense, because they had done rough stuff in reliance on a legal opinion that was now withdrawn. The interrogators weren't lawyers; they had a right to rely on the advice of government counsel. But they had acted based on bad advice from the Justice Department, and that shouldn't continue. A new legal opinion had to be written that was legally sound and firmly grounded in the facts.

Though it was not our role to judge the program's value to the country, Goldsmith and I both were familiar with the world of FBI interrogations. The Bureau had long ago concluded that coercive interrogations were of no utility, the information obtained largely useless or unreliable. Instead, over decades, the FBI had perfected the art of "rapport-building interrogation" — forming a trusting relationship with those in its custody. The FBI had succeeded time after time in getting lifesaving and timely information from terrorists, mobsters, and serial killers. As a result, we were deeply skeptical of what we were told about the effectiveness of the CIA's coercive tactics. It struck me as the kind of stuff pushed by chicken hawks — aggressive-sounding administration officials who had seen plenty of movies but had never actually been in the storm.

The CIA leadership, and the powerful administration officials who backed them up, like Vice President Dick Cheney, held a starkly different view. They were driven by one of the most powerful and disconcerting forces in human nature — confirmation bias. Our brains have evolved to crave information consistent with what we already believe. We seek out and focus on facts and arguments that support our beliefs. More worrisome, when we are trapped in confirmation bias, we may not consciously perceive facts that challenge us, that are inconsistent with what we have already concluded. In a complicated, changing, and integrated world, our confirmation bias makes us very difficult people. We simply can't change our minds.

But there was more to it than biology. The president, the vice president, and those around them also labored under our political culture, where uncertainty is intolerable, where doubt is derided as weakness. Then and now, leaders feel a special pressure to be certain, a pressure that reinforces their natural confirmation bias.

Of course, in a healthy organization, doubt is not weakness, it is wisdom, because people are at their most dangerous when they are certain that their cause is just and their facts are right. And I'm not talking about finger-in-the-wind, I'm-afraid-to-make-a-decision kind of doubt. Decisions have to be made, often quickly, even the hardest decisions. And the hardest ones always seem to need to be made the fastest and on the least information. But those decisions must be made with the recognition that they could be wrong. That humility leaves the leader open to better information until the last possible moment.

In fairness to the president and vice president, our modern culture makes this incredibly hard for leaders — especially those in government — even if they possess enough confidence to be humble. Admitting doubt or mistakes is career suicide. And that's the way we want it, right? We want strong, certain leaders. Imagine supporting a leader who, as he finished his time at the helm, told us that, although he didn't do anything intentionally wrong, he is sure he made many mistakes, prays his mistakes haven't hurt people, and hopes we will forgive and forget the times when he was incompetent. That weakling would be run out of town on a rail. But America's first president said exactly that in his farewell to the country in 1796:

Though, in reviewing the incidents of my administration, I am unconscious of intentional error, I am nevertheless too sensible of my defects not to think it probable that I may have committed many errors. Whatever they may be, I fervently beseech the Almighty to avert or mitigate the evils to which they may tend. I shall also carry with me the hope that my country will never cease to view them with indulgence; and that, after forty five years of my life dedicated to its service with an upright zeal, the faults of incompetent abilities will be consigned to oblivion, as myself must soon be to the mansions of rest.

In the Bush administration, Dick Cheney, David Addington, and others had decided that "enhanced interrogations" — acts that fit any normal person's definition of torture — worked. They simply couldn't admit that evidence contradicting their conclusion was valid, maybe most of all to themselves. And so, in their view, people standing in the way of allowing these activities — lawyers like me — were needlessly putting lives at risk.

I understood why people like Vice President Cheney were frustrated when the Department of Justice changed its legal opinions. But much of the responsibility for the original flawed legal work could be laid at the feet of policymakers like the vice president — powerful leaders who were absolutely certain what needed to be done and who demanded quick answers from a tiny group of lawyers. Their actions guaranteed the very problems we were forced to deal with down the road.

From my perspective, it was simple. The United States Department of Justice had made serious legal mistakes in advising the president and his administration about surveillance and interrogation. If the institution was to continue to be useful to the country and its presidents — including President Bush — the department simply had to fix its errors. To do otherwise, even in the face of angry leaders, would mean the Justice Department had become just another member of the partisan tribe, willing to say what needed to be said to help our side win.

It makes good sense that the leaders of the Department of Justice are appointed by the president, with the advice and consent of the Senate. The department has important discretion on policy questions — like what kinds of crimes to prioritize or how to approach antitrust disputes — and should be responsive in its policy choices to the will of the people, expressed through election of the president. But there is a tension in having political leaders atop the Justice Department, because the administration of justice must be evenhanded.

The Constitution and the rule of law are not partisan political tools. Lady Justice wears a blindfold. She is not supposed to peek out to see how her political master wishes her to weigh a matter.

There is a place I have visited on the coast of North Carolina where two barrier islands come close together. In the narrow passageway between them, the waters of the Atlantic Ocean meet the waters of the huge and shallow sound that lies behind the islands. There is turbulence in that place and waves appear to break even though no land is visible. I imagine that the leaders of the Department of Justice stand at that spot, between the turbulent waters of the political world and the placid waters of the apolitical sound. Their job is to respond to the political imperatives of the president and the voters who elected him, while also protecting the apolitical work of the thousands of agents, prosecutors, and staff who make up the bulk of the institution. So long as the leaders understand the turbulence, they can find their footing. If they stumble, the ocean water overruns the sound and the department has become just another political organ. Its independent role in American life has been lost and the guardians of justice have drowned.

One evening after work in spring 2004, Patrice looked at me. She obviously knew I was involved in something that was wearing me down. She had seen all the media coverage of the treatment of captives. She simply said to me, "Torture is wrong. Don't be the torture guy."

"What?" I protested. "You know I can't talk about that stuff."

"I don't want to talk about it," she said. "Just don't be the torture guy." She would periodically repeat that admonition over the next year.

The prospect of being the "torture guy" disturbed my sleep for many nights. I couldn't get away from the mental pictures of naked men chained to the ceiling in a cold, blazingly lit cell for endless days, defecating in their diapers, unchained only to be further abused and convinced they were drowning, before being rechained.

In June 2004, Goldsmith, with my support, formally withdrew the Department of Justice legal opinions that had supported the 2002 and 2003 interrogations. True to form, the vice president's counsel, David Addington, was furious. At a meeting I didn't attend, he pulled out a card he said listed all the classified opinions Justice had written since 9/11 and sarcastically asked Goldsmith to tell him which ones Justice still stood by. I reminded Goldsmith that

Addington's anger was an increasingly reliable indicator that we were on the right track. I don't think my assessment made Jack feel any better. Nor did Patrick Philbin take any comfort in the thought. Addington spoke to Philbin privately and told him that, based on the withdrawal of the Stellar Wind and torture legal opinions, Addington believed Philbin had violated his oath to support and defend the Constitution of the United States. He suggested that Philbin resign and vowed that he personally would prevent him from being promoted anywhere else in the government.

Jack Goldsmith was a step ahead of him. After nine months as head of the Office of Legal Counsel, Jack's cherubic glow was gone. He had been through brutal battles over electronic surveillance and interrogation. At the same moment as he withdrew the torture opinion, he announced he was leaving to return to academia.

Reworking the interrogation advice would fall to Dan Levin, the new acting head of the Office of Legal Counsel. Levin was another gifted and careful lawyer, with a somber look that masked a dark sense of humor. There was nothing cherubic about Levin. In an earlier role supporting Bob Mueller at the FBI, where Mueller was called "the director," Levin, with his gloomy countenance, was privately referred to as "the funeral director." Levin threw himself into the huge job of reworking the legal guidance supporting so-called enhanced interrogations. I didn't know it at the time, but he quite literally threw himself into it — undergoing the simulated drowning technique known as waterboarding. He later told me it was the worst experience of his life.

In late December 2004, Levin and the Office of Legal Counsel finally finished the interrogation opinion. It was an impressive piece of scholarship — careful, thoughtful, tethered tightly to the CIA's statements about how things actually worked. It did something significant that was overlooked by most people who read the lengthy, unclassified opinion. Levin concluded that intentionally inflicting severe *mental* suffering was a separate category of prohibited conduct under the law against torture. This was a big deal. The original 2002 Justice opinions had focused largely on defining severe *physical* pain. Suddenly, it was obvious (to me and Levin, at least) that the accumulation of CIA techniques could quickly become illegal because mental suffering was a broad category. Taking a naked, cold, severely sleep-deprived and calorie-deprived person, slamming him against a wall, putting him in stress positions, slapping him around, waterboarding him, and then sticking him in a small box could easily produce great mental suffering, especially if the CIA did those things more than once.

There were two additional opinions that needed to follow Levin's general opinion. First, each of the CIA's techniques needed to be evaluated individually under the standards Levin had announced. That would be fairly straightforward, because a single technique, viewed in isolation, was unlikely to cause severe physical pain or severe mental suffering. The second opinion would be the whole ball game. In that one, the CIA and White House wanted to apply Levin's standards to the "combined effects" of all the techniques. They needed this because nobody was interrogated using just one technique. At actual black sites, they did a whole lot of brutal stuff to their subjects. Those actions could add up very quickly to the prohibited severe mental suffering. It was going to be difficult to sustain the program once Justice was asked to evaluate combined effects.

Levin worked long hours trying to document exactly what was going on at these black-site interrogations. To support the 2002 legal opinion, the interrogations had been presented to the Department of Justice as if they were highly regulated and conducted in almost surgical, clinical environments. Although Levin had moved heaven and earth in 2004 to nail down exactly what was going on, it was still like nailing Jell-O to the wall; he got it up there, but it sure looked shaky.

I never asked Dan Levin this, but I suspect he shared my hope that the entire CIA interrogation program would crater under the weight of these requirements. But this, of course, was not what we were asked to do. Justice Department lawyers were only being asked to provide legal opinions based on factual representations from the CIA. Although our internal voices screamed that this was terrible stuff and was based on inflated claims of success, those voices had to stay trapped inside us. But I heard one voice many times. "Don't be the torture guy," it said.

After George W. Bush won reelection in 2004, John Ashcroft had gone through the motions, like all cabinet officers, of tendering his resignation letter to the president. The tradition allowed the president flexibility to change his administration for a new term. But the hope was that cabinet officers who performed well would be asked to stay. To Ashcroft's surprise, the president accepted his resignation. To add to the sting, Bush gave Ashcroft just a few hours' notice before publicly announcing his successor. The person he had in mind as a replacement was another slap at all of us at Justice.

On November 10, 2004, President Bush announced that his pick to be the next attorney general of the United States was Alberto Gonzales. I was getting a new boss who had actively opposed what I viewed as the department's responsibility to enforce the law as it was written, not as the administration wanted it to be. One who seemed to prefer satisfying his boss more than focusing on hard truths. I don't know why Bush picked Gonzales, but I suspect it was the age-old presidential mistake I would try, years later, to warn Donald Trump about — because "problems" often come from Justice, some presidents think they will benefit from a close relationship with the attorney general. It almost always makes things worse.

Later that day, I was home for Patrice's birthday when my cell phone rang. To my surprise, Gonzales was on the line. He said he was calling to tell me he really looked forward to working with me and hoped I would stay because he would need the help. I congratulated him on his appointment and said I looked forward to working with him. It seemed like the right thing to say, and I had nothing against Gonzales personally, despite the challenges we had been through. If he was going to be attorney general, I wanted to help him succeed. My main concern was not that he was evil, but that he was weak and would easily be over-matched by Addington and Cheney and their view that the war on terrorism justi-fied stretching, if not breaking, the written law.

I found out later that President Bush called Gonzales immediately after the an-nouncement and suggested that he call me. I didn't realize it at the time, but after what I knew — and had not talked about — from the Ashcroft hospital scene, I was something of a loaded gun in the Bush administration's eyes, one that could go off at any moment. Because I was a loaded weapon, they han-dled me with care, but it was obvious to me that serving as Gonzales's deputy was not the right thing for me. In the spring of 2005, I announced I would be leaving that August. We had a new attorney general who needed his own deputy, I reasoned. I was tired and disappointed with the choice of my new boss. Without the support of Ashcroft, I didn't have the stomach for what were certain to be more losing battles within the administration. More important, my financial situation had not improved and our oldest was headed to college. It was time to leave. I sent the president my resignation letter, making it effective in August to ensure a responsible transition.

Just as I was preparing to leave the Department of Justice, Vice President Cheney began leaning on Gonzales to produce the two remaining opinions he needed on interrogation policies. In addition to a new attorney general, the Justice Department also had a new acting leader of the Office of Legal Counsel, a bright and affable lawyer named Stephen Bradbury. Steve, who had no background in national security matters, wanted to be formally nominated for the job and he was being pushed to produce the two opinions the way Cheney's tribe wanted. Patrick Philbin and I were disappointed to see that his opinions were overbroad, untethered to an actual case, and, to our minds, deeply irresponsible.

We had suggested Bradbury consider the actual, recent case of someone who had been interrogated by the CIA. We knew of a terrorist who had recently been in CIA custody and whose interrogation was finished. We suggested he describe precisely what had been done to that captive, and then offer an opinion as to whether that actual, real-world combination of actions crossed the legal threshold. That was the only way to responsibly give an opinion. And, as it happened, this actual case was one where, given what we understood had been done to that guy, we did not think it would add up to severe pain or suffering as the statute defined it and the Department of Justice interpreted that statute, even though anyone in their right mind would say the man had been tortured. But even though the opinion would likely approve what had been done to that prisoner, that wasn't what the vice president wanted. He wanted Bradbury to rule on the legality of a hypothetical scenario — a "typical" interrogation — not what the CIA actually was doing to a real human being.

I met with Attorney General Gonzales to explain to him why I thought it was so irresponsible to write a hypothetical opinion that way — and immediately saw the difference between the attorney general I knew and respected, John Ashcroft, and his replacement. Wearily, Gonzales complained that the vice president was putting enormous pressure on him and that Cheney had even prompted the president to ask when the opinions would be ready. I said that I understood the pressure, but there were no prototypical interrogations. They all involved real interrogators reacting to real subjects, slapping them, chilling them, cramping them, and on and on, in permutations and combinations that were all unique. It was impossible to write a forward-looking opinion without making it look like Justice was writing a blank check. Someday when all this came out, I warned him, it would look like the attorney general had just caved in response to White House pressure and done something we would all deeply regret.

If one thing motivates people in Washington, it's being on the receiving end of bad headlines. And on that thought, Gonzales paused. It wasn't clear to me that this had ever occurred to him. "I agree with you, Jim," he said. He instructed me to work with Bradbury to try to fix the approach.

My relief proved short-lived. The next evening, I spoke by telephone with Gonzales's chief of staff. He told me the interrogation opinions were to be formalized and sent the next day. There was no more time.

I reminded him that the attorney general had told me the opposite only the day before. His chief of staff told me things had changed.

Bradbury finalized and signed both opinions, as he and the White House wanted it. A week after that, the White House began the background check process to formally nominate him as assistant attorney general. The legal battle was over.

Now that we were no longer acting as lawyers on the torture question, I felt free to do what I hadn't done before. I went to the attorney general to seek permission to request a policy review of the entire program by the National Security Council. Typically this would lead to a full review by what is called the NSC's Deputies Committee, of which I was a member, along with the deputies of the other relevant departments and agencies in the Bush administration. The deputies would frequently hash out policy issues and tough questions before their bosses grasped the issues personally. I knew I could make my case in that setting. We would have an honest, administration-wide discussion of whether we should be doing this stuff to human beings. Unfortunately, I never got that chance.

The next thing I knew, strangely, the

policy discussion on torture was elevated from the Deputies Committee to the Principals Committee, comprised only of the top leadership of the major defense and intelligence agencies — such as the secretary of defense, secretary of state, CIA director, and attorney general. That meant my team and I would have to prepare Gonzales to voice our concerns for us — because nobody else from Justice was allowed to go with him. Oh boy.

As Pat Philbin and I sat down to prepare Gonzales for the May 31, 2005, White House policy discussion, the attorney general began by showing us the writing on the wall. He said Condi Rice, who had been national security adviser when the interrogation program was conceived and was now the secretary of state, replacing Colin Powell, "was not interested in discussing the details." He added that Rice believed, "If Justice says it's legal and CIA says it's effective, that ends it. There is no need for a detailed policy discussion."

Knowing I'd never be able to plead the case to others on the National Security Council, Philbin and I did our best to buck up Gonzales to make the case on the department's behalf. We protested that just because something was deemed to be legal —

based on an opinion we disagreed with — and allegedly effective did not mean it was appropriate. I again reminded him, and hoped he would remind the others in the cabinet, that someday the interrogation methods used, and the shaky legal support for them, would all become public — adding that I had heard there was a videotape of one of these CIA interrogations — and this would reflect very poorly on the president and the country.

Then I showed Gonzales a heavy-stock, cream-colored three-by-five card I'd compiled. On it I had written a list of the things that could be done to another human being under the CIA program as currently written and authorized by the Gonzales Justice Department. Reading from the card, I painted a picture for him of a human being standing naked for days in a cold room with hands chained overhead to the ceiling, defecating and urinating in his diaper, engulfed in deafening heavy metal music, and spending hours under a constant bright light. He is then unchained to be slapped in the face and abdomen, slammed against a wall, sprayed with cold water, and then, even though weak from a severely reduced-calorie liquid diet, made to stand and squat in positions that put extreme stress on his muscles and tendons. When he can't move any longer, he will be put in a coffin-sized box for hours before being returned to the ceiling chain. And, of course, in special cases, he may be made to believe he is drowning on the waterboard.

"That's what this is," I told the attorney general, holding the card aloft. "The details matter." I urged him to make sure that all of the principals on the National Security Council stared at those details while deciding our country's future interrogation policy.

Gonzales paused for a long time, as he often did. He then thanked me for coming to him with this and asked whether he could keep my card with the handwritten list, so he could use it at the meeting. I handed it to him and left, praying that I had made a difference.

I heard nothing immediately after the Principals Committee meeting. Late in the afternoon, I attended a meeting on sentencing policy with the attorney general and others. In front of the others, unprompted, the attorney general told me the White House meeting had gone very well, that he had told them just what I had asked, but all the principals were entirely supportive of the current interrogation policy and all parts of it.

No policy changes were made. CIA enhanced interrogations could continue. Human beings in the custody of the United States government would be subjected to harsh and horrible treatment. And I never got my card back. I left government service two months later. I was never going to return.

CHAPTER 8
IN HOOVER'S SHADOW

The supreme quality for leadership
is unquestionably integrity. Without it,
no real success is possible, whether it is
on a section gang, a football field,
in an army, or in an office.
— DWIGHT D. EISENHOWER

On the first day of summer in 2013, I found myself where I never thought I'd be again.

On the bright day when President Barack Obama announced my nomination in the Rose Garden to replace FBI Director Bob Mueller, the president, Mueller, and I stood alone in the Oval Office, waiting to walk out the glass door and into the garden, where the White House press pool already had gathered.

As we turned to step into view of the cameras, the president stopped us. With a serious look on his face, Obama turned to me and said, "Jim, there's one thing I forgot to talk to you about."

While I looked confused, the president nodded toward Mueller. "Bob long ago made a commitment to me, and I need you to honor it." What could this possibly be? The president had assured me of my independence. Now I was being asked for secret assurances?

The president paused to signal the gravity of the moment. Then he went on. "Bob has always allowed me to use the FBI gym to play basketball, and I need you to commit to continuing that."

I laughed. "Of course, Mr. President. It *is* your gym, in a way."

Though I love basketball, I knew I would never join him in the FBI gym. I also love golf, but knew we would never play. FBI directors can't be that way with presidents. Everybody knows why. Or at least I thought they did.

After leaving the Bush Justice Department in August 2005, I worked in the private sector. With five kids approaching college at about two-year intervals and fifteen years of government salary that hadn't exactly been conducive to saving, it was time to save some money. I went to work as the chief lawyer — general counsel — at the defense contractor Lockheed Martin for five years, and then at an investment firm called Bridgewater Associates in Connecticut for three years. In early 2013, I left Bridgewater and joined the faculty at Columbia Law School as a fellow focused on national security, because I have always found teaching deeply rewarding.

That March, Attorney General Eric Holder called out of the blue to ask whether I would interview for FBI director. He wasn't guaranteeing me the job, but said he wouldn't be calling personally if I wasn't going to be very seriously considered.

I was surprised. Maybe it was because I had become so hardened to the tribal loyalties of Washington, D.C., that it was difficult to believe a Democrat would choose someone who had been a political appointee of his Republican predecessor for such an important post. I also was on record as having financially contributed to President Obama's political opponents.

I was cold to the idea. It would be too much for my family. I didn't tell him why I said that, but Patrice was in graduate school and working as a counselor at a walk-in mental health clinic in Bridgeport; one of our kids was a senior in high school; and we were foster parents with continuing connections and obligations to young people who had been in our home. Holder asked me to think about it. I told him I would sleep on it, but the answer was likely to be no.

I woke up the next morning and Patrice was missing from our bedroom. I went downstairs and found her in the kitchen on her laptop. She was looking at houses for sale in the Washington, D.C., area.

"What are you doing?" I asked.

"I've known you since you were nineteen. This is who you are, this is what you love. So go down there and do your best." Then she paused and added, "But they're not going to pick you anyway." She liked President Obama and had voted for him, but she still thought this was just an exercise. Her interest, she later confessed, was in not having my sad face moping around for years afterward talking about what might have been. She, like me, doubted he'd pick someone who'd worked in the Bush administration.

After preliminary interviews with his staff, I met President Obama in the Oval Office. He sat in the same position President Bush always had — in an armchair with his back to the fireplace, on the side closest to the grandfather clock. I sat on the couch to his left, on the cushion closest to him. We were joined by the White House counsel, Kathy Ruemmler, who sat across from me.

I had never met President Obama before and was struck by two things: how much thinner he appeared in person and his ability to focus. As Ruemmler and I stood just outside the Oval Office waiting for the meeting to begin, I could see the president standing at his desk holding the phone. Kathy said he was talking with the governor of Oklahoma about the historic tornadoes that had torn through that state, killing two dozen people and injuring hundreds. Obama hung up the phone, waved me into the room, spoke briefly about the terrible tragedy in Oklahoma, and then shifted entirely to the new subject — the FBI.

The president was almost grave in explaining why he took the selection of the FBI director so seriously. "In a way, this and the Supreme Court are the two most important personnel decisions a president makes, because I'm choosing for the future," he said. "You will be here after I'm gone." He said he thought there was great value in that long tenure and hoped that if I were the director, I could help a new president. For example, he said he had been pushed to make military decisions as a new and inexperienced president and under great pressure from military leaders. Without saying so, he seemed to be expressing regret that he didn't have the experienced counsel around him that he needed at the time. He thought it was good that I would be around to help a future, perhaps similarly inexperienced leader think about national security decisions better.

We talked about the natural tension between the need to investigate leaks of classified information and the need to support a free press. Recent Department of Justice efforts to investigate leak cases were much in the news at that point and the press was assailing the alleged "Obama administration crackdown." We didn't talk about particular cases, but I shared my view that the balance could be struck by thoughtful leadership; it simply was not sustainable to say the investigators would never seek information from reporters, and it was an exaggeration to say that we couldn't have a free press if we investigated leaks. We could protect a free press and classified information at the same time.

What surprised me most — and led me in the moment to realize Patrice was likely wrong about this being a waste of time — was the president's view of the FBI job. It turns out he had a different conception of the FBI director than either I or most partisans assumed. He said, "I don't want help from the FBI on policy. I need competence and independence. I need to sleep at night knowing the place is well run and the American people protected." Contrary to my assumption, the fact that I was politically independent from him might actually have worked in my favor.

I replied that I saw it the same way. The FBI should be independent and totally divorced from politics, which was what the ten-year term for a director was designed to ensure.

After my meeting with President Obama, I called Patrice with the wise-ass comment, "Your faith in their poor judgment may be misplaced." Feeling good about my conversation with Obama, I agreed to the nomination when it was offered. My family would stay in Connecticut for two years to wind up all the things they were involved in, but I fully intended to serve as director of the FBI through the year 2023. What, I wondered, could possibly interfere with that?

After deciding I was his choice, but before he announced the nomination, President Obama surprised me by inviting me back to the Oval Office. We sat in the same seats and were again joined by the White House counsel. The president opened the conversation by explaining, "Once you are director, we won't be able to talk like this." What he meant was that for over forty years, the leaders of our government had understood that a president and an FBI director must be at arm's length. The FBI is often called upon to investigate cases that touch on the president's senior aides and affect the course of his presidency. To be credible — both in reality and in perception — the FBI and its director cannot be close with the president. So one final time, President Obama and I had the kind of conversation two college classmates might. We discussed and debated hard issues that were not under the FBI director's purview, like using drones to kill terrorists. I was struck by the way he could see and evaluate a variety of angles on a complicated issue. And I suppose he wanted to make one last assessment of me and the way I thought through problems before my nomination was a done deal.

On the way out the door, I told Kathy Ruemmler how surprised I was by the interesting discussion, telling her, "I can't believe someone with such a supple mind actually got elected president."

President Obama and I would never have another casual conversation.

■ ■ ■ ■

Before I took the job, the FBI had had only six directors since 1935, when it was officially named as the Federal Bureau of Investigation. Its first, the legendary J. Edgar Hoover, had led the organization for nearly fifty years (including its predecessor organization, the Bureau of Investigation) and built a culture around himself that profoundly shaped the Bureau and its agents. For decades, Hoover used an iron hand to drive the agency and strike fear in the hearts of political leaders. He had "personal files" on many of them, something he let them know. He dined and drank with presidents and senators, letting them use the FBI when it suited him, and frightening them with the FBI when that suited him.

Inside the FBI, the director was the absolute center. His approach brought tremendous fame, attention, and power to the organization. It also created an environment in which the goal of most agents and supervisors in the FBI was to avoid being noticed by Mr. Hoover. Tell him what he wants to hear, then get on with your work. That mentality was hard to displace, even decades after Hoover's death.

Before I was sworn in as FBI director in 2013, I spent a week shadowing Bob Mueller. Bob, a former marine, was a bit old-school as director, not given to what he saw as touchy-feely stuff. In the grueling days immediately after September 11, 2001, for example, his wife had prodded Bob to be sure his people were holding up under the stress. Early the next morning, or so I was told, he dutifully telephoned key members of his staff — whose offices were all within a ten-second walk of his — asking, "How're you doing?" When each offered the perfunctory reply of "Fine, sir," he replied, "Good," and hung up.

Mueller was characteristically disciplined about preparing me to follow him as director. During the first morning of my week of shadowing, he explained that he had arranged for me to talk with the leaders of the FBI's major divisions. I was to meet with them one-on-one, he said, and they would each brief me on their area's challenges and opportunities. Then, Mueller explained, without a hint of a smile, he would meet with me after each of these sessions, "to tell you what's really going on." That comment rocked me. The FBI is an institution devoted to finding the truth. Why would the director need to tell me "what's really going on" after each meeting? The assumption in Bob's comment was that senior officials either weren't aware of what was happening at the FBI or weren't going to be truthful to me, their new boss, about it. My guess was the latter.

Many people, in my experience, hesitate to tell the whole truth and nothing but the truth to their bosses — and for reasons that may make sense. I could hear the voices of jaded FBI veterans channeling a character in the movie *The Departed:* "What's the upside to doing that? It can only hurt you. Bosses are like mushrooms; you keep 'em in the dark and feed 'em shit." I admired Bob and marveled at the way he had transformed the FBI in the aftermath of 9/11, driving the organization to break down walls, overcome its heritage as solely a detective culture, and become a fully integrated member of the intelligence community. Bob had proven that it would be a mistake to break the FBI into a criminal investigative agency and a counterterrorism agency by making the FBI great at both. I was in awe of what he had done, but I also wanted to signal a more open style of leadership.

I was officially sworn in as the seventh director of the FBI on September 4, 2013.

After delays caused by a congressional budget fight — complete with a shutdown of the federal government for lack of funds — we held a public installation at FBI headquarters in October. President Obama was present at the ceremony, and I caught an early glimpse at what made him a compelling leader.

Patrice and our kids were, of course, in attendance at the ceremony. My two older girls had brought their serious boyfriends along, and we all joined the president for a commemorative photo of the occasion. Remembering what he had learned about our group during the introductions, President Obama smiled for the first photo and then, gesturing toward the boyfriends, said, "Hey, why don't we take another without the guys. You know, just in case." He was playful as he said it, and he did it in a way that no one was offended. But I could tell he was also being thoughtful in a way few leaders are. What if things didn't work out with one or the other of these guys? Would having them in a picture with the president ruin it for the Comeys forever? So Obama gestured the boyfriends out of the shot, to our great amusement. (I'm happy to report that one of the guys is now our son-in-law and the other soon will be.)

Though it was a small moment, what struck me about President Obama's remark is that it displayed a sense of humor, insight, and an ability to connect with an audience, which I would later come to appreciate in the president even more. These are all qualities that are indispensable in good leaders. A sense of humor in particular strikes me as an important indicator — or "tell" — about someone's ego. Having a balance of confidence and humility is essential to effective leadership. Laughing in a genuine way requires a certain level of confidence, because we all look a little silly laughing; that makes us vulnerable, a state insecure people fear. And laughing is also frequently an appreciation of others, who have said something that is funny. That is, you didn't say it, and by laughing you acknowledge the other, something else insecure people can't do.

President Bush had a good sense of humor, but often at other people's expense. He teased people in a slightly edgy way, which seemed to betray some insecurity in his personality. His teasing was used as a way to ensure that the hierarchy in his relationship with others was understood, a strange thing given that he was president of the United States, and it was a sure way to deter his people from challenging the leader's reasoning.

President Obama could laugh with others, and, as with President Bush, poke fun at himself in some circumstances, such as when Bush told fellow "C students" at a commencement address, "you, too, can be president of the United States." Unlike Bush, though, I never saw a belittling edge to Obama's humor, which in my view reflected his confidence.

The FBI director's job is much broader than may be apparent from the outside, or as depicted in the movies, where most of the director's work seems entirely focused on individual cases and capturing bad guys. The director is the CEO of an extraordinarily complex organization. Each day began very early, when the director's protective detail would pick me up for the drive to work. Though I had a security detail of Deputy U.S. Marshals when I served as deputy attorney general during the Bush administration, my new team was made up of specially trained FBI special agents and was much larger and more intense, because the threat to the FBI director is greater.

Like the U.S. Marshals who protected me as deputy attorney general, the special agents who watched over me and my family became family. Which is a good thing, because we tested them as only relatives can. Once we were in Iowa for a wedding on Patrice's side. I went to bed while Patrice stayed up late playing cards with our kids and their cousins. As it typically was, my hotel room was alarmed in all kinds of ways, and all around me in the hotel were agents. And as they typically did, the agents gave me a device with a button to push in the event of dire emergency. I was afraid of this thing and always put it far away from me in a hotel room, so I didn't accidentally touch it during the night. This night, I put it on a countertop in the outer room and went to sleep in the bedroom, far away from it.

I didn't tell Patrice I had put the button on the counter in the outer room, the exact place where she was changing quietly at 2:00 A.M. so as not to wake me. She must have put something on top of the button, because there was pounding on the door about five seconds later. She opened the door a crack to see the lead agent standing at an odd angle, wearing a T-shirt and boxer shorts. He was holding his arm so she couldn't see his hand behind his back. He looked very tense.

"Is everything all right, ma'am?"

"Yes. I'm just getting ready for bed."

"Are you sure everything is all right, ma'am?"

"Yes."

"Can I see the director, ma'am?"

"He's sleeping in the other room."

"Will you check on him, please?"

Patrice walked to the bedroom door, saw me, and reported back. "I see him there sleeping. He's fine."

"Thank you, ma'am. Sorry to bother you."

What Patrice couldn't see, but I learned the next morning, was that there were agents stacked down the wall on either side of the door, guns held low and behind their backs. She had touched the button. My bad.

The FBI boasts a strong gun culture. Guns, in the hands of the good guys, were a regular feature of FBI life. In every staff meeting, 80 percent of the attendees had a gun on them. I eventually grew accustomed to seeing a pistol in an ankle holster when the deputy director crossed his legs during a meeting. After all, the deputy director is the senior special agent in the organization and is always armed, except when he goes to the White House. As director, I too was permitted to carry a gun, but I figured that would only complicate my life. Bob Mueller had seen it the same way. Besides, I was surrounded by armed people all day long. If I wasn't safe in the hands of the FBI, then our country was really in trouble. Sean Joyce, who served as my first deputy director, became famous in the organization for hitting "reply all" when some bureaucrat within the Bureau sent an all-employee message instructing personnel to shelter in place or flee in the event of an "active shooter" in the workplace. Sean replied that any special agent who took that advice and hid or failed to run *toward* an active shooter would be fired.

On my morning drives to work, I would read in the back of the fully armored black Suburban, preparing myself for the first two meetings of the day. But before any meetings, I would sit at my desk and read more, starting with the applications the Department of Justice was submitting to the court for electronic surveillance in FBI national security cases. Each application must be personally approved by the director or, in his absence, the deputy director. I would review the inch-thick applications, pulling from a stack that, on many mornings, was a foot high. After reviewing and signing the applications, I would read my classified intelligence briefing, bringing me up to speed on intelligence relevant to the FBI's missions to prevent terrorism and defeat foreign intelligence threats in the United States. Then I would read unclassified material relevant to our many other responsibilities. With that homework done, I was ready to meet my senior team, starting with the six to ten most senior people to discuss the most sensitive classified matters, followed by a meeting where more of the FBI's leaders were admitted.

I would ask the group questions and get their morning reports on subjects that covered the FBI's span: personnel (including injuries to our agents), budget, counterterrorism, counterintelligence, weapons of mass destruction, cyber, criminal cases (including kidnapping, serial-killer, gang, and corruption cases), Hostage Rescue Team deployments, congressional affairs, press, legal, training, the FBI lab, international affairs, and on and on. Most days I would then go meet with the attorney general to brief her, or him, on the most important matters.

During the Obama administration, I worked with two attorneys general — Eric Holder and Loretta Lynch. They were each intelligent and personable lawyers and I liked them both. Holder was close to President Obama and his senior team, and very attentive to the policy and political implications of the department's work. By the time I became director, his relationship with Republicans in Congress was toxic, with the Republican-led House of Representatives having voted to hold him in contempt for his failure to provide information to their satisfaction about an ATF gun-trafficking investigation on the southwest border, known as "Fast and Furious." The feeling of contempt seemed to be mutual.

Loretta Lynch was much quieter and new to Washington. She spoke little and when she did, frequently seemed tightly scripted. It always takes time to become comfortable in a high-profile job; I'm not sure Lynch's brief tenure gave her that time. And where Holder had a close working relationship with his deputy attorney general, Lynch's relationship with Deputy Attorney General Sally Yates seemed distant and strained. It was as if they and their staffs simply didn't talk to each other.

My days were consumed by both emergencies and the disciplined execution of priority programs. I was trying to transform the way the FBI approached leadership, cyber, diversity, and intelligence, among other things, which required regular CEO — or director — focus to drive them forward. And the FBI is also an international enterprise, with people in every state and more than eighty other countries. That meant I needed to travel to see, listen to, and speak to the people of the FBI.

In my first fifteen months as director, I visited all fifty-six FBI offices in the United States and more than a dozen overseas. I went there to listen and learn about the people of the FBI. What are they like, what do they want, what do they need? I spent hours and hours meeting them and listening to them. The first thing that struck me was that two-thirds of the FBI's employees are not gun-carrying special agents. They are an extraordinarily diverse array of talented people, from all walks of life, serving in the FBI as intelligence analysts, linguists, computer scientists, hostage negotiators, surveillance specialists, lab experts, victim specialists, bomb technicians, and in many other roles. The one-third who are special agents, especially the thousands who were drawn by love of country after 9/11 to service in the FBI, are similarly diverse: former cops and marines, but also former teachers, chemists, therapists, clergy, accountants, software engineers, and professional athletes. Many of them look like TV special agents — tall, attractive men and women in business dress — but they come in all shapes and sizes, from crew cuts to ponytails, from ankle tattoos to hijabs, from six foot ten to four foot ten. What drives them all is a palpable sense of mission. They helped me rewrite the organization's mission statement to match what was already written on their hearts: they exist to "protect the American people and uphold the Constitution of the United States."

I was amazed at the talent, but I was frightened by one trend. The special agent workforce since 9/11 had been growing steadily more white. When I became director, 83 percent of the special agents were non-Hispanic Caucasians. As I explained to the workforce, I had no problem with white people, but that trend is a serious threat to our effectiveness. In a country that is growing more diverse, which, in my view, is wonderful, if every agent looks like me, we are less effective. Eighty-three percent could become 100 percent very quickly, if the FBI became known as "that place where white people work." I told the workforce that the challenge and the opportunity were captured in something one of my daughters said when I told her about our diversity crisis. "The problem, Dad, is that you are The Man. Who wants to work for The Man?"

My daughter was right, but also wrong. Because if people knew what the men and women of the FBI are really like, and what the work is really like, they would want to be a part of it. Almost nobody leaves the FBI after becoming a special agent. Whether white or black, Latino or Asian, male or female, the annual turnover is about the same — 0.5 percent. Once people experience the environment and the mission at the FBI, they become addicted to it and stay until retirement, despite being paid government salaries and working under incredible stress. Our challenge, I told the FBI, is to simply get out there and show more people of color and more women (that number had been stuck just below 20 percent for years) what the place is like and dare them to try to be part of it. It's not rocket science, I said; the talent is out there. They just don't know what they are missing. So we made it our passion to show them, and in just three years, the numbers started to change in a material way. During my third year at the FBI, a huge new-agent class at Quantico was 38 percent nonwhite.

Our standards hadn't changed; we were just doing a better job of showing people the life they could make by joining us, which is contagious in a positive way.

My travels around the country and the world taught me something else: the FBI's leaders weren't good enough. In the private sector, I had learned that the best organizations obsess over leadership talent — they hunt for it, test it, train it, and make it part of every conversation. They treat leadership talent like money. At the FBI, though, leadership was largely an afterthought. For decades, the organization counted on good people volunteering to be leaders and then putting up with all the family moves and time at Washington headquarters that required. Fortunately, many good people volunteered. But that kind of approach was also a recipe for people becoming leaders to escape a job they weren't doing well or people being promoted by their bosses to get rid of them. I discovered from listening to the employees that we had some great leaders, some crappy leaders, and everything in between. That was simply not acceptable for an organization as important as the FBI.

I told the organization that I had an ambitious goal: the FBI would one day be the government's premier leadership factory, and private employers would count the days until an FBI leader could retire (age fifty for special agents) so they could hire them to lead. The FBI would become so good at identifying and growing leaders that all the burdens of government leadership borne by FBI families would be repaid by successful second careers in the private sector. I told our employees that the military services were great organizations, but there was no reason why the FBI shouldn't be the dominant government supplier of America's corporate leaders. I said we were going to paint a picture of what great leadership looks like, find and grow those who could be great, and teach or remove those already in leadership jobs who weren't getting it done.

With broad support across the organization, I was going to drive leadership into every corner and every conversation in the FBI, until we were consistently excellent, across all roles and at all levels. We would teach that great leaders are (1) people of integrity and decency; (2) confident enough to be humble; (3) both kind and tough; (4) transparent; and (5) aware that we all seek meaning in work. We would also teach them that (6) what they say is important, but what they do is far more important, because their people are always watching them. In short, we would demand and develop ethical leaders.

I knew a bit about this because I arrived at the FBI having spent decades watching leaders, reading about leaders, and trying to lead. From all that learning and all those mistakes, I knew the kind of leader I wanted to follow and the kind I wanted to be. And I set out immediately to try to set that example.

On my first full day as FBI director, for example, I sat in an auditorium in front of a camera and spoke to all employees about my expectations for them and their expectations for me. I gave the talk sitting on a stool, wearing a tie but no jacket. I also wore a blue shirt. This might not seem like a big deal to outsiders, but Bob Mueller wore a white shirt every day for twelve years (Congress had extended his ten-year term for two extra years). Not some days, or most days — every day. That was the culture, and I thought shirt color was one early, small way to set a different tone. I said nothing about my shirt, but people noticed.

I laid out my five expectations that first day and many times thereafter. Every new employee heard them, and I repeated them wherever I went in the organization:

- I expected they would find joy in their work. They were part of an organization devoted to doing good, protecting the weak, rescuing the taken, and catching criminals. That was work with moral content. Doing it should be a source of great joy.
- I expected they would treat all people with respect and dignity, without regard to position or station in life.
- I expected they would protect the institution's reservoir of trust and credibility that makes possible all their work.
- I expected they would work hard, because they owe that to the taxpayer.
- I expected they would fight for balance in their lives.

I emphasized that last one because I worried many people in the FBI worked too hard, driven by the mission, and absorbed too much stress from what they saw. I talked about what I had learned from a year of watching Dick Cates in Madison, Wisconsin. I expected them to fight to keep a life, to fight for the balance of other interests, other activities, other people, outside of work. I explained that judgment was essential to the sound exercise of power.

Because they would have great power to do good or, if they abused that power, to do harm, I needed sound judgment, which is the ability to orbit a problem and see it well, including through the eyes of people very different from you. I told them that although I wasn't sure where it came from, I knew the ability to exercise judgment was protected by getting away from the work and refreshing yourself. That physical distance made perspective possible when they returned to work.

And then I got personal. "There are people in your lives called 'loved ones' because *you* are supposed to love *them.*" In our work, I warned, there is a disease called "get-back-itis." That is, you may tell yourself, "I am trying to protect a country, so I will get back to" my spouse, my kids, my parents, my siblings, my friends. "There is no getting back," I said. "In this line of work, you will learn that bad things happen to good people. You will turn to get back and they will be gone. I order you to love somebody. It's the right thing to do and it's also good for you."

I added something I learned from Stellar Wind and the torture struggle. When someone is tired, their judgment can be impaired. When they are dragging, it is hard for them to float above a problem and picture themselves and the problem in another place and time, so I gave them another directive: sleep. When you sleep, your brain is actually engaged in the neurochemical process of judgment. It is mapping connections and finding meaning among all the data you took in during the day. Tired people tend not to have the best judgment. And it is not as hard as you may think, I added with a smile. "You can multitask. You can sleep with people you love. In appropriate circumstances."

One day during my first week, around noon, I walked out of my huge office, through my huge conference room, and past the desk of Bob Mueller's administrative assistant, who would work with me for another few months. She had been there for decades and was an invaluable resource to me but was much more familiar with a different style of leadership.

"Where are you going?" she asked.

"To get a sandwich," I said.

"Why are you doing that?"

"Because I'm hungry. I'm just gonna run up to the cafeteria."

"What if people try to talk to you?" she asked with a bewildered look.

"I *hope* they talk to me."

Whenever I possibly could during my three years, eight months, and five days as FBI director, I walked down a long hall and up a flight of stairs to the FBI headquarters cafeteria. I never wore my jacket. I asked my security detail to stay far enough away from me that people would think I was walking alone. I didn't want FBI employees to think I needed to be protected from them.

No matter how I felt inside, I tried to walk with a bounce in my step, standing straight and smiling at those I passed. The way I looked at it, when the director of the FBI stepped into that cafeteria, hundreds of pairs of eyes turned to look, and every pair was asking, in some form, the same question: "So how are we doing?" The answer from my face and posture had to be: "We're doing just fine. It's all going to be okay."

I also never cut the line. Even when I wished I could, or even when I was in a hurry. I stood and waited as people in front of me ordered panini (which take forever, by the way). I thought it was very important to show people that I'm not better than anyone else. So I waited.

The wait in line allowed me to interview people. I would turn to the person next to me and ask them to tell me their story, including what they liked about their job at the FBI. I learned a tremendous amount from these many conversations. One lesson was that I wasn't the big deal I thought I was. One day after I had been on the job for close to a year, I turned to the guy behind me and asked him about himself. I learned that he worked on computer servers. He said he had been with the FBI for three years, and what he liked best about the agency was that he could get experience and responsibility far beyond what the private sector offered someone his age. There was an awkward pause, and he probably thought he needed to be polite. So he asked, "How 'bout yourself?"

"I'm the director," I replied.

Bobbing his head side to side to emphasize his question, he asked, "Director of . . . ?"

"Dude," I said, "I'm the director of the FBI. You work for me."

Another awkward pause. Finally, he said, "Oh, you look so different online."

That evening I went home and told Patrice that story. "That should happen to you *every* day," she said with a laugh.

Before I became FBI director, I worked at Bridgewater Associates — which aspires to build a culture of complete transparency and honesty. I learned there that I could sometimes be a selfish and poor leader. Most often, that was because I was hesitant to tell people who worked for me when I thought they needed to improve. The best leaders are both kind and tough. Without both, people don't thrive. Bridgewater's founder, Ray Dalio, believes there is no such thing as negative feedback or positive feedback; there is only accurate feedback, and we should care enough about each other to be accurate. By avoiding hard conversations and not telling people where they were struggling and how they could improve, I was depriving them of the chance to grow. My squeamishness was not only cowardly, it was selfish. If I really care about the people who work for me — if I create the atmosphere of deep personal consideration I want — I should care enough to be honest, even if it makes me uncomfortable. I should, of course, still consider the best way to deliver the message. There is a right time, and a right way, for every conversation. If someone's mom just died, that is not the day to be accurate, but I was honor bound to find a way to have that conversation.

Effective leaders almost never need to yell. The leader will have created an environment where disappointing him causes his people to be disappointed in themselves. Guilt and affection are far more powerful motivators than fear. The great coaches of team sports are almost always people who simply need to say, in a quiet voice, "That wasn't our best, now was it?" and his players melt. They love this man, know he loves them, and will work tirelessly not to disappoint him. People are drawn to this kind of leader, as I was drawn all those years ago to Harry Howell, the grocer. A leader who screams at his employees or belittles them will not attract and retain great talent over the long term.

At the FBI, I spoke often about LeBron James. Even though I don't know the man personally, I talked about him for two reasons. First, I believe he is the best basketball player in the world today. Second, he is never satisfied he is good enough. I have read that he spends every off-season working on some part of his game to improve it. At first glance, that seems crazy; he's already better than everybody else. But it makes complete sense when you consider his perspective: he isn't measuring himself against the other players; he is measuring himself against himself. The best leaders don't care much about "benchmarking," comparing their organization to others.

They know theirs is not good enough, and constantly push to get better.

Early in my term as director, when I had declared that the FBI's leadership culture needed to improve, someone handed me a survey showing we had the second-best leadership survey results among the seventeen agencies in the United States intelligence community. I returned the survey, explaining that I didn't care; I wasn't measuring us against them. I was measuring us against us, and we weren't nearly good enough. The tough and kind leader loves her people enough to know they can always improve their game. She lights a fire in them to always get better.

I knew there were other areas where we could improve, and I suggested to the entire workforce that they read Martin Luther King Jr.'s "Letter from Birmingham Jail," one of the most important things I ever read. Inspired in part by theologian Reinhold Niebuhr, King's letter is about seeking justice in a deeply flawed world. I have reread it several times since first encountering it in college. Because I knew that the FBI's interaction with the civil rights movement, and Dr. King in particular, was a dark chapter in the Bureau's history, I wanted to do something more. I ordered the creation of a curriculum at the FBI's Quantico training academy. I wanted all agent and analyst trainees to learn the history of the FBI's interaction with King, how the legitimate counterintelligence mission against Communist infiltration of our government had morphed into an unchecked, vicious campaign of harassment and extralegal attack on the civil rights leader and others. I wanted them to remember that well-meaning people lost their way. I wanted them to know that the FBI sent King a letter blackmailing him and suggesting he commit suicide. I wanted them to stare at that history, visit the inspiring King Memorial in Washington, D.C., with its long arcs of stone bearing King's words, and reflect on the FBI's values and our responsibility to always do better.

The FBI Training Division created a curriculum that does just that. All FBI trainees study that painful history and complete the course by visiting the memorial. There, they choose one of Dr. King's quotations from the wall — maybe "Injustice anywhere is a threat to justice everywhere" or "The ultimate measure of a man is not where he stands in moments of comfort and convenience, but where he stands at times of challenge and controversy" — and then write an essay about the intersection of that quotation and the FBI's values. The course doesn't tell the trainees what to think. It only tells them they must think, about history and institutional values. Last I checked, the course remains one of the highest-rated portions of their many weeks at Quantico.

To drive the message home, I obtained a copy of the October 1963 memo from J. Edgar Hoover to Attorney General Robert F. Kennedy seeking permission to conduct electronic surveillance of Dr. King. At the bottom of the single-page memo, which is only five sentences long and without meaningful facts, Kennedy's signature grants that authority, without limit as to time and place. I put the memo under the glass on the corner of the desk where every morning I reviewed applications by the FBI and the Department of Justice to conduct national security electronic surveillance in the United States. As Hoover did, I was required to personally sign an application. The difference was that our applications went to a court and were often thicker than my arm. As I would explain to employees, it is a pain in the neck to get permission to conduct that kind of surveillance, and it should be.

I kept the Hoover memo there not to make a critical statement about Hoover or

Kennedy, but to make a statement about the value of oversight and constraint. I have no doubt that Hoover and Kennedy thought they were doing the right thing. What they lacked was meaningful testing of their assumptions. There was nothing to check them. It is painful to stare openly at ourselves, but it is the only way to change the future.

The FBI rank and file reacted very positively to this and other initiatives, something I could see in their annual anonymous rating of me across the organization. But I knew some FBI alumni were confused as to why I seemed to be "attacking" the organization I led. But transparency is almost always the best course. Getting problems, pain, hopes, and doubts out on the table so we can talk honestly about them and work to improve is the best way to lead. By acknowledging our issues, we have the best chance of resolving them in a healthy way. Buried pain never gets better with age. And by remembering and being open and truthful about our mistakes, we reduce the chance we will repeat them.

Harry Truman once said, "The only thing new in the world is the history you don't know." Humans tend to do the same dumb things, and the same evil things, again and again, because we forget.

CHAPTER 9
THE WASHINGTON LISTEN

Let me not seek as much . . .
to be understood as to understand.
— PEACE PRAYER OF ST. FRANCIS

Eric Garner. Tamir Rice. Walter Scott.
Freddie Gray.

Those are the names of some of the black
civilians who died during encounters with
the police in 2014 and 2015. Those encounters were captured on video, and those
videos went viral, igniting communities that
had been soaked in the flammable liquid of
discrimination and mistreatment. And
although it didn't involve video of the shooting, one death, in particular, rocked the
country. On August 9, 2014, a young black
man named Michael Brown was shot and
killed by a white police officer in Ferguson,
Missouri, touching off weeks of unrest in
that community and bringing unprecedented attention in America to the use of

deadly force by police against black people.

In the months after the shooting, the federal investigation discovered some important truths. The Ferguson police had been engaged in a pattern of discriminatory behavior directed at African Americans, and the town governance — from ticketing practices to the bail system — operated to oppress black people. As in so many American towns and cities, the police needed to change before African Americans would trust them. It was understandable that Michael Brown's death was a tragic spark that ignited a powder keg built by oppressive policing in that community.

But in the end, the Department of Justice found there wasn't sufficient evidence to charge that police officer with federal civil rights crimes for shooting Michael Brown. FBI agents knocked on hundreds of doors throughout Ferguson and discovered not only that there was not sufficient evidence but also that early media accounts of the shooting were factually wrong and misleading.

Contrary to what most of the public had heard or thought they had seen, there was reliable evidence that Michael Brown was not surrendering when he was shot, and there was DNA evidence that he had assaulted the officer and tried to take his gun. In one sense, those conclusions by federal investigators — reached months after Michael Brown's death — didn't matter; most of the world had already heard false reports and believed Brown was gunned down while surrendering with his hands up. In the time it took for the truth to get its boots on, false information had circled the earth many times.

The Department of Justice's conclusions were important, but late. By spring 2015, when the department completed its work and publicly released a detailed account of the investigation and its conclusions, several highly publicized videotaped encounters between police and African Americans had dramatically increased the focus on police use of force. Millions watched videos of violent police encounters, including NYPD officers killing Eric Garner with a chokehold and Cleveland police officers shooting twelve-year-old Tamir Rice in a city park. Millions more watched as Walter Scott was murdered by a South Carolina police officer, who, after shooting Scott in the back, was then captured on video appearing to alter the crime scene to cover up what he had done. Still more watched Baltimore officers drag Freddie Gray into the back of a police van for a ride he did not survive. These tragic deaths dominated perceptions of the police. They swamped and overshadowed millions of positive, professional encounters between citizens and police officers, and extraordinary anger was building toward all uniformed law enforcement.

During this volatile period, in December 2014, two NYPD officers were executed by a killer claiming to be acting in retaliation by "putting wings on pigs." President Obama asked me to attend one of the NYPD funerals as his representative. As I spoke to the family of Officer Wenjian Liu in a small Brooklyn funeral home, the grief was so thick as to be suffocating. Outside, thousands of stone-faced police officers stood for miles in a cold wind.

I had felt the pain and anger of black communities since Ferguson, and now I could feel the pain and anger of law enforcement. Police officers didn't feel safe or appreciated on streets they were trying to protect, and communities didn't trust the police.

Law enforcement and the black community in America have long been separate parallel lines — closer in some communities, farther apart in others — but now those lines were arcing away from each other everywhere, each video depicting the death of a civilian at the hands of police driving one line away, each killing of a police officer arcing the other line away.

I struggled with whether there was something I could say or do that would make a difference, to help bend the lines back toward each other. The FBI was a federal investigative agency, but we were deeply involved in local policing, both as a trainer of police leaders and as a key partner to uniformed law enforcement. I decided I could do two things. I could use the high profile of the director's job to say some things I believed to be true, in the hope it would foster better dialogue. And then I could use the FBI's nationwide presence to drive that dialogue. So, in February 2015, I went to Georgetown University and talked about four "hard truths" that all of us need to know.

First, I said, we in law enforcement need to acknowledge the truth that we have long been the enforcers of a status quo in America that abused black people; we need to acknowledge our history because the people we serve and protect cannot forget it. Second, we all need to acknowledge that we carry implicit biases inside us, and if we aren't careful, they can lead to assumptions and injustice. Third, something can happen

241

to people in law enforcement who must respond to incidents resulting in the arrest of so many young men of color; it can warp perspectives and lead to cynicism. Finally, I said, we all must acknowledge that the police are not the root cause of the most challenging problems in our country's worst neighborhoods, but that the actual causes and solutions are so hard that it is easier to talk only about the police. I then ordered all fifty-six FBI offices around the country to convene meetings between law enforcement and communities to talk about what is true and how to build the trust needed to bend those lines back toward each other. It is hard to hate up close, and the FBI could bring people up close.

The public reaction to the Georgetown speech was positive. As a white FBI director with long law enforcement experience, I could say things about law enforcement history and biases that others couldn't, and many police chiefs were privately grateful. But the lines stayed far apart, and by the middle of 2015, something ominous was happening. In late summer, more than forty of the country's largest cities reported to the FBI that they were experiencing jumps in the number of murders, starting in late 2014. What was particularly unusual about the numbers was that the rise in the murder rate wasn't uniform and didn't follow any obvious pattern. In fact, about twenty of the sixty largest cities in America were not seeing increases. Some had seen fewer murders. And the cities, some with huge increases, some without, were mixed together on the American map.

Even while I was speaking at Georgetown, murders were climbing, and the victims were overwhelmingly young black men. The cities with dramatic increases had different gang problems and different illegal drug patterns. What they appeared to have in common were large and concentrated poor black neighborhoods where more young black men were being shot and killed by other young black men.

I was hearing from police leaders that the increases might be connected to changes in behavior, among police and civilians, connected to the narratives driven by viral videos. I didn't know for sure, and didn't have the expertise or the data to figure it out, but I was determined to raise the issue. It would be too easy for the country to ignore more deaths of black men, too easy for the country to "drive around" the problem because it was happening to "those people, over there." Somebody had to say something to force a conversation about what was happening. My fondest wish was to be wrong and find out that something simple explained the numbers, or that this was some random but widespread statistical anomaly.

At the same time, the Obama administration and an interesting alliance of liberal Democrats and libertarian Republicans in Congress were working together to reduce punishments for some federal criminal offenses. It was one of the only policy areas on which some self-described Tea Party Republicans and President Obama could agree. I had no heartburn with the specific proposals, which all seemed quite modest and reasonable to me. But a national conversation about murder spikes — and what might be causing it — was the last thing advocates of criminal justice reform wanted. I understood that. But I just couldn't bear to be silent about the deaths of so many young black men and the possibility that broad changes in human behavior might be some part of that.

So I talked about the subject again, in Chicago, in late October 2015. I talked about the lines of community and police arcing away from each other and the competing narratives pushing the lines apart, and used two popular Twitter hashtags to make my point:

> I actually see an example and a demonstration of that arcing through hashtags, through the hashtag #blacklivesmatter and the hashtag #policelivesmatter. Of course, each of those hashtags and what they represent adds a voice to an important conversation. But each time somebody interprets the hashtag #blacklivesmatter as anti–law enforcement, one line moves away. And each time that someone interprets the hashtag #policelivesmatter as antiblack, the other line moves away. I actually feel the lines continuing to arc away and maybe accelerating, incident by incident, video by video, hashtag by hashtag. And that's a terrible place for us to be.

Then I turned to the rising murders, saying that "just as those lines are arcing away from each other, and maybe, just maybe, in some places *because* those lines are arcing away from each other," we are seeing huge jumps in homicide in vulnerable neighborhoods, and the dead are almost all young black men. I said that communities, academics, and law enforcement need to demand answers. I reviewed some of the theories I had heard — guns, drugs, gangs, release of jailed offenders — and said none of them seemed to explain the map and the calendar: all over the United States and all at the same time.

I then said I had heard another theory: "Almost nobody says it on the record, but police and elected officials are saying it quietly to themselves all over the country. And it's the one theory that to my mind, to my common sense, does explain the map and the calendar. And of the explanations I have heard, it's the one that makes the most sense to me. Maybe something has changed in policing."

I said, "I don't know for sure whether that's the case. I don't know for sure that even if it is the case it explains it entirely. But I do have a strong sense that some part of what's going on is likely a chill wind that has blown through law enforcement over the last year."

I finished with a plea:

We need to figure out what's happening and deal with it now. I have heard some folks suggest that it's too early, it's only October, we should wait to the end of the year and then see what the crime stats look like. I refuse to wait. Especially given the information that we have from all the big-city chiefs and especially because these are not just data points, these are lives. Law enforcement leaders must not wait to push their folks to police well. By that I mean firmly, fairly, and professionally. And as important, community leaders must not wait to demand and assist those officers in policing well. And to insist those officers get the space, time, and respect to do it effectively and professionally.

I knew these comments would anger some people in the Obama administration, but I felt strongly that the FBI director should be an independent voice on criminal justice issues like this. Independence was what President Obama told me he was looking for when he selected me. Issues of crime, race, and law enforcement are complicated and emotional, but they don't get better by not talking about them.

I was right about one thing. Everybody was upset by my comments. In fact, more people than I expected. My goal had been to highlight a serious problem, give a nuanced treatment of it, and ignite a discussion about possible causes and solutions. I wanted to force a conversation about a hard thing. I wanted to stimulate people to ask difficult questions about what could be true, to drive collection of data, and to push for the study of that data. And I hoped that it might even change behavior and save lives by encouraging both better policing and more supportive community relationships. Instead, I got to see another demonstration of tribalism in America.

Police unions complained I was blaming cops and calling them cowards. Voices from the left said I was asserting a "Ferguson effect" without evidence and it couldn't possibly be true. They said I was against scrutiny of the police. Voices from the right said the country was experiencing a murder epidemic and blamed President Obama. Too few people asked, "What is true?" Too few people actually considered the possibilities and asked what might be going on, even if they believed I was out to lunch. Instead, folks rushed to their team, their side. Very few voices in the public square took the time to ask, "So what is this guy worried about and what is he saying, exactly?"

One person — in the very center of the public square — did. A day or two after I returned from Chicago, my chief of staff came in to tell me the president would like to speak with me in the Oval Office. No topic was given and no information on who else would be there. It turned out to be just the two of us, my first meeting alone with President Obama.

Until I met my wife, I didn't know what listening really was. Neither, at least in my experience, do most people in Washington, D.C. To them, listening is a period of silence, where someone else talks before you say what you were planning to say all along. We see these exchanges in nearly every "debate" on television. It's the candidate sitting on the stool, waiting for the light to go on, then standing up and saying their prearranged talking points, while someone else says their prearranged talking points back at them. It's just words reaching ears, but not getting into a conscious brain. That's the "Washington listen."

My marriage has taught me that what I thought of as listening really isn't listening, either. Like a lot of people, I thought that listening involved sitting silently as someone else talked, and then perceiving what they say.

I was wrong. True listening is actually that period of silence and allowing someone's words to reach your conscious brain, but it also includes something else that's a little weird: with your posture, your face, and your sounds, you signal to someone, "I want what you have, I need to know what you know, and I want you to keep telling me the things you're telling me." Two good friends talking to each other is a stenographer's worst nightmare. They are talking over each other. When one is speaking formed words, the other is making sounds — "Uh-huh." "Ooh." "I know." "Yup, yup, oh, I've seen it, yup. They'll do that." They're listening to each other in a way where each is both pushing information to the other and pulling information out of the other. Push, pull, push, pull. When they are really connecting, it actually runs together — pushpullpushpull. That's real listening.

To be effective at the FBI, I spent a lot of time listening, something we all struggle to do well. It is hard for leaders to listen well because it requires us to be vulnerable, to risk our superior position. Barack Obama surprised me by picking me as FBI director. And this is where Barack Obama surprised me yet again. He was an extraordinary listener, as good as any I've seen in leadership. In various meetings with the president, I watched him work hard to draw as many viewpoints as possible into a conversation, frequently disregarding the hierarchy reflected in seating arrangements

— principals at the table, lower-ranked folks in chairs against the wall. I can recall a meeting in the Situation Room about a classified technology topic where President Obama asked some Silicon Valley whiz kid without a tie sitting against the wall what he thought of the discussion the formally dressed leaders of the nation's military and intelligence agencies had just had at the table. The shaggy dude then contradicted several of us. Obama hunted for points of view. Maybe it was a legacy of his life as a professor, cold-calling someone in the back row. This approach often led to chaotic conversations, but it allowed him to hear views that, in the Bush administration, would have been watered down by rank or by fear of being teased. No guy without a tie would have been in the Bush Situation Room, and if he somehow snuck into a back-row seat, he would not be called upon, and if he spoke anyway, he would be mocked for his attire.

Obama had the ability to really discuss something, leveling the field to draw out perspectives different from his own. He would turn and face the speaker, giving them long periods without interruption to share their view. And although he was quiet, he was using his face, his posture, and sometimes small sounds to draw the person out. He was carefully tracking what they said, something he would prove by asking questions when they finished; the questions were often drawn from throughout the minutes he had been listening.

President Obama was also more than willing to discuss things that people weren't sure he wanted to hear. I learned this firsthand after I made those controversial comments about law enforcement and race. It turns out they caused considerable concern at the White House. When I joined President Obama in the Oval Office after returning from Chicago, I discovered that he had intentionally excluded his senior staff and the Justice Department from the room. It was to be our first one-on-one meeting in the twenty-six months I had been FBI director. As I walked through the door by the grandfather clock and saw nobody else, I thought maybe I was about to get an ass-chewing. The president sat in his usual seat — the armchair to the right of the fireplace. I sat on the couch just to his left.

There was no chewing out. Instead, the president began the meeting by saying, "I asked you to come because I know your head and your heart and I want to understand what you are seeing and thinking." We then spoke with each other for about an hour. And I use the word "with" intentionally. It was a true conversation, with pushing and pulling, pushing and pulling.

The president asked a question that invited an open-ended response: "What are you seeing and what's worrying you?" I talked for about ten minutes. I talked about the map and the calendar — more than forty of the nation's sixty largest cities seeing rises in killings of young black men, all coming at the same time, in a pattern that didn't line up with other crime trends, and mixed geographically with large cities that were not seeing a murder increase. I explained my worry that most of the country could just ignore the problem because it was black men dying, and only in "those" neighborhoods. I also noted my concern that the increases were connected to changes in behavior following the viral videos. I said my goal was to call it out, raise the question of whether the police and the communities were pulling back from each other in small ways that added up to something big. I said my hope was that by raising the question, I could help change behaviors if that was what was happening.

When I was done, he expressed appreciation for my focus on the issue, then laid out some of the things I had said publicly that struck a discordant note with him. For example, I had used the term "weed and seed" to describe what I thought was needed — pulling out the bad guys and working to grow something healthy in the space created by the arrests. He asked, "Can you see how that might sound to black people? Calling young men in their community 'weeds'?" He spoke of how black people often resented a trade-off that their circumstances forced them to make: they welcomed the security police bring, but resented the conditions that make that police presence necessary in their neighborhoods — poor schools, few jobs, addiction, and broken families.

I responded that it hadn't occurred to me that people of color might hear my words that way. I hadn't taken the time to consider how the term "weed and seed" — one we had been using in law enforcement for decades — might strike people, especially black people at a challenging time. I was trapped in my own perspective. A black person — who happened to be president of the United States — helped me see through other eyes.

We talked about the impact on black communities from the extraordinarily high percentage of black men in the criminal justice system, and how poor a job our country has done to prepare those in prison to return to productive lives. Although I agreed that the jailing of so many black men was a tragedy, I also shared how a term he used, "mass incarceration" — to describe what, in his view, was a national epidemic of locking up too many people — struck the ears of those of us who had dedicated much of our lives to trying to reduce crime in minority neighborhoods. To my ears, the term "mass incarceration" conjures an image of World War II Japanese internment camps, where vast numbers of people were herded behind barbed wire. I thought the term was both inaccurate and insulting to a lot of good people in law enforcement who cared deeply about helping people trapped in dangerous neighborhoods. It was inaccurate in the sense that there was nothing "mass" about the incarceration: every defendant was charged individually, represented individually by counsel, convicted by a court individually, sentenced individually, reviewed on appeal individually, and incarcerated. That added up to a lot of people in jail, but there was nothing "mass" about it, I said. And the insulting part, I explained, was the way it cast as illegitimate the efforts by cops, agents, and prosecutors — joined by the black community — to rescue hard-hit neighborhoods.

He responded by urging me to see how black people might experience law enforcement and the courts very differently, and that it was hard to blame them for seeing the jailing of so many black men, in numbers wildly greater than their proportion of the population, as anything other than "mass."

When we were done, I was smarter. And I hoped that in some small way I'd helped him see things from a different perspective as well. Our discussion was the total opposite of the Washington listen: each of us actually took the time to really understand a different way of looking at something and with a mind open to being convinced.

President Obama would never have considered such a conversation if he did not have enough confidence in himself to show humility. In fact, if I saw any hint of imbalance with President Obama as a leader, it was on the confidence side of the scale. And I would see it in grappling with the hardest problem I encountered in government — encryption.

■ ■ ■ ■

Before I became FBI director, Edward Snowden, a contractor at the National Security Agency, stole a huge trove of classified data about the NSA's activities and then shared a very large amount of that data with the press. One obvious result of this theft was that it dealt a devastating blow to our country's ability to collect intelligence. Another result was that, in the year after his disclosures, bad actors across the world began moving their communications to devices and channels that were protected by strong encryption, thwarting government surveillance, including the kind of court-authorized electronic surveillance the FBI did. We watched as terrorist networks we long had been monitoring slowly went dark, which is a scary thing.

In September 2014, after a year of watching our legal capabilities diminish, I saw Apple and Google announce that they would be moving their mobile devices to default encryption. They announced it in such a way as to suggest — at least to my ears — that making devices immune to judicial orders was an important social value. This drove me crazy. I just couldn't understand how smart people could not see the social costs to stopping judges, in appropriate cases, from ordering access to electronic devices. The Apple and Google announcement came on the eve of one of my regular quarterly sessions with the press corps that covered the FBI and the Department of Justice. I hadn't planned to talk about encryption, but I couldn't help myself. I expressed my frustration with the move to default encryption:

> I am a huge believer in the rule of law, but I also believe that no one in this country is beyond the law. What concerns me about this is companies marketing something expressly to allow people to place themselves beyond the law.

With those comments, I joined an incredibly complicated and emotional battle.

The divide between the FBI and companies like Apple can be explained, in large measure, by how each sees the world, and the limitations of each of those perspectives. And, frankly, there is not a lot of true listening going on between the parties. The leaders of tech companies don't see the darkness the FBI sees. Our days are dominated by the hunt for people planning terrorist attacks, hurting children, and engaging in organized crime. We see humankind at its most depraved, day in and day out. Horrific, unthinkable acts are what the men and women of the FBI live, breathe, and try to stop. I found it appalling that the tech types couldn't see this. I would frequently joke with the FBI "Going Dark" team assigned to seek solutions, "Of course the Silicon Valley types don't see the darkness — they live where it's sunny all the time and everybody is rich and smart." Theirs was a world where technology made human connections and relationships stronger. Who doesn't love sharing cat GIFs with grandma? Or ordering coffee on your app so it's ready when you walk into the Starbucks? Although I was joking, I thought the tech community did not fully appreciate the costs when good people from law enforcement were unable to use judicial orders to get evidence. I also think it would be fair criticism to say we focused too much on those costs, given the darkness outside our windows all day long.

Because both sides are biased by our places in the world, I thought it critical that the resolution shouldn't be dictated by either Apple or the FBI; the American people should decide how they want to live and govern themselves. But what exactly that means as a practical matter is an incredibly hard question to answer. The collision between privacy and public safety in the encryption context touches on not just privacy and public safety but also issues of technology, law, economics, philosophy, innovation, and international relations, and probably other interests and values.

The bargain at the heart of our government has always been that privacy matters enormously, but it must yield when, with appropriate evidence and oversight, the government needs to see into private spaces to protect the community. No large part of America has ever been entirely off-limits to judicial authority. President Obama was, by background and instinct, a civil libertarian, but he could see the darkness and the danger in talking about privacy as an absolute value, as he explained publicly in Austin, Texas, in spring 2016:

But the dangers are real. Maintaining law and order and a civilized society is important. Protecting our kids is important. And so I would just caution against taking an absolutist perspective on this. Because we make compromises all the time. . . . And this notion that somehow our data is different and can be walled off from those other trade-offs we make I believe is incorrect.

He dove into the issue, ordering unprecedented White House scrutiny of the clash between privacy and security. At one of several meetings he personally led on the topic in the White House Situation Room, he said that if we were headed to a place where wide swaths of American life would be judge-proof, that wasn't a decision a company should make. That would be a change in the way we live; only the people of the United States should make such a decision.

Unfortunately, President Obama ran out of time. Though the administration made some progress on the issue, including developing a technical plan — called a "proof-of-concept" — to show it was possible to build secure mobile devices and still permit judges to order access in appropriate cases, he left office without deciding what to do next, including whether to seek legislation or regulation of some kind.

One thing about those discussions stayed with me. In the summer of 2016, I sat in the White House Situation Room, where various leaders and staffers were laying out and discussing the many dimensions of the problem with the president. The Situation Room is actually the name for a collection of offices and conference rooms that support the president and his National Security Council. But it is also the name commonly used for the conference room in which the president normally holds national security meetings. The room looks nothing like it does on television. It is really small. If the leather, wheeled office chairs are jammed together, maybe ten people can join the president at the table, and they will all need breath mints.

The seating arrangement for each meeting was dictated by nameplates put on the table by the Situation Room staff before the meeting began. I have been there dozens of times under three presidents and still can't explain the placement of the nameplates. In back-to-back meetings, I have moved to another seat because there was a different design for the second meeting and my nameplate moved. Nobody sat at the opposite end of the table from the president because that would block the video screen and camera that allowed senior leaders to join from the road. They would appear on the screen in a *Hollywood Squares* setup, visible only from the waist up. (Knowing this, I once "attended" from Hawaii wearing a suit jacket and tie, and my bathing suit.) From time to time, the Sit Room staff would pull smaller wood chairs up to the end of the table farthest from the president. I called these the "kids' chairs," and, because I was not a cabinet secretary, I was often assigned one. Kind colleagues would sometimes offer me their big-kid seats to avoid the hilarious spectacle of the FBI giraffe sitting on a tiny chair. Around the walls there was room for another ten or twelve participants, but the room was so small that their knees nearly touched chairs at the table.

And so, here we were, in the waning days of the Obama administration, packed in to talk about encryption. Near the end of the meeting, the president spoke up. He had a look of discovery on his face. "You know, this is really hard," he said to no one in particular. "Normally I can figure these things out, but this one is really hard."

I had two reactions to the comment, both of which I kept to myself. "No kidding" was the first reaction. A whole lot of smart people had been banging on this incredibly complicated issue for years. My second reaction was to be struck by the president's breathtaking confidence. To my eye, at least, he wasn't puffing or trying to show off. He also wasn't being self-deprecating or sarcastic in the way President Bush might have. He really did believe that he, Barack Obama, could always figure out the hardest stuff. He couldn't figure this one out, which surprised him. Wow, I thought.

I really didn't know what to make of it. That much confidence — the belief that he personally can solve even the hardest problems — can be worrisome in a leader because it tends to close off other views. I had seen it in myself. One of my weaknesses, especially when I was younger, was overconfidence, a tendency to reach a conclusion quickly and cling to it too tightly. Or to make a decision too quickly, telling myself I was being "decisive," when I was really being impulsive and arrogant. I have struggled with it my entire life. But in Obama, I had also seen the humility to learn from others, which doesn't often exist alongside overconfidence. I still don't know what to make of it, and can't think of a national security issue on which we interacted in which he showed an imbalance of confidence and humility. Instead, I consistently saw President Obama work to get people to relax and tell him what he needed to know.

I tried very hard to do the same at the FBI, never forgetting that we are all downhill from our leaders. No matter how "flat" an organization, there is a hierarchy, and everyone knows what it is. Even if everyone in the room is wearing a hooded sweatshirt, ripped jeans, and flip-flops. Even if we are all sitting on beanbags eating trail mix and spitballing ideas on a whiteboard, if anyone in the room is a boss or owner, everyone knows it. Someone in the room is "above" the others, whether that rank is explicit or not.

Speaking uphill takes courage. It takes overcoming a universal human affliction — the impostor complex. All of us labor, to one degree or another, under the belief that if other people really knew us, if they knew us the way we know ourselves, they would think less of us. That's the impostor complex — the fear that by showing ourselves we will be exposed as the flawed person we are. If you don't have this, in some measure, you are an incredible jerk and should stop reading immediately.

Speaking candidly to a peer requires us to risk exposure. Speaking uphill to a leader is scarier. Speaking to the top leader of the organization is scarier still. And in a paramilitary organization of many layers like the FBI, dominated for its first half-century by a single person, J. Edgar Hoover, the hill is mighty steep. And it is harder than that, because getting the speakers to overcome their impostor complex is only half the answer. The leaders must also overcome their own impostor complex — their fear of being less than perfect.

I tried to foster an atmosphere at the FBI where people would tell me the truth. I did things that probably struck people as silly, but they were all carefully thought out. I began by attempting to encourage less formal attire at my regular meetings. I discovered that people dressed to come see the director as if they were going to a funeral. I never wore a jacket to internal meetings, but that wasn't enough. If people are formally dressed, they will think and act in that formal, restrictive box. That is not a recipe for great debate and conversations. Changing the dress code took some doing.

I told my senior staff of about twenty people, men and women, not to wear suit jackets to my morning meetings unless they were leaving my meeting directly for a meeting with outsiders where they needed to be dressed up. I had success early on, and then about three weeks later nearly everyone was wearing suit jackets again. I made the clothing announcement again, which got me about six weeks of compliance. I kept at it.

I worked to build an atmosphere of trust by encouraging leaders to tell the truth about something personal. I asked an entire conference room of FBI senior executives to tell the group something about themselves that would surprise the room, quickly adding, to much laughter, that it should ideally not be something that would jeopardize their security clearance. Weeks later, I went around the room and asked them to tell me their favorite Halloween candy as a child. In November, I requested their favorite food at Thanksgiving, and, in December, their favorite gift of the holiday season. Of course, these could be seen as childish techniques, the kind a teacher might urge on an elementary school classroom, but children open up and trust one another in amazing ways. We were in need of a little more childlike behavior in our lives, because children tend to tell each other the truth more often than adults do.

I would need that culture of truth, and habit of true listening, when the FBI ended up, improbably and unexpectedly, in the middle of the 2016 election between Hillary Clinton and Donald Trump.

CHAPTER 10
ROADKILL

Standing in the middle of the road is
very dangerous; you get knocked down
by the traffic from both sides.
— MARGARET THATCHER

I have never met Hillary Clinton, although
I tried. When I became the United States
Attorney for the Southern District of New
York in January 2002, I asked my assistant
to arrange an introduction to the state's
junior senator. I thought it was a standard
thing for the United States Attorney —
there were four of us representing the
federal government in New York State — to
know the senators in the state, and I didn't
want to be rude. I had met the other senator, Chuck Schumer, during the Senate
confirmation process, but for some reason I
had not met Clinton. After a number of at-
tempts and multiple messages with Clinton's office, we gave up. It wasn't a big deal

at the time, but I found it odd.

To this day, I don't know why the meeting never happened. I suppose it could be the result of poor administrative support at Clinton's office, or she was simply too busy. I suppose it also could have been due to the fact that seven years earlier, I had worked for five months for the Senate committee investigating the Clintons for a variety of things grouped under the heading "Whitewater." I was a junior lawyer for the committee, still working at a Richmond law firm and charging the Senate by the hour. My focus was largely on the suicide of the former deputy White House counsel, Vincent Foster, and the handling of documents in his office. But my role on the Whitewater committee was so minor and so short — I left the assignment when our son Collin died in August 1995 — that it seemed unlikely that was the reason the senator wasn't returning my calls.

The unreturned messages in early 2002 were more likely due to the fact that my office was then supervising an investigation into Senator Clinton's husband's pardon of fugitive oil trader Marc Rich a year earlier, in the final hours of the Clinton presidency. In 1983, Rich and his codefendant, Pincus Green, had been indicted on sixty-five

criminal counts by then–United States Attorney Rudy Giuliani. Among the counts
were income tax evasion, wire fraud, racketeering, and trading with an enemy of the
United States — Iran — while it held
dozens of Americans hostage. Rich fled the
United States shortly before the indictment
(then the biggest tax evasion case in U.S.
history). He was given safe haven in Switzerland, which refused to extradite him for
what the Swiss considered essentially tax
crimes.

Nearly two decades later, on his final day
in office, President Clinton had issued Rich
a highly unusual pardon. It was unusual
because the pardon was given to a fugitive,
which was, to my knowledge, unprecedented. It was also unusual, and suspicious,
because it had not gone through the normal
review process at the Department of Justice.
The pardon had only been seen by then–
Deputy Attorney General Eric Holder, who,
without seeking input from the prosecutors
or agents who knew the case, cryptically
told the White House he was "neutral, leaning positive." The *New York Times* editorial
board called the pardon "a shocking abuse
of federal power." Amid allegations the
pardon had been issued in exchange for
promises of contributions by Marc Rich's

ex-wife to Bill Clinton's presidential library, my predecessor as United States Attorney in Manhattan, Mary Jo White, had opened an investigation focused on whether there was evidence of a corrupt bargain. When I became United States Attorney in January 2002, I inherited the investigation, which had been the subject of media stories.

I knew something about the case because I had actually been in charge of the fugitive hunt for Marc Rich when I was a federal prosecutor in Manhattan a decade earlier. Rich was then represented by prominent lawyers, among them Scooter Libby, well before his tenure as Dick Cheney's chief of staff. In 1992, I flew to Zurich with other law enforcement officials for what we were told by Rich's attorneys would be negotiations for his surrender. According to his lawyers, Rich would turn himself in once he saw that his prosecutors were honorable people. Along with my boss, United States Attorney Otto Obermaier, I met Rich and Pincus Green in the presidential suite of a grand hotel overlooking Lake Zurich to make arrangements for them to surrender in New York. That was when we discovered that Rich actually had no intention of surrendering without first negotiating a deal that promised him no prison time. He went into a long discourse about his charitable works and the merits of his case, saying, "I don't want to spend a day in jail." Obermaier replied, "We won't make that promise." He explained that we would not negotiate cases with fugitives and Rich was welcome to make all these arguments after he had appeared in federal court in Manhattan. We had no power under Swiss law to arrest him, so we left Switzerland and continued our efforts to capture Rich when he traveled.

Bill Clinton ended that fugitive hunt with a stroke of his pen. Now I was the United States Attorney investigating whether that pen stroke had been bought. I could see why that would have made Senator Clinton feel awkward about meeting me. In the end, we did not find sufficient evidence to bring any charges and closed the case. Our paths, I assumed, were unlikely to cross again.

On July 6, 2015, the Bureau received a referral from the inspector general of the intelligence community, a congressionally created independent office focused on finding risks and vulnerabilities across the nation's vast intelligence community. The referral raised the issue of whether Secretary of State Hillary Clinton had mishandled classified information while using her personal email system. On July 10, the FBI opened a criminal investigation. The Obama administration's Justice Department, then run by Attorney General Loretta Lynch, assigned prosecutors to support the investigation. As with hundreds of other investigations, the case was opened at the FBI far below my level, and I learned of it when the deputy director briefed me on it.

The facts of the case were straightforward: Hillary Clinton had used her personal email system, on a server and with an email address that was entirely of her own creation, to conduct her work as secretary of state. She set the server up several months after taking office. For the first few months of her tenure, she had used a personal AT&T BlackBerry email address before switching to a Clintonemail.com domain. In the course of doing her work, she emailed with other State employees. In the course of emailing those people, the inspector general discovered, she and they talked about classified topics in the body of dozens of their emails.

Though much has been made since of Hillary Clinton's emails and the FBI's investigation, the focus of the Bureau's investigation is often lost. The criminal investigation was *not* centered on the fact that Secretary Clinton decided to use nongovernmental email to do her work. In an attempt to blur the seriousness of the case, her defenders often cite the fact that one of her predecessors, Colin Powell, also used nongovernmental email, in his case AOL, as if that were relevant to the investigation. In fact, it entirely misses the point. I have never seen any indication that Powell discussed on his AOL account information that was classified at the time, but there were numerous examples of Secretary Clinton having done so.

Our investigation required us to answer two questions. The first question was whether classified documents were moved outside of classified systems or whether classified topics were discussed outside of a classified system. If so, the second question was what the subject of the investigation was thinking when she mishandled that classified information.

Information is classified based on its potential for harm to the United States if it is disclosed. Information marked at the lower classification level of "Confidential" refers to information that can cause some damage to the security of the United States if released. Information labeled "Secret" refers to material expected to cause "serious" damage to national security. "Top Secret" information is material that, if disclosed, could be expected to cause "exceptionally grave" damage to the security of the United States. This system is enforced by a variety of possible administrative punishments, including possible loss of a person's security clearance or loss of their job. For the most serious cases, criminal prosecution is a possibility. A variety of espionage statutes make it a felony to steal or to disclose national security information to people not permitted to receive it. Those statutes are used most often when someone is a spy or gives classified information to journalists for publication. More commonly used is a statute making it a misdemeanor — punishable by up to a year in jail — to mishandle classified information by removing it from appropriate facilities or systems. Even with the misdemeanor, the Department of Justice has long required that investigators develop strong evidence to indicate government employees *knew* they were doing something improper in their handling of the classified information.

In Secretary Clinton's case, the answer to the first question — was classified information mishandled? — was obviously "yes." In all, there were thirty-six email chains that discussed topics that were classified as "Secret" at the time. Eight times in those thousands of email exchanges across four years, Clinton and her team talked about topics designated as "Top Secret," sometimes cryptically, sometimes obviously. They didn't send each other classified documents, but that didn't matter. Even though the people involved in the emails all had appropriate clearances and a need to know, anyone who had ever been granted a security clearance should have known that talking about top-secret information on an unclassified system was a breach of rules governing classified materials. Although just a small slice of Clinton's emails, those exchanges on top-secret topics were, by all appearances, improper. Put another way, there were thirty-six email chains about topics that could cause "serious" damage to national security and eight that could be expected to cause "exceptionally grave" damage to the security of the United States if released. The heart of the case, then, was the second question: What was she thinking when she did this? Was it sloppy or was there criminal intent? Could we prove that she knew she was doing something she shouldn't be doing?

Knowing and proving what is in someone's head is always a hard task. At the front of my mind from the start of this investigation was the recent case of former CIA Director David Petraeus, which had concluded only a few months earlier. In 2011, Petraeus had given multiple notebooks containing troves of highly sensitive, top-secret information to an author with whom he was having an affair. In contrast to those Hillary Clinton corresponded with, the author did not have the appropriate clearance or a legitimate need to know the information, which included notes of discussions with President Obama about very sensitive programs. Petraeus was the CIA director, for heaven's sake — in charge of the nation's secrets. He knew as well as anyone in government that what he did was wrong. He even allowed the woman to photograph key pages from classified documents. And then, as if to underscore that he knew he shouldn't do what he did, he lied to FBI agents about what he had done. Despite all of this clear and powerful evidence, on facts far worse for him than for Secretary Clinton, and after he demonstrably lied to the FBI, the Department of Justice charged him only with a misdemeanor after he reached a plea-bargain agreement. In April 2015, he admitted guilt and agreed to a forty-thousand-dollar fine and probation for two years.

The misdemeanor charge Petraeus received for mishandling classified material was reasonable and consistent with past cases, but I argued strongly to Attorney General Holder that Petraeus also should be charged with a felony for lying to the Bureau. Replaying in my mind the Martha Stewart, Leonidas Young, and Scooter Libby cases, I argued that if we weren't going to hold retired generals and CIA directors accountable for blatantly lying during investigations, how could we justify jailing thousands of others for doing the same thing? I believed, and still believe, that Petraeus was treated under a double standard based on class. A poor person, an unknown person — say a young black Baptist minister from Richmond — would be charged with a felony and sent to jail.

Despite the endless drumbeat in the conservative media, filled with exaggerated scandals and breathless revelations of little practical import, Hillary Clinton's case, at least as far as we knew at the start, did not appear to come anywhere near General Petraeus's in the volume and classification level of the material mishandled. Although she seemed to be using an unclassified system for some classified topics, everyone she emailed appeared to have both the appropriate clearance and a legitimate need to know the information. So although we were not going to prejudge the result, we started the Clinton investigation aware that it was unlikely to be a case that the career prosecutors at the Department of Justice would prosecute. That might change, of course, if we could find a smoking-gun email where someone in government told Secretary Clinton not to do what she was doing, or if we could prove she obstructed justice, or if she, like Petraeus, lied to us during an interview. It would all turn on what we could prove beyond a reasonable doubt, a very different standard from that of television talk shows or Congressional sound bites.

Washington being a tribal city, prominent Republicans immediately and predictably began chanting that the Obama administration couldn't be trusted to investigate the Democratic Party's presidential front-runner and a former official in the Obama administration. Many Republicans, prodded by self-appointed legal and investigative experts on their favored media outlets, and often reacting to inaccurate or misleading news reporting, seemed certain the former secretary of state had committed the worst crimes since the Rosenbergs gave our nuclear secrets to the Russians in the 1950s and were executed for it. The Democrats, in turn, were dismissive of the case from the outset, claiming the examination of the emails wasn't even an "investigation" but merely a "review" or some other tortured euphemism.

Under intense pressure from the Clinton presidential campaign, *The New York Times* walked back a story, published on July 23, 2015, reporting that the Justice Department was considering opening a criminal investigation into Clinton's handling of her emails. As a result of the Clinton team's tenacious pushback, the *Times* appended two separate corrections to its original article — first claiming that Mrs. Clinton herself was not the focus of any investigation and then, a day later, changing the description of the inspector general's transmission to the FBI from "criminal referral" to "security referral." Though the *Times* may have thought those clarifications were necessary, their original story was much closer to the mark. It was true that the transmission to the FBI from the inspector general did not use the word "criminal," but by the time of the news story we had a full criminal investigation open, focused on the secretary's conduct. We didn't correct the *Times* and contradict the Clinton campaign because — consistent with our practice — we were not yet to a point where it was appropriate to confirm an investigation. Still, the bitterly fought episode, parsing word choices, was only a small taste of what was to come, and many within the FBI knew it.

"You know you are totally screwed, right?"

The FBI deputy director in the summer of 2015 was a plainspoken, smart, and darkly funny career special agent named Mark Giuliano.

I smiled tightly. "Yup," I said. "Nobody gets out alive."

This of course was not my first time in the middle of something guaranteed to antagonize, even outrage, some very powerful people. In a way I couldn't have imagined then, Martha Stewart, Scooter Libby, Stellar Wind, and the Bush administration's torture policy were all preparation for what lay ahead. Under great pressure in all those situations, we had tried to push outside voices aside, and to follow the law and the facts. Even in hindsight, I still thought we had done the right thing.

The Clinton investigation, or inquiry, or referral, or whatever people on either side of the political spectrum chose to call it, was already a major topic in the emerging presidential campaign. Giuliano's point, which I saw clearly, was that this was a no-win scenario for the FBI. At the core of Mark's gallows humor was a gallows. No matter what the honest outcome, the institution's credibility — and mine — would be damaged; the only question was how much. As strange as it might sound, there is a certain freedom in being totally screwed, in knowing you will be attacked no matter what you do. Half the country will howl either way, so tune out the critics and let only the facts and the law dictate which half. At the time, of course, it never occurred to me that our decisions could outrage *both* halves.

To handle the case, the FBI's Counterintelligence Division brought together a group of about twenty experts — made up of agents, analysts, and support personnel. As the division normally did, they gave the case an obscure code name: Midyear Exam. The group I regularly dealt with about Midyear ranged from the senior-most FBI executives to the supervisory agent and analyst supervising the case together day-to-day, and

282

included lawyers from three different levels in the general counsel's office. I frequently referred to this collection of twelve people as "the Midyear team." I didn't meet with the "line-level" agents, analysts, and support folks except to periodically thank them for their hard work.

Over the next eighteen months, I relied on the twelve-member Midyear team to help me make decisions on the case — though the ultimate decisions would be mine. Some members moved in and out as a few senior executives retired, but the group remained a collection of very bright people with strong personalities, who frequently clashed with one another, as siblings might. I liked that. One of the junior lawyers was given to exhaling in disgust at statements she didn't like and then interrupting aggressively, no matter who was speaking. This annoyed many of her colleagues. I loved it. I wanted her on the team because I knew she didn't care about rank at all. Her directness added value even when she was wrong. I wanted to hear her perspective and knew it would come without prompting, even if she interrupted a senior official to offer it. That interruption would stimulate great conversation.

Each of my advisers undoubtedly had

their own political opinions and views. They were human beings, after all. They also had spouses, friends, or family members who had their own points of view as well. But I didn't know what those views were. I never heard anyone on our team — not one — take a position that seemed driven by their personal political motivations. And more than that: I never heard an argument or observation I thought came from a political bias. Never. Instead we debated, argued, listened, reflected, agonized, played devil's advocate, and even found opportunities to laugh as we hashed out major decisions. I ordered the team to keep me closely informed so I could make sure the investigators had all the resources they needed and all possible protection from outside pressure. And so I could make all the major decisions, which was ultimately my job.

The first decision that had to be made was whether to talk about the case publicly. As was customary, the FBI refused to confirm the existence of any investigation concerning Secretary Clinton's email usage after we opened it that July. But by late September 2015, almost three months into the case, that "no comment" seemed increasingly silly. The investigation, after all, had started with a public referral from an inspector general. The campaigns themselves and both parties in Congress were talking about our work. Agents were out doing interviews with people connected to the case and interacting with people who could, and did, tell the press about it. Congress also wanted some on-the-record assurance that we were looking into the issues, especially because the press was clamoring.

Department of Justice and FBI policies contained established exceptions to our no-comment policy, for investigations of extraordinary public interest or where our investigative activity is apparent to the public. We had already utilized this exception a number of times in my tenure as director, confirming a criminal investigation into whether there had been unlawful targeting by the IRS of so-called Tea Party political organizations, as well as confirming a criminal civil rights investigation in Ferguson, Missouri. In each of those situations, as in many others during my career, the department made a judgment that the public needed to be assured that law-enforcement professionals were investigating those controversial cases.

As it happened, Attorney General Loretta Lynch and I had scheduled appearances with reporters at the beginning of October where it was obvious that we each would be pressed on whether the Justice Department was acting on the referral we'd received from the intelligence community inspector general. If we were going to confirm an investigation, I thought this would be a sensible time to do it. So, in late September, I scheduled a meeting with the attorney general to discuss this possibility. The senior leadership of DOJ and the FBI also attended the meeting, which was held in a conference room in the Justice Department's Command Center.

I had known Loretta Lynch since the early 1990s, when we worked a case together as prosecutors in New York. Drug dealers we were investigating in Manhattan were plotting to kill a federal judge in Brooklyn, where she was an Assistant United States Attorney, so we joined forces on the case. She was a smart lawyer and honest person, open to hearing others' points of view. In the Justice Command Center, I explained that I thought we had reached a point where at my regular quarterly press roundtable, set for October 1, I should confirm we had a Clinton email investigation open, which the whole world knew anyway, but then offer no further details.

Attorney General Lynch agreed that it

made sense to do that. But then she quickly added, "Call it 'a matter.' "

"Why would I do that?" I asked.

"Just call it 'a matter,' " came her answer.

It occurred to me in the moment that this issue of semantics was strikingly similar to the fight the Clinton campaign had waged against *The New York Times* in July. Ever since then, the Clinton team had been employing a variety of euphemisms to avoid using the word "investigation." The attorney general seemed to be directing me to align with that Clinton campaign strategy. Her "just do it" response to my question indicated that she had no legal or procedural justification for her request, at least not one grounded in our practices or traditions. Otherwise, I assume, she would have said so.

The FBI didn't do "matters." The term means nothing in our language, and it was misleading to suggest otherwise. It was probably a mistake that I didn't challenge this harder. But in that moment, I decided that her request was too frivolous to take issue with, especially as my first battle with a new boss. I also was confident the press, and the public, would totally miss the distinction between a "matter" and an "investigation" anyway. Maybe she knew that, too. I know the FBI attendees at our meeting saw her request as overtly political when we talked about it afterward. So did at least one of Lynch's senior leaders. George Toscas, then the number-three person in the department's National Security Division and someone I liked, smiled at the FBI team as we filed out, saying sarcastically, "Well, you are the Federal Bureau of *Matters.*"

I followed the attorney general's direction at my regular quarterly press roundtable on October 1, 2015. When a reporter asked a question about the "investigation," I replied that I was following it closely. I said I was confident we had "the resources and the personnel assigned to the matter, as we do all our work, so that we are able to do it in a professional, prompt, and independent way."

I did what my boss ordered me to do. I said "matter." As expected, the press uniformly missed the distinction and reported that I had confirmed the existence of an investigation. From then on, I called it by its true name — we had an open "investigation" and I wouldn't comment on it any further. Until I had to, many months later.

The Midyear Exam investigators worked

hard all winter, digging for evidence that would help us determine what Secretary Clinton was thinking when she set up her email system and when she used it. They read every email they could find, they searched for emails in the mailboxes of others she might have written to, they tracked down the people who created her system, maintained it, and supplied her mobile devices, and they interviewed everyone who worked around her at the State Department. The supervisory investigator and analyst met with me about every two weeks to update me on their team's work, much of which involved painstaking reconstruction of electronic records. For example, agents found a decommissioned server that had once hosted her personal email domain, but the email software had been removed by technical personnel as a routine matter when the server was replaced, which was like dropping millions of tiny email fragments into the bottom of the server. With incredible, painstaking skill, the FBI team put much of that mind-boggling jigsaw puzzle back together.

Still, by early 2016, it was starting to look like we did not have a prosecutable case. We had more work to do, and needed to interview Secretary Clinton — something the investigators, as was typical in cases like this, were saving for late in the investigation, after we had gathered all available information. But so far we had not found evidence that would form a prosecutable case. We knew that the Department of Justice would never bring — and had never brought — criminal charges in such a situation without strong evidence that the subject of our investigation knew she was doing something she shouldn't be doing. Accidents, sloppiness, and even extreme carelessness with regard to classified information were not things that were prosecuted. Ever. For a current government employee, of course, there would be severe consequences for such carelessness, including the real possibility of losing access to classified information or getting fired, but there would be no criminal prosecution.

If the investigation continued on the same trajectory, the challenge was going to be closing the case in a way that maintained the confidence of the American people that their justice system was working in an honest, competent, and nonpolitical manner. We'd never convince extreme Clinton haters in the news media of that, of course, but hopefully we could persuade a majority of fair-and open-minded Americans.

But in early 2016, there was a development that threatened to challenge that effort significantly. A development still unknown to the American public to this day. At that time, we were alerted to some materials that had come into the possession of the United States government. They came from a classified source — the source and content of that material remains classified as I write this. Had it become public, the unverified material would undoubtedly have been used by political opponents to cast serious doubt on the attorney general's independence in connection with the Clinton investigation.

I, for one, didn't see any instance when Attorney General Lynch interfered with the conduct of the investigation. In fact, I had not spoken to her about the case at all since our "call it a matter" conversation in late September. Though I had been concerned about her direction to me at that point, I saw no indication afterward that she had any contact with the investigators or prosecutors on the case. But it bothered me that there was classified information that would someday become public — likely decades from now — and be used to attack the integrity of the investigation and, more important, call into question the independence of the FBI.

Contributing to this problem, regrettably, was President Obama. He had jeopardized the Department of Justice's credibility in the investigation by saying in a *60 Minutes* interview on October 11, 2015, that Clinton's email use was "a mistake" that had not endangered national security. Then on Fox News on April 10, 2016, he said that Clinton may have been careless but did not do anything to intentionally harm national security, suggesting that the case involved overclassification of material in the government. President Obama is a very smart man who understands the law very well. To this day, I don't know why he spoke about the case publicly and seemed to absolve her before a final determination was made. If the president had already decided the matter, an outside observer could reasonably wonder, how on earth could his Department of Justice do anything other than follow his lead? The truth was that the president — as far as I knew, anyway — had only as much information as anyone following it in the media. He had not been briefed on our work at all. And if he was following the media, he knew nothing, because there had been no leaks at all up until that point. But his comments still set all of us up for corrosive attacks if the case were completed with no charges brought.

In early spring, as I began to see the end of the investigation coming with insufficient evidence to support a prosecution, I urged the deputy attorney general — my immediate boss — to give thought to what the endgame might look like if the case were to be closed without charges. Sally Yates was a career prosecutor whom I had known casually for years. She and one of my close friends had been federal prosecutors together in Atlanta, where she earned a reputation as tough, thoughtful, and independent. Everything I saw as FBI director was consistent with that reputation. Because this was not a normal case, and 2016 was not a normal year, I suggested to Yates that unusual transparency might be necessary to reassure the American people and to protect the institutions of justice. I said I hoped she would put people to work researching what was possible under the law. I never heard back.

Any investigator or prosecutor who doesn't have a sense, after nearly a year of investigation, where their case is likely headed, is incompetent. Prosecutors routinely begin drafting indictments before an investigation is finished if it looks likely to end up there, and competent ones also begin thinking about how to end investigations that seem likely to end without charges. In neither case are minds closed to a different outcome if subsequent evidence dictates, but competent people think ahead.

One weekend in early May, I typed a draft statement laying out the findings of this case with the most aggressive transparency possible assuming the investigation ended in the current position. Unless we suddenly found a smoking-gun email or directive clearly pointing to Clinton's intent, or unless she lied to us in an FBI interview, both of which were possibilities, this was the way I expected the case to end. In such a poisonous political environment, I knew we needed to think far in advance how best to present our decision. Many changes were made to those early drafts. I tried out different ways to most accurately describe the nature of Secretary Clinton's conduct. Her actions in regard to her emails seemed really sloppy to us, more than ordinary carelessness. At one point the draft used the term "grossly negligent," and also explained that in this case those words should not be interpreted the way a hundred-year-old criminal statute used the term. One part of that 1917 law made it a felony if a person "through gross negligence permits [classified material] to be removed from its proper place of custody or delivered to anyone in violation of his trust, or to be lost, stolen, abstracted, or destroyed."

The history of that provision strongly indicated that Congress in 1917 meant the statute to apply only to conduct that was very close to willful — that is, driven by bad intent — and members of Congress who voted for it back then were very concerned that they not make merely careless behavior a felony. I was told that the Department of Justice had only charged one person under this statute since 1917 — a corrupt FBI agent whose conduct was far worse than gross negligence — and no one had ever been convicted under it. This context strongly reinforced my sense that the statute simply did not apply in the Clinton email case and made use of the term "grossly negligent" inappropriate and potentially confusing, given the old statute. So I directed our team to consider other terms that more accurately captured her behavior. After looking at multiple drafts, I settled on "extremely careless" as the best way to describe the conduct.

I gave my draft statement to senior FBI personnel and asked them to think about three things: the accuracy of the facts laid out in the draft; any policy or other limitations around making such a statement; and the wisdom and mechanics of presenting it to the American people. This was the farthest I could imagine us going. I have made no final decision, I said, but let's use this draft to start our discussions. What is possible under the law? What makes sense? If we were going to provide some kind of public statement, how would we do it? Standing with the attorney general? In some kind of written report to Congress? Alone? Let's talk about it.

The FBI leadership team chewed on it, marked it up, debated it, and slept on it. I wanted as much feedback as possible, with one big exception: to protect the FBI's independence if necessary down the line, I didn't want the Department of Justice to know what we were doing. The most aggressive step to demonstrate the independence of our investigation would be for the FBI to announce something without involving the Justice Department at all. I didn't know whether that made sense — and at times the idea struck me as crazy — but this would no longer be even a theoretical option if we told anyone at Justice about our deliberations. They might well direct me not even to consider such a thing, and I would be bound to follow that order, as I had when ordered to call it "a matter." So we kept it inside the FBI and continued debating it as the investigation moved toward the final step — interviewing Hillary Clinton.

But at that point the investigation got bogged down. A big issue in the case, and in the public debate over the case, was Secretary Clinton's process for deciding which of her emails to return to the State Department after State requested she turn over work-related emails. By her account, there were about sixty thousand total emails on her personal server as of late 2014, when State asked for the work emails. The secretary's personal lawyers reviewed those emails, producing about half of them and deleting the rest. I, and the entire FBI Midyear team, believed our investigation would not be credible if we did not dive into that culling process. We weren't just going to take their word for it. We needed to know firsthand how the lawyers made those decisions and we wanted to see the devices they used so our experts could look for traces of the deleted emails.

For understandable reasons, this made the Justice Department lawyers very nervous. The laptops that the Clinton lawyers used to review Secretary Clinton's emails also contained their work for other clients. Our examination of those laptops could potentially violate the attorney-client privilege and attorney work-product protections, not just for their client Hillary Clinton but for other, unrelated clients as well. The attorney representing Clinton's lawyers, Beth Wilkinson, was talking tough to the Justice Department: there was no way she and those lawyers were going to talk about work for a client, and no way they were going to produce their laptops so the FBI could look at them. That was something that Wilkinson intimated she would fight until the bitter end. FBI General Counsel Jim Baker knew Wilkinson, so I asked him to speak to her and emphasize our determination to get those laptops. He did so, and she promptly told the Department of Justice lawyers the FBI was going around them. A chill descended on the relationship between the FBI and the department attorneys.

We were at an impasse. The FBI could not, with a straight face, tell the American people we had done a competent investigation if we didn't move heaven and earth to understand that email review and deletion process. It didn't matter to us that it involved her lawyers. I would not agree to

298

complete the investigation without seeing those laptops and interviewing those lawyers. Period. If Secretary Clinton wanted to still be under criminal investigation for the next two years, fine. Despite the force of that argument, by mid-May, we still had not gotten access to the laptops. We faced the real prospect of the investigation going on into the summer and after the political conventions, when the presidential candidates would be nominated.

In May, I went to Sally Yates and told her this was dragging on too long. We were now weeks from the conventions and I was close to the point where I was going to recommend the appointment of a special prosecutor. My predecessors had done that from time to time, most prominently when Director Louis Freeh recommended in writing that the attorney general appoint one to investigate then–President Bill Clinton's fund-raising activities. I said that soon it would be too late for this Department of Justice to complete the investigation without grievous damage to public faith in our work. It would require a prosecutor outside the control of the political leadership of the department. I didn't know the date I would recommend such a thing, I said, but we were getting close, unless we got those laptops.

Yates understood. I don't know what she did, but almost immediately the Midyear team could feel an injection of energy and backbone into the junior lawyers at the Justice Department. Suddenly they were hell-bent on getting those laptops. Within a week or two, the lawyers had negotiated a deal that got us what we needed — the physical laptop devices and interviews of the lawyers who used them to sort Clinton's emails. I don't know how they convinced the private lawyers to make the deal, because the FBI was not involved in the negotiations. We got the access we wanted and found nothing that changed our view of the case, but I was now satisfied that we had done what a credible investigation required.

While all this wrestling over the lawyer laptops was going on, I spent June still struggling with what I thought was the endgame. How do we close the Clinton email case — six weeks before the Democratic Convention — in a way that maximizes public confidence that the institutions of justice have acted justly? Two things happened that brought me back to the crazy idea of personally offering the American people unusual transparency, and doing it without the leadership of the Justice Department.

First, in mid-June, the Russian government began dumping emails stolen from institutions associated with the Democratic Party. It began with entities calling themselves DCLeaks and Guccifer 2.0. They were stolen emails intended to harm Clinton and the Democrats. This made very real the prospect that the classified material relating to Loretta Lynch might drop at any moment, not decades from now. As noted earlier, the release of that material, the truth of which we had not verified, would allow partisans to argue, powerfully, that the Clinton campaign, through Lynch, had been controlling the FBI's investigation.

Then, on Monday, June 27, on a hot Phoenix airport tarmac, Bill Clinton and Attorney General Lynch met privately aboard an FBI Gulfstream 5 jet for about twenty minutes. When I first heard about this impromptu meeting, I didn't pay much attention to it. I didn't have any idea what they talked about. But to my eye, the notion that this conversation would impact the investigation was ridiculous. If Bill Clinton were going to try to influence the attorney general, he wouldn't do it by walking across a busy tarmac, in broad daylight, and up a flight of stairs past a group of FBI special agents. Besides, Lynch wasn't running the investigation anyway. But none of these basic realities had any impact on the cable news punditry. As the firestorm grew in the media, I paid more attention, watching it become another corrosive talking point about how the Obama Justice Department couldn't be trusted to complete the Clinton email investigation.

In the middle of that firestorm, the attorney general rejected calls that she recuse herself from the Hillary Clinton investigation altogether. Instead, on Friday, July 1, she chose a very strange position — that she would not remove herself, but she would accept my recommendation about the case and that of the career prosecutors at Justice. In effect, she was removing herself but not removing herself. Again, very strange.

Given the attorney general's tortured half-out, half-in approach, I again considered calling for the appointment of a special prosecutor. The appointment of a special prosecutor — someone outside the normal chain of command and with powers to ensure independence — was, as noted, a rare step. But I decided it would be brutally unfair to do that. This was not a political decision, but an ethical one, driven by our values. Any subject of an investigation is entitled to be treated fairly. A world-class FBI team had investigated Hillary Clinton for a year, and all of them — to a person — believed there was no prosecutable case. Calling for a special prosecutor now would wrongly imply there was something to the case, which would then drag on for many months, if not longer. And it would give a false impression to the American people; in other words, it would be a lie.

For years, I have spoken of the reservoir of trust and credibility that makes possible all the good we do at the FBI and the Department of Justice. When we stand up, whether in a courtroom or at a cookout, and identify ourselves as part of those institutions, total strangers believe what we say, because of that reservoir. Without it, we are just another partisan player in a polarized world. When we tell a judge or a jury or Congress what we saw, or found, or heard, they are not hearing it from a Republican or a Democrat. They are hearing it from an entity that is separate and apart in American life. The FBI must be an "other" in this country or we are lost. I have always used the reservoir metaphor because it captures both the immensity of it and how quickly it can be drained away by a hole in the dam. How could I protect the reservoir standing behind an attorney general who appeared politically compromised? The FBI was independent and apolitical, and the American people needed to see that.

To protect that reservoir, I made a decision. I needed to visibly step away from Loretta Lynch and do something I never could have imagined before 2016: have the FBI separately offer its views to the American people as soon as possible, by making public my recommendation and the thinking behind it. I knew this was going to suck for me. From the Democratic side would come predictable stuff about my wanting the spotlight, being out of control, driven by ego. From the Republican side would come more allegations of Justice Department incompetence or corruption. And it could forever sour my relationship with the leadership of the Justice Department. But I believed — and still believe, even in hindsight — it was the best thing for the FBI and for the Department of Justice.

The American people needed and deserved transparency, and I believed that I had the independent reputation to step out front and take the hits to protect the reservoir.

As things stood, I was going to step to a podium on Tuesday morning, July 5, in FBI headquarters and end this case. Unless, of course, Hillary Clinton lied to us when we finally conducted our interview with her, on July 2, 2016.

Many pundits have questioned why the FBI waited so long to interrogate Secretary Clinton when she was the subject of the inquiry. That is exactly the reason. Experienced investigators always avoid conducting interviews with subjects who know more about the facts than they do. That knowledge imbalance favors the subject, not the investigator. Especially in white-collar crime cases, investigators prefer to master all of the facts before questioning the subject, so that interrogators can ask smart questions and so the subject can be confronted, as necessary, with documents or statements made by other witnesses. That is what the FBI did in every standard investigation; and that is what the Midyear team did with Hillary Clinton. The agents and analysts of the FBI spent a year learning all they could about how Secretary Clinton set up and used her personal email system. Now we were ready to see if, under extensive questioning, she would lie to us about any of it and whether we could prove she had lied. In white-collar criminal cases, we often find that a subject will lie to cover up bad behavior, offering us a way to prosecute even where we can't make a case on the substantive charges that started the case. It is unlikely that a sophisticated, well-represented person will lie in a way we can prove, but Stewart and Libby show it can happen. The Clinton interview, while coming at the end of our investigation, was extremely important.

The Department of Justice prosecutors and Secretary Clinton's lawyers set the Saturday morning of the Independence Day three-day weekend for her interview, which would take place at FBI headquarters in Washington.

There has been so much misinformation spread about the nature of this interview that the actual events that took place merit discussion. After being discreetly delivered by the Secret Service to the FBI's basement garage, Hillary Clinton was interviewed by a five-member joint FBI and Department of Justice team. She was accompanied by five members of her legal team. None of Clinton's lawyers who were there remained investigative subjects in the case at that point. The interview, which went on for more than three hours, was conducted in a secure conference room deep inside FBI headquarters and led by the two senior special agents on the case. With the exception of the secret entry to the FBI building, they treated her like any other interview subject. I was not there, which only surprises those who don't know the FBI and its work. The director does not attend these kinds of interviews. My job was to make final decisions on the case, not to conduct the investigation. We had professional investigators, schooled on all of the intricacies of the case, assigned to do that. We also as a matter of procedure don't tape interviews of people not under arrest. We instead have professionals who take detailed notes. Secretary Clinton was not placed under oath during the interview, but this too was standard procedure. The FBI doesn't administer oaths during voluntary interviews. Regardless, under federal law, it would still have been a felony if Clinton was found to have lied to the FBI during her interview, whether she was under oath or not. In short, despite a whole lot of noise in the media and Congress after the fact, the agents interviewed Hillary Clinton following the

FBI's standard operating procedures.

I spent a long time on the phone with the Midyear team leaders that afternoon hearing their report of what Secretary Clinton had said. None of it surprised the professionals who had spent hundreds if not thousands of hours over the past year circling the former secretary, reading thousands of her emails and interviewing all those around her. By Clinton's account, she was unsophisticated both about technology and security, used the personal account for convenience to avoid maintaining dual government and personal email accounts, and still didn't consider the contents of the emails to be classified. Her lack of technological sophistication is evident in her memoir, *What Happened,* in which she seems to intimate that her private server in Chappaqua was protected from hacking because it was contained in a home guarded by the Secret Service. Hacking a server is done through the internet, not by breaking the glass in a basement window. She also said in her interview that she believed she and her staff had successfully "talked around" sensitive topics, a method of operating made necessary by the State Department's poor communications infrastructure, which didn't provide secure and reliable email and phone for her and her senior staff. There was some truth to this, but although frustrating to her team, it didn't change the rules around classified information. Also in her interview, Clinton said she delegated the review and deletion of her emails to others, believed they were only deleting purely personal emails, and had no knowledge of any efforts to obstruct justice.

After discussion and careful review of her answers, there was nothing in her comments that we could prove was a lie beyond a reasonable doubt. There was no moment when investigators caught her in a lie. She did not at any point confess wrongdoing or indicate that she knew what she had done with her emails was wrong. Whether we believed her or not, we had no significant proof otherwise. And there was no additional work the investigators thought they should do. This case was done. Now the American people needed to know what the FBI had found.

I spent Sunday and Monday with the team, working on the announcement. We decided to do it live and in person so that people heard it all at once, and we worked hard to maintain the professional, nonpartisan tone we intended. We would keep it short and take no questions, but try to offer as much detail and transparency as possible. We believed that the details of what we did and what we found were essential to the credibility of the investigation and the announcement. Every word of the statement was reviewed by the FBI legal team to ensure it was consistent with the law and Department of Justice policy.

I was nervous on the morning of July 5, for a bunch of reasons. It felt like I was about to damage my career. That's okay, I told myself; you are fifty-five years old, you have money in the bank and a ten-year term, and you don't want to be anything else; you aren't trying to climb anyplace. I was also nervous because I liked both the attorney general and the deputy attorney general and I was about to piss them off by not coordinating with them on a public statement about a high-profile case because any coordination could be perceived as political influence. Although I felt duty bound to call them before my announcement to tell them I was doing it, I was also not going to tell them what I was about to say. Awkward.

When I called Sally Yates, I told her I was about to make an announcement on the Clinton case and that I was not coordinating my statement with the Justice Department.

When I gave her this news, she asked no questions. Although I have never spoken to her about it, I think Yates understood what I was doing and why, and appreciated it. Attorney General Lynch's response was a little different. She asked only, "What will you be recommending?"

"I'm sorry, but I'm not going to answer that," I replied. "It's very important that I not have coordinated this in any way with the department. I hope someday you will understand why." She said nothing.

I hung up and walked out of my office. I stopped on the way to authorize the release of an email to the entire FBI. I wanted them to hear from me first:

To all:
As I send this, I am about to walk downstairs to deliver a statement to the media about our investigation of Secretary Clinton's use of a personal email server during her time as Secretary of State. I have attached a copy of the statement I intend to give. You will notice immediately that I am going to provide more detail about our process than we normally would in connection with an investigation, including our recommendation to Justice that no charges be

brought. I am doing that because I think the confidence of the American people in the FBI is a precious thing, and I want them to understand that we did this investigation in a competent, honest, and independent way. Folks outside the FBI may disagree about the result, but I don't want there to be any doubt that this was done in an apolitical and professional way and that our conclusion is honestly held, carefully considered, and ours alone. I have not coordinated or reviewed my statement with anyone except a small group of FBI officials who worked on the investigation. Nobody elsewhere in government has any idea what I am about to say, and that's the way it should be.

There is a lot of the pronoun "I" above, but this investigation and the conclusion are the product of a large and talented FBI team, made up of agents, analysts, technical experts, lawyers, and others. I have stayed close to it simply to ensure that the team had the resources they needed and that nobody interfered with them. Nobody did. I am proud to represent their work, and the entire FBI. We have done it the way the American people expect and deserve.

I was intentionally wearing a gold tie so I wasn't displaying either of the normal political gang colors, red or blue. I thought about trying to memorize the statement, but we kept making little word changes up to the end, making that impossible. My crack public affairs team figured out how to project the text on the back wall of the room so I could track it as I spoke.

I've taken some abuse, including from my beloved family, for "Seacresting it," by which they mean imitating the dramatic tease — "but first, this commercial" — of TV host Ryan Seacrest. I didn't intend to, but I can see what they meant. My thinking was that if I started with the conclusion that we were recommending no charges, nobody would listen to the rest of what I said. And the rest of what I said was critical to the American people having confidence that the FBI had been competent, honest, and independent.

As I expected, people on both sides of the partisan divide in Washington were very angry. Republicans were furious that I had failed to recommend prosecution in a case that "obviously" warranted it. This, as I've noted, was absurd. No fair-minded person with any experience in the counterespionage world (where "spills" of classified informa-

313

tion are investigated and prosecuted) could think this was a case the career prosecutors at the Department of Justice might pursue. There was literally zero chance of that. Democrats were furious because I had "defamed" Hillary Clinton by describing and criticizing her conduct in detail and yet recommending no charges.

There was shouting from both sides about my "violation" of Department of Justice policies. But in appropriate cases, where the public interest requires it, the Department of Justice has long revealed details about the conduct of uncharged people. The department had done so in the spring of 2015 after the FBI's investigation of the killing of Michael Brown in Ferguson, Missouri — including releasing an eighty-page memo detailing the entire investigation. They did it again in October 2015, in the case against IRS supervisor Lois Lerner, when the department laid out evidence gathered during a criminal investigation into whether the IRS had targeted and harassed Tea Party groups. The department said Lerner had used "poor judgment," but that "ineffective management is not a crime. . . . What occurred is disquieting and may necessitate corrective action — but it does not warrant criminal prosecution." Like those recent examples, this was a case where public interest and public confidence required that we explain what we had learned about Secretary Clinton's conduct. The result would have been far less credible and transparent without those details, causing damage to our Justice institutions' reservoir of trust with the American people. What made this unusual was that the FBI director — to protect both institutions — was stepping out front to make the announcement separate from the Department of Justice leadership. That decision was made knowing it put me and my professional reputation directly in the line of fire from all sides of the political spectrum.

Hindsight is always helpful, and if I had it to do over again, I would do some things differently. I would avoid the "Seacresting" mistake by saying at the beginning of my statement that we weren't recommending charges. At the time, I thought there was a risk people wouldn't listen carefully after the headline, but looking back, the risk of confusion from me delaying the conclusion was greater. More important, I would have tried to find a better way to describe Secretary Clinton's conduct than "extremely careless." Republicans jumped on the old statute making it a felony to handle classified information in a "grossly negligent" way — a statute that Justice would never use in this case. But my use of "extremely careless" naturally sounded to many ears like the statutory language — "grossly negligent" — even though thoughtful lawyers could see why it wasn't the same. I spent hours responding to congressional questions about it, and it became a talking point for those interested in attacking the FBI and the Department of Justice. Other than those two things, and in spite of the political shots directed at me since — and my supposedly being fired because of it — I would do the same thing again at that announcement, because I still believe it was the best available alternative to protect and preserve the Department of Justice's and the FBI's reservoir of trust with the American people.

After a September congressional hearing, despite all of the criticism, at least I could say the Bureau was rid of this awful case. We had offered transparency, tried to show the American people competence, honesty, and independence, and now the presidential campaign could run its course. Months later, during our January 27, 2017, dinner, President Trump told me that I had "saved her" with my July press conference. That was not my intention, just as I did not intend to "save him" with what came later. The goal was to tell the truth and demonstrate what higher loyalty — to the institutions of justice — looks like.

So my deputy director was right; we really were screwed, and it was as painful as anticipated. We had tasted the poison of our political system, and I had taken all the hits I anticipated, but I also felt great relief because the FBI and I were finished with Hillary Clinton and her emails.

If only.

CHAPTER 11
SPEAK OR CONCEAL

Safety lies in the prosecutor who tempers zeal with human kindness, who seeks truth and not victims, who serves the law and not factional purposes, and who approaches his task with humility.
— ROBERT H. JACKSON,
SUPREME COURT JUSTICE

Although the Clinton email case seemed like the center of the universe to the Washington political class, the FBI was actually involved in many other important matters. During the summer of 2016, we were working like crazy to understand what the Russians were up to. Evidence within the intelligence community strongly suggested that the Russian government was trying to interfere in the election in three ways.

First, they sought to undermine confidence in the American democratic enterprise — to dirty us up so that our election process would no longer be an inspiration to the rest of the world.

Second, the Russians wanted to hurt Hillary Clinton. Putin hated her, blaming her personally for large street demonstrations against him in Moscow in December 2011. Putin believed Clinton had given "a signal" to demonstrators by publicly criticizing what she called "troubling practices" before and during the parliamentary vote in Russia that year. She said, "The Russian people, like people everywhere, deserve the right to have their voices heard and their votes counted." Putin took that as an unforgivable personal attack.

Third, Putin wanted to help Donald Trump win. Trump had been saying favorable things about the Russian government and Putin had shown a long-standing appreciation for business leaders who cut deals rather than stand on principle.

At the heart of the Russian interference campaign was the release of damaging emails stolen from organizations and individuals associated with the Democratic Party. There were also indications of an extensive Russian effort to penetrate voter registration databases maintained by the states. In late July, the FBI learned that a Trump campaign foreign policy advisor named George Papadopoulos had been discussing, months earlier, obtaining from the Russian government emails damaging to Hillary Clinton. Based on this information, the FBI opened an investigation to try to understand whether Americans, including any associated with the Trump campaign, were working in any way with the Russians in their influence effort.

As with the Clinton email investigation, for months the Bureau resisted all calls from reporters and other outside observers to confirm an investigation was under way. It was simply too early, we didn't know whether we had anything to go on, and we wouldn't want to tip off any of the individuals we were examining. The FBI and the Department of Justice did not officially confirm our investigation — and then only in a general way — until March 2017.

A harder question was whether, during the heat of a presidential campaign, to tell the American people more about the overall Russian effort to influence the election. President Obama and his national security team wrestled with that question throughout August and September. At one meeting with the president, we discussed whether some kind of public "inoculation" made sense. That is, arming the American people with knowledge of the hostile effort to influence their voting decisions might help blunt its impact. I said I was tired of being the guy at the podium with controversial news — especially after the beating I had taken since the July 5 announcement — but I was willing to be the voice on this, absent any alternatives. I also acknowledged to the president that an inoculation effort might accidentally accomplish the Russians' goal of undermining confidence in our election system. If you tell Americans that the Russians are tampering with the election, have you just sowed doubt about the outcome, or given one side an excuse for why they lost? This was very tricky. President Obama saw the dilemma clearly and said he was determined not to help the Russians achieve their goal of undermining faith in our process. The administration continued to consider the idea of inoculation and what that might look like.

A few days later, to offer an option as the Obama team deliberated, I followed up on the idea of providing a "voice of inoculation" by drafting and sharing within the administration a newspaper opinion piece in my name. It laid out what the Russians were doing with the dumping of stolen emails, highlighted hacking aimed at state

321

voter databases, and placed those activities in the context of historical Russian election disruption efforts. I intended that as a warning to the American people. But there was no decision. The Obama team's deliberations were, as usual, extensive, thoughtful, and very slow. I suspected a major factor in their deliberations was the universal view of pollsters that Donald Trump had no chance. During a September meeting about the Russian effort, I remember President Obama reflecting that confidence in the outcome, saying of Putin, "He backed the wrong horse." Why risk undermining faith in our electoral process, he seemed to conclude, when the Russian efforts were making no difference? And why give Donald Trump the excuse to blame Obama for frightening the American people? He was going to lose anyway.

Finally, a month later, in early October, the Obama team decided some kind of formal statement from the administration was in order after all. The director of national intelligence, Jim Clapper, and the secretary of Homeland Security, Jeh Johnson, were prepared to sign it. The FBI leadership team and I decided that there was not an adequate reason for us to also sign on. By that point, there was widespread media coverage of a Russian campaign to influence the election. Numerous unnamed government officials were identified as sources in those stories. Prominent legislators issued statements and told the media they had been briefed about the Russian interference campaign. Candidate Clinton herself was talking about the Russian effort to elect her opponent. The websites and social media outlets pushing out stolen emails — including WikiLeaks and the Twitter page of its founder, Julian Assange — were widely and publicly associated with Russia. Given all of that, the administration's October statement was at best a marginal addition to the public's knowledge. Adding the FBI's name would change nothing and be inconsistent with the way we hoped to operate on the eve of an election.

Despite what politicians and pundits may say, there are no written rules about how the FBI and the Department of Justice should handle investigations as elections draw near. But there is a powerful norm that I always tried to follow: we should try to avoid, if possible, any action in the run-up to an election that could have an impact on the election result. In October 2016, there was no good reason for the FBI to speak about the Russians and the election. Americans already knew what was happening, so the FBI could reasonably avoid action.

But "avoid action" was not an option when the Clinton email investigation came back to my office in October in a powerful and unexpected way, four months after I had declared in front of cameras that the FBI had done a thorough investigation and was finished.

At some point in early October, someone at FBI headquarters (I think it was Deputy Director Andrew McCabe) mentioned to me that former Congressman Anthony Weiner had a laptop that might have some connection to the Clinton email case. I don't remember the conversation clearly. I suspect that is because it seemed like a passing comment and the notion that Anthony Weiner's computer might connect to Midyear and Hillary Clinton made no sense to me.

Weiner was a disgraced former Democratic congressman from New York, who resigned in 2011 after revelations that he was sending naked pictures of himself to a variety of women. He was also the estranged husband of Huma Abedin, one of Secretary Clinton's closest aides. The FBI had come into possession of the content of Weiner's laptop as part of a criminal investigation into Weiner's alleged improper contact with underage girls. The criminal investigators in New York had a search warrant that allowed them to review certain files from the laptop. In the course of their work, the criminal team saw other file names, but they could not open those under the authority of their search warrant, which was confined to materials directly relevant to the sex case. And some of the names on those thousands of email files led the criminal team in New York to think they might be related to the Clinton case.

At 5:30 A.M. on Thursday, October 27 — twelve days before the election — McCabe sent me an email saying the Midyear team needed to meet with me. I had no idea what that was about, but of course asked my staff to set something up as soon as possible. Later that morning, I walked into my conference room and smiled broadly at the team leaders, lawyers, and executives from the Midyear case, each sitting in the same seats they had occupied so many times in the year of the Clinton email investigation.

"The band is back together," I said, as I slid into my seat. "What's up?"

It would be a long time before I smiled like that again.

Members of the team explained that it appeared Weiner's laptop contained hundreds of thousands of emails from Hillary Clinton's personal email domain. This was an enormous trove of Secretary Clinton's emails. In 2014, Clinton had turned over to the State Department about thirty thousand emails and deleted about thirty thousand others as personal. This was far higher than those totals. But there was something else that caught their attention. The Midyear team had never been able to find Secretary Clinton's emails from her first few months as secretary of state, a period during which she was using an AT&T BlackBerry email domain. The investigators had been keen to find those early emails because if there were so-called smoking-gun emails — perhaps in which the secretary had been instructed not to use her personal email system or in which she had acknowledged doing something improper with classified materials — those emails were likely to be at the beginning of her tenure at State, when she first set up her own email address. But we had never found those early BlackBerry emails.

For reasons no one around the table could explain, the Weiner laptop held thousands of emails from the AT&T BlackBerry domain. They told me those might well include the missing emails from the start of Clinton's time at the Department of State. The team said there was no prospect of getting Weiner's consent to search the rest of the laptop, given the deep legal trouble he was in.

"We would like your permission to seek a search warrant."

Of course, I replied quickly. Go get a warrant.

"How fast can you review and assess this?" I asked.

Everyone in the room said that this review would take many weeks. There was, they said, simply too much material to do it more quickly. They needed to individually read tens of thousands of emails, and it had to be done by people who knew the context. This was not a situation where we could bring in hundreds of FBI employees to do the work. They wouldn't know what they were reading or looking for. The team told me there was no chance the survey of the emails could be completed before the November 8 election, now less than two weeks away.

"Okay," I said. "Do it as quickly as you can, but do it well, always well, no matter how long that takes."

After the meeting, the team contacted lawyers at the Justice Department, who agreed we needed to immediately get a search warrant for the Clinton emails on Weiner's laptop. Now we had another decision to make.

In July, and in the period since, I had repeatedly told the country and Congress that the FBI had done an honest, competent, and independent investigation and we were finished. There was no case here. People could take that to the bank. Yet, on October 27, the FBI and the Department of Justice had just decided to seek a search warrant to review a huge trove of Hillary Clinton's emails, including information that conceivably could change our view of the investigation. And, as I was assured by top investigators at the Bureau, there was no prospect of finishing the review before the election. What was our responsibility?

As I've noted, our long-standing tradition is to avoid, if at all possible, taking any action that might have an impact on an election. That tradition, that norm, was part of my identity. It was why the FBI hadn't signed the October Obama administration statement about Russian election interference. If this was a brand-new investigation, doing nothing would have been an option. But in the Clinton email case, I saw only two choices, only two doors, and they were both actions.

One door was marked "Speak." By speaking, I would tell Congress that the FBI's prior statements about the investigation being over were no longer true. That would be really, really bad. It would put the Bureau, and me, in a place where we might have an impact on an election. Really bad, nauseating even. To be avoided if humanly possible.

What was that other door? "Conceal," is what it read to my eyes. On behalf of the Federal Bureau of Investigation, an organization whose success relies on the public trust, I had testified under oath in public hearings to Congress and the American people that this case was finished. Now I knew that was no longer true. To remain silent at this point, while taking the step of getting a search warrant to review thousands of Hillary Clinton's emails, including possibly the missing early emails, would be an affirmative act of concealment, which would mean the director of the FBI had misled — and was continuing to mislead — Congress and the American people.

Speak or conceal — both terrible options. The Midyear senior team debated them both. We talked, then broke so people could think, then we talked again. We sat around my conference table and looked at it from every direction we could think of. My chief of staff, Jim Rybicki, took his normal seat at the opposite end of the oblong table from me, so he could quietly watch all the participants and their body language; his job was to make sure I was hearing from everyone, with nothing held back. He has unusual emotional intelligence, and if he saw something concerning — someone hesitating or being talked over — he would speak to the person privately and alert me so I could draw that person into a later discussion. The FBI's general counsel, Jim Baker, played a similar role. He was a longtime and wise friend, and I could count on him to bring arguments and concerns to me if they weren't being adequately voiced. He would often come to me privately and play devil's advocate because he knew we needed every view, every concern, every argument.

We made arguments against our arguments, but even with a dozen perspectives, we kept coming back to the same place: the credibility of the institutions of justice was at stake. Assuming, as nearly everyone did, that Hillary Clinton would be elected president of the United States in less than two weeks, what would happen to the FBI, the Justice Department, or her own presidency if it later was revealed, after the fact, that she was still a subject of an FBI investigation? What if, after the election, we actually found information that demonstrated prosecutable criminal activity? No matter what we found, that act of concealment would be catastrophic to the integrity of the FBI and the Department of Justice. Put that way, the choice between a "really bad" option and a "catastrophic" option was not that hard a call. We had to tell Congress that things had changed.

As we were arriving at this decision, one of the lawyers on the team asked a searing question. She was a brilliant and quiet person, whom I sometimes had to invite into the conversation. "Should you consider that what you are about to do may help elect Donald Trump president?" she asked.

I paused for several seconds. It was of course the question that was on everyone's mind, whether they expressed it out loud or not.

I began my reply by thanking her for asking that question. "It is a great question," I said, "but not for a moment can I consider it. Because down that path lies the death of the FBI as an independent force in American life. If we start making decisions based on whose political fortunes will be affected, we are lost."

In other words, if we at the FBI started to think like every other partisan in Washington thought — what's good for my "side" or whose political futures we might help or hurt — then the FBI would no longer have, and would no longer deserve, the public trust. The reservoir would be empty.

I instructed the team to tell the senior staff at Justice that I believed it was my duty to inform Congress that we were restarting the investigation. I would say as little as possible, but the FBI had to speak. I said I would be happy to discuss the matter with the attorney general and the deputy attorney general. I'm not sure exactly why I opened the door to them in a way I hadn't in July. I think part of it was a human reaction; I had taken an enormous amount of criticism for freezing them out in July. Part of it was also that I thought they would see the issue as I did and support me in what was to be a brutal situation. After all, the attorney general had publicly testified in July that the email investigation had been done well and was complete. Now her own prosecutors were seeking a search warrant. Surely, she would see that concealing that would be dishonest and a catastrophe for the Department of Justice. But, through their staffs, Lynch and Yates communicated that they thought this was a bad idea, that they would advise against it, but that it was my call and they didn't see a need to speak with me about it. They didn't order me not to do it, an order I would have followed.

They didn't want to choose a door: Speak or Conceal?

After I got this answer, I briefly toyed with the idea of communicating to them that I had decided not to tell Congress, just to see what they would do if I shifted the responsibility entirely to them, but decided that would be cowardly and stupid. Once again it became my responsibility to take the hit. I told the Midyear team to offer Justice the chance to review my draft letter to Congress and suggest any changes. They took that opportunity and, while preserving their advice against my doing it, offered some useful suggestions for how to describe what was going on, and in just a few sentences.

On Friday morning, October 28, which oddly enough stuck in my head as the thirty-ninth anniversary of the Ramsey Rapist attack, I sent the letter to the chairpersons and the ranking members of each committee to which the Bureau had provided information in the wake of the "completion" of the Clinton email investigation. As I did in July, I again emailed the entire FBI workforce about what was happening:

To all:
This morning I sent a letter to Congress in connection with the Secretary Clinton email investigation. Yesterday, the investigative team briefed me on their recommendation with respect to seeking access to emails that have recently been found in an unrelated case. Because those emails appear to be pertinent to our investigation, I agreed that we should take appropriate steps to obtain and review them.

Of course, we don't ordinarily tell Congress about ongoing investigations, but here I feel an obligation to do so given that I testified repeatedly in recent months that our investigation was completed. I also think it would be misleading to the American people were we not to supplement the record. At the same time, however, given that we don't know the significance of this newly discovered collection of emails, I don't want to create a misleading impression. In trying to strike that balance, in a brief letter and in the middle of an election season, there is significant risk of being misunderstood, but I wanted you to hear directly from me about it.

My letter to Congress was released to the press in about ten minutes, which in Washington was about nine minutes later than I expected. And my world caught back on fire.

The lovers and the haters from July largely switched positions. The fear that my letter was going to bring a Trump victory drove some normally thoughtful people around the bend. There was much hysteria about how we were violating Justice Department rules and policies. Of course, there were no such rules and there had never been another situation in the middle of an election like this. I suppose reasonable people might have decided not to speak about the renewed investigation, but the notion that we were out there breaking rules was offensive. "Tell me what you would do in my shoes and why you would do that," I asked, unheard, of op-ed writers and talking heads on television. I knew the answer, of course: most of them would do what would be best for their favorite team. Well, the FBI can't have a favorite team. The FBI represents the blindfolded Lady Justice and has to do the right thing outside the world of politics.

On Sunday night, October 30, I received an email from the attorney general, asking if she could meet with me privately after our Monday morning intelligence briefing at FBI headquarters.

"Of course," I replied.

As the briefing drew to a close, the attorney general, in front of the full conference room of our staffs, asked if she could meet with me. Which was a little odd, since I'd already agreed to the private meeting over email. But our staffs all noticed her request, which I suppose was the point. We went into a private office reserved for the attorney general, just off the morning briefing room. Her staff and mine waited outside, and we were finally alone.

During the last few days, the outcry in the media had been so intense, especially and understandably among supporters of Hillary Clinton, that I didn't know what I was about to hear from Loretta Lynch. Was she going to scream at me? Threaten me? Warn me? Deliver a message from the president? Everyone in the Obama administration almost certainly was angry at me and fearful that I'd jeopardized Clinton's election. I had every reason to believe that Loretta was among that group.

I walked into the room first. I turned and waited as the attorney general closed the door. She then turned, lowered her head, and walked toward me with arms out wide. This was awkward in a number of respects. Perhaps mostly because I am about eighteen inches taller than Loretta Lynch. When our bodies came together, her face went into my solar plexus as she wrapped her arms around me. I reached down and pressed both forearms, also awkwardly, against her back.

"I thought you needed a hug," she said as we separated. She was probably right. Although I'm not a hugger by nature, I felt physically beaten after the last few days. I also probably looked that way.

She then sat down on the couch and gestured for me to sit in an armchair near her. "How are you doing?" she asked. I detected genuine concern in her voice.

I told her this had been a nightmare. I explained how I saw the choices I faced and that "really bad" was better than "catastrophic." And then she floored me with another surprise.

"Would they feel better if it leaked on November 4?" she asked, referring to the Friday before the election.

"Exactly, Loretta," I answered.

I hadn't made my decision based on the prospect of a leak, but she was right. Once Justice approved the search warrant, it was likely the world would find out we had restarted the investigation anyhow, and we would look dishonest. Was she telling me I had done the right thing? Was she in some way thanking me for taking this brutal hit? She wasn't going to answer those questions for me.

Moments later, our conversation concluded. Loretta rose and reached for the door, but paused. Turning her head slightly toward me, she said, with just the slightest hint of a smile, "Try to look beat up." She had told somebody she was going to chew me out for what I had done. What a world.

I found the whole nightmare very painful. So much so that it actually made me a bit numb. Even people who liked me were confused by what I had done. Many others were downright nasty. I understood. My wife, who wanted Hillary Clinton to be elected the first woman president, was mostly concerned that I was back in the middle again. She said she understood why I did what I did, but resented the fact that I had to stand out front and take another hit. "It's like you keep stepping in front of the institution to get shot," she said. "I get it, but I wish it wasn't you, and I wish other people would get it."

Emotions were extraordinarily raw, and it

looked like the FBI had just put a finger on the scale for Donald Trump. And there was no hearing, no press conference, no chance to explain why we were doing what we were doing or to add anything to the letter we'd sent. Because we didn't know what we had and what we might find, any further public statement would be inherently limited and misleading and only add confusion and damage the FBI. For that reason, we chose the wording in my letter carefully:

In connection with an unrelated case, the FBI has learned of the existence of emails that appear to be pertinent to the investigation. I am writing to inform you that the investigative team briefed me on this yesterday, and I agreed that the FBI should take appropriate investigative steps designed to allow investigators to review these emails to determine whether they contain classified information, as well as to assess their importance to our investigation.

Although the FBI cannot yet assess whether or not this material may be significant, and I cannot predict how long it will take us to complete this additional work, I believe it is important to update your Committees about our efforts in light of my previous testimony.

Early the next week, while the Weiner laptop email review was under way, I attended a meeting in the White House Situation Room. As I walked down the White House halls and even when I was sitting in the meeting room, I felt like Bruce Willis in *The Sixth Sense,* where (spoiler alert) he doesn't realize he's dead. I imagined I could see my breath as I sat around the Sit Room table. Only Director of National Intelligence Jim Clapper and CIA Director John Brennan acknowledged me, each coming to me in the hallway as I waited for the meeting to start, putting a hand on my arm, and urging me to hang in there. With those two exceptions, nobody else in the room even met my eye.

Jim Clapper was the leader I admired most in government. His bald head and grouchy, deep, often mumbling voice masked a person who almost perfectly embodied the balances of kindness and toughness, confidence and humility. As the leader of the FBI, which is part of the American intelligence community, I reported to Director Clapper as well as the attorney general. I had come to treasure our quarterly evening meetings — "vespers," he called them — where we would sit in a secure room at his office and talk about work and life. Joined by our deputies, we would hoist wine for me, a vodka martini with two olives for him, and I would learn from someone who had led for nearly as long as I had been alive. To seal our friendship, I regifted to him a tie my brother-in-law had given me. It was solid red and decorated with little martini glasses. Because we considered ourselves people of integrity, I disclosed it was a regift as I handed him the tie. Clapper would invariably change into the martini tie for our vespers.

As we headed into the final week before the election, I checked on the Midyear team every day. They were working constantly, reading hundreds of new Clinton emails that we had never seen before. In a huge breakthrough, one I had been assured was not possible, the wizards at the FBI's Operational Technology Division figured out a way to do some of the de-duplicating electronically so agents and analysts didn't need to read hundreds of thousands of emails. Commercially available software wouldn't work for us. But the custom software program cut it down to mere thousands, which they read night after night. Despite what the team had told me on October 27, there might be a way after all to finish the review before the election.

On November 5, the Saturday before the election, the team told me they would be finished reviewing emails by the next morning and would be prepared to meet with me to offer their views. We met Sunday morning, two days before the election. There were indeed thousands of new Clinton emails from the BlackBerry domain, but none from the relevant time period. There were new work-related emails to and from Secretary Clinton. There were emails with classified content, but none of it was new to us. None of the new emails changed their view of the case. I pressed and pressed, wanting to be sure this wasn't their fatigue talking. No, they pushed back, we are tired, but we are also sure this is the right answer.

We then began debating what to do next. The group's overall view was that, having written to Congress on October 28, I was obligated to write to Congress again. There was one dissenter. The head of the National Security Branch of the FBI argued that it was just too late to speak again. He didn't offer much reasoning, only that he thought it was simply too close to the election. I think he was reacting to the pain our first letter had caused. We listened, kicked it around for a while, and decided we had to write to Congress again. If our rule in this unique context — Speak or Conceal — was to be as transparent as possible about the Bureau's activities, then it made no sense to act any differently on November 6 than we had on October 28. As before, we offered the Department of Justice senior staff the chance to edit my draft letter, and they gave us suggestions.

On Sunday, November 6, we sent a short letter to Congress informing them that the Clinton investigation was complete and our view had not changed. We didn't consider further public statement because it could only add more confusion two days before the election were I to stand before cameras to talk about what we found on Anthony Weiner's laptop. For reasons I couldn't yet explain, the FBI found that Weiner's laptop contained large numbers of new work-related Clinton emails (after she had previously claimed to have produced all work-related emails to the State Department) and also many of the emails we had seen previously about classified topics. The team had additional investigative work to do with respect to Huma Abedin and Anthony Weiner to figure out how they ended up with classified emails. Better, we concluded, to mirror the first notification to Congress with a similarly short closing notification. There was no time to send an email to the FBI workforce; they would hear about it on the news before turning on their computers Monday morning. The FBI had chosen not to conceal important information from Congress and the American people, and we had worked incredibly hard to competently close the case prior to Election Day. I thanked the Midyear team, telling them I had never worked with a finer group of people and that they had helped me deal with really hard problems in a great way.

That night, Patrice and I and one of our girls went out to a local Tex-Mex restaurant. The news about the second letter, closing the case again, was everywhere. A patron walked past my table and whispered, "Go Hillary." I was too tired to care. I wasn't going to vote. I didn't want anything more to do with the whole thing. I was deeply sorry we were part of it. I wanted a drink, so I had a delicious margarita on the rocks with salt, and even that made the news: *The Washington Post* reported that I was spotted drinking a "giant" margarita.

I have spent a great deal of time looking

back at 2016. And even though hindsight doesn't always offer a perfect view, it offers a unique and valuable perspective.

Like many others, I was surprised when Donald Trump was elected president. I had assumed from media polling that Hillary Clinton was going to win. I have asked myself many times since if I was influenced by that assumption. I don't know. Certainly not consciously, but I would be a fool to say it couldn't have had an impact on me. It is entirely possible that, because I was making decisions in an environment where Hillary Clinton was sure to be the next president, my concern about making her an illegitimate president by concealing the restarted investigation bore greater weight than it would have if the election appeared closer or if Donald Trump were ahead in all polls. But I don't know.

I have seen and read reports that Hillary Clinton blames me, at least in part, for her surprising election defeat. I know that at one point in her book she wrote that she felt she'd been "shivved" by me. She had worked for much of her professional life to become the first woman president of the United States, and quite understandably that loss, as unexpected and unpredicted as it was, hurt her badly. I have read she has felt anger toward me personally, and I'm sorry for that. I'm sorry that I couldn't do a better job explaining to her and her supporters why I made the decisions I made. I also know many Democrats are similarly baffled — even outraged — by the actions I took.

After the election, I attended a classified briefing with a group of senators from both parties. Toward the end of our meeting, which was not about Hillary Clinton's emails, one of the Democrats, then–Senator Al Franken, blurted out what probably many were thinking. He said he wanted to address "the elephant in the room," which was "what you did to Hillary Clinton." I asked Senate leader Mitch McConnell, who was also present, whether I could have an opportunity to respond to that. With a tone that seemed close to enjoyment, McConnell sat back and said, "Sure. Take all the time you need."

What I said to the senators gathered was that I wished they could go back in time with me and look at what happened from my perspective — from the FBI's perspective. "Come with me to October 28," I said. Even if I couldn't persuade them that I made the right decision, I hoped that at least I could explain what I was thinking, the doors I saw, and why I chose the one labeled "Speak" rather than the one labeled "Conceal." I didn't handle everything in the investigation perfectly, but I did my best with the facts before me. That was the point I was trying to convey that day, and I convinced at least one person in attendance. When I finished speaking, Senator Chuck Schumer came up to me. With tears in his eyes, he grabbed my hand with one of his and reached out with the other hand to repeatedly tap the center of my chest. "I know you," he said. "I know you. You were in an impossible position."

I hope very much that what we did — what I did — wasn't a deciding factor in the election. I say that with a wife and daughters who voted for Hillary Clinton and walked in the 2017 Women's March in D.C. the day after Donald Trump's inauguration. As I said in testimony, the very idea that my decision had any impact on the outcome leaves me feeling mildly nauseous (or, as one of my grammatically minded daughters later corrected me, "nauseated"). That's not because Donald Trump is such a deeply flawed person and leader (so flawed that he likely misunderstood what I meant when I testified that the notion of impact on the election left me "mildly nauseous").

It leaves me feeling sick because I have devoted my life to serving institutions I love precisely because they play no role in politics, because they operate independently of the passions of the electoral process. But 2016 was an election like no other. One of my kids showed me a tweet that seemed to capture the feelings at the time. It said, "That Comey is such a political hack. I just can't figure out which party."

I don't like being criticized, but I have to pay attention to the criticism because all human beings can be wrong sometimes. Still, to avoid being paralyzed and crushed by second-guessing, I use a rule of thumb: if the criticism is coming from a person I know to be thoughtful, I pay close attention to it. I even pay attention to anonymous critics and even savage partisans if their logic or factual presentation tell me they may be seeing something I missed. The rest of the crazies, and there were a lot of crazies, I ignore.

The stuff that gets me the most is the claim that I am in love with my own righteousness, my own virtue. I have long worried about my ego. I am proud of the fact that I try to do the right thing. I am proud of the fact that I try to be truthful and transparent. I do think my way is better than that of the lying partisans who crowd our public life today. But there is danger that all that pride can make me blind and closed off to other views of what the right thing is.

I have replayed the Clinton email case hundreds of times in my mind. Other than mistakes in the way I presented myself in the July 5 public statement in front of the television cameras, I am convinced that if I could do it all again, I would do the same thing, given my role and what I knew at the time. But I also think reasonable people might well have handled it differently.

For example, had I been a Democrat who had served in prior Democratic administrations, I'm not sure stepping away from the attorney general for the July 5 announcement would have been a helpful option. If I had a Democratic pedigree, I would have been painted as a conflicted partisan, and I would not have been able to credibly step away from the Justice political leadership to represent the institution independently. Of course, even an FBI director with a Democratic pedigree who didn't make a separate announcement would have faced the same decision to speak or conceal in late October because he or she would have informed Congress, in some fashion, that the investigation was completed in July.

Had I not served so long in the Department of Justice and led the organization in the Bush administration, I don't know that I would have felt the need to protect more than the FBI. I also don't know that I would have had the nerve to step away from the attorney general if I hadn't seen the negative side of deferring — about torture — in my last days as deputy attorney general in 2005. My public speaking experience also made it an option to do a live press conference. Another director, with different experiences behind him, might have deferred to Justice, letting that institution sort out its issues.

A different FBI director might have called for the appointment of a special prosecutor in late June, after Bill Clinton's visit to the attorney general's plane. I still think that would have been unfair to Hillary Clinton, but I can imagine another director doing it that way rather than trying to protect the institutions in the way I did.

Another person might have decided to wait to see what the investigators could see once they got a search warrant for the Clinton emails on Anthony Weiner's computer. That's a tricky one, because the Midyear team was saying there was no way to complete the review before the election, but I could imagine another director deciding to gamble a bit by investigating secretly in the week before the election. That, of course, walks into Loretta Lynch's point after our awkward hug. Had I not said something, what was the prospect of a leak during that week? Pretty high. Although the Midyear team had proven itself leakproof through a year of investigation, people in the criminal investigation section of the FBI in New York knew something was going on that touched Hillary Clinton, and a search warrant was a big step. The circle was now larger than it had ever been, and included New York, where we'd had Clinton-related leaks in prior months. Concealing the new investigation and then having it leak right before the election might have been even worse, if worse can be imagined. But a reasonable person might have done it.

I've also asked myself a hundred times whether I should have pressed for faster action after hearing something about Weiner's laptop around the beginning of October. But I did not understand what it meant until October 27. I had moved on to other cases and problems, and assumed if it was important, the team would bring it to me. Had I been told about it earlier, I'm sure I would have had the same reaction I had on

October 27 — we need to go get those emails, immediately. Whether I should have, or could have, been told the details earlier than October 27 is a question I can't answer.

The 2016 presidential election was like no other for the FBI, and even knowing what I know now, I wouldn't have done it differently, but I can imagine good and principled people in my shoes making different choices about some things. I think different choices would have resulted in greater damage to our country's institutions of justice, but I'm not certain of that. I pray no future FBI director is forced to find out.

In late November, after the election, I was in the Oval Office for a national security meeting with the president and other senior leaders. I still had that *Sixth Sense* feeling, especially among people who likely had thought they were going to continue their time in the White House under a new Democratic president. But President Obama was not among them. He greeted me as he always had and was professional and welcoming.

Extraordinary observer of body language that he was, maybe President Obama sensed I felt ill at ease, or maybe he just felt it was important to say something to me for a variety of reasons. As the meeting broke up, he asked me to stay behind. I sat on the couch, back to the grandfather clock. He sat in his normal chair, back to the fireplace. The White House photographer Pete Souza lingered to record the moment, but the president shooed him away. Within seconds, it was just the two of us.

President Obama then leaned forward, forearms on his knees. He started with a long preamble, explaining that he wasn't going to talk to me about any particular case or particular investigation.

"I just want to tell you something," he said.

I knew how badly Obama had wanted Hillary Clinton to win the White House. He had campaigned tirelessly for her and, by some accounts, harder for her than any other president had for their hoped-for successor. I knew he took the loss hard, as did the entire White House staff. But I respected President Obama and was very open to whatever it was he had to say.

"I picked you to be FBI director because of your integrity and your ability," he said. Then he added something that struck me as remarkable. "I want you to know that nothing — nothing — has happened in the last year to change my view."

He wasn't telling me he agreed with my decisions. He wasn't talking about the decisions. He was saying he understood where they came from. Boy, were those words I needed to hear.

I felt a wave of emotion, almost to the verge of tears. President Obama was not an outwardly emotional man in these kinds of meetings, but still I spoke in unusually emotional terms to him.

"That means a lot to me, Mr. President. I have hated the last year. The last thing we want is to be involved in an election. I'm just trying to do the right thing."

"I know, I know," he said.

I paused and then decided to add something. Maybe it was what I believe a large proportion of the country was feeling.

"Mr. President, my wife would kill me if I didn't take the opportunity to thank you and to tell you how much I'm going to miss you."

Although I hadn't supported President Obama when he ran for office, I had developed great respect for him as a leader and a person, and it was only at that moment that I felt the full weight of his imminent departure and what it would mean.

Unable to help myself, I added, "I dread the next four years, but in some ways, I feel more pressure to stay now."

He said nothing to this. There was no hint of what he thought of the incoming president or the future of the country, though undoubtedly there was much he could have said in both respects. Instead he patted me on the arm, then we rose and shook hands, and I walked out of the Oval Office. Soon that same office would have a new and very different occupant.

CHAPTER 12
TRUMP TOWER

And because seeking the truth is what
we are all about . . . the possibility —
even the perception — that that quest
may be tainted deeply troubles us, as it
long has and as it should.
— ROBERT M. GATES,
DIRECTOR OF CENTRAL INTELLIGENCE

A small fleet of fully armored SUVs — carrying the directors of national intelligence, the Central Intelligence Agency, the National Security Agency, and the Federal Bureau of Investigation — made its way toward the tall, shining gold tower in the middle of Manhattan. It was January 6, 2017, two weeks before Inauguration Day, and we had all flown up that morning. The NYPD led our cars through the barricade and onto the side street between Madison and Fifth Avenues in Manhattan. We walked in a group, surrounded by our security

people, and entered the side-street entrance for the Trump Tower residences.

The press, in their holding area on Fifth Avenue, couldn't see us arrive, nor could the protesters, in their own holding area not far away. Still, it was quite the scene in the comparatively quiet Trump Tower residences lobby. We were a two-elevator crowd of leaders and protectors. One elevator discharged a lady going to walk her tiny dog. She and her dog, both wearing expensive coats against a cold Fifth Avenue day, passed through our tight pack of dark suits and armed men. Chief spies holding locked bags with our nation's secrets politely mumbled, " 'Scuse us."

After all the live TV images of job applicants and dignitaries coming and going through the gilded Fifth Avenue lobby as though on a reality TV show, the leaders of our country's biggest intelligence agencies were sneaking in to see the president-elect. We were sneaking in to tell him what Russia had done to try to help elect him.

This was to be the third and final briefing session by the leadership of the intelligence community — referred to inside the government as the IC — to describe the classified findings of an intelligence community assessment (ICA) of Russia's actions during

the presidential election. At President Obama's direction, analysts from the CIA, NSA, and FBI, coordinated by senior analysts from ODNI — the Office of the Director of National Intelligence — had spent a month pulling together all sources of information to offer government officials, as well as the incoming Trump administration, a complete picture of the level of Russian interference in the 2016 presidential campaign. A watered-down, unclassified version of the ICA had been prepared for public release. But this was the meaty stuff. This was about sharing the most sensitive information, including sources and methods — precisely how we knew what we knew — spelling out in great detail why we had achieved the unusual state of a joint high-confidence opinion that Russia had intervened extensively in an American presidential election.

The four agencies had joined in the assessment, which was both stunning and straightforward: Russian president Vladimir Putin ordered an extensive effort to influence the 2016 presidential election. That effort, which came through cyber activity, social media, and Russian state media, had a variety of goals: undermining public faith in the American democratic process, deni-

grating Hillary Clinton and harming her electability and potential presidency, and helping Donald Trump get elected.

Our first briefing on the assessment had occurred the day before, January 5, 2017, with the incumbent of the Oval Office. In front of President Obama, Vice President Biden, and their senior aides, Jim Clapper, the director of national intelligence, laid out the work that had been done, the conclusions reached, and the basis for those conclusions. The president asked a variety of questions, as did the vice president.

It was at moments like these when I occasionally caught a glimpse of the warm, brotherly, and sometimes exasperating relationship between Barack Obama and Joe Biden, two very different personalities. The pattern was usually the same: President Obama would have a series of exchanges heading a conversation very clearly and crisply in Direction A. Then, at some point, Biden would jump in with, "Can I ask something, Mr. President?" Obama would politely agree, but something in his expression suggested he knew full well that for the next five or ten minutes we would all be heading in Direction Z. After listening and patiently waiting, President Obama would then bring the conversation back on course.

In this instance, we stayed on track. After an extended discussion on the intelligence assessment, the president asked what the plan was for further briefings. Director Clapper explained that we were to meet the Gang of Eight the next morning — the top officials in Congress, both Democrats and Republicans, briefed on intelligence matters — and then we would go immediately to New York City to brief the president-elect and his senior team.

Clapper explained to Obama that there was an unusual matter that needed to be brought to Mr. Trump's attention: additional material — what would become commonly called "the Steele dossier" — that contained a variety of allegations about Trump. The material had been assembled by an individual considered reliable, a former allied intelligence officer, but it had not been fully validated. The material included some wild stuff. Among that stuff were unconfirmed allegations that the president-elect had been engaged in unusual sexual activities with prostitutes in Russia while on a trip to Moscow in 2013, activities that at one point involved prostitutes urinating on a hotel bed in the presidential suite of the Ritz-Carlton that the Obamas had used while on a visit there. Another allegation was that these activities were filmed by Russian intelligence for the possible purpose of blackmail against the president-elect. Director Clapper explained that we believed the media were about to report on this material and therefore we had concluded it was important for the intelligence community to alert the incoming president.

Obama did not appear to have any reaction to any of this — at least none he would share with us. In a level voice, he asked, "What's the plan for that briefing?"

With just the briefest of sidelong glances at me, Clapper took a breath, then said, "We have decided that Director Comey will meet alone with the president-elect to brief him on this material following the completion of the full ICA briefing."

The president did not say a word. Instead he turned his head to his left and looked directly at me. He raised and lowered both of his eyebrows with emphasis, and then looked away. I suppose you can read whatever you want into a wordless expression, but to my mind his Groucho Marx eyebrow raise was both subtle humor and an expression of concern. It was almost as if he were saying, "Good luck with *that.*" I began to feel a lump in my stomach.

As the meeting broke up, my eyes fixed

on the bowl of apples on the Oval Office coffee table. Because the president and Mrs. Obama were very health conscious — the First Lady had run a campaign in schools about exchanging junk food for fruits and vegetables — the apples had been a fixture of the Oval Office for years. I wasn't entirely certain they were edible, but I once saw Chief of Staff Denis McDonough grab two at a time. He surely wasn't eating plastic fruit replicas. My youngest daughter long ago had asked me to get her a presidential apple, and this was surely the last time the Oval Office, an apple, and I would ever be together. Now or never. Swipe an apple at the close of a meeting about Russian interference? So tacky. But fatherhood beats tacky. I scooped an apple. Nobody stopped me. I photographed it in the car and texted the picture to my daughter, delivering the product that evening. She let me taste a slice. Not plastic.

Later that day, I received a call from Jeh Johnson, the secretary of Homeland Security, who had been a friend since we were federal prosecutors together in Manhattan in the 1980s. He had been in the Oval Office that morning for the briefing. I have no idea whether he was calling me at President

Obama's suggestion, or if the two even spoke about the matter, but he gave voice to how I viewed the Oval Office eyebrow raise.

"Jim, I'm worried about this plan for you to privately brief the president-elect," he said.

"Me, too," I replied.

"Have you ever met Donald Trump?" he asked.

"No."

"Jim, please be careful. Be very careful. This may not go well."

I thanked Jeh for the concern and the call. This was not making me feel better.

Still, I could see no way out of it. The FBI was aware of the material. Two United States senators separately contacted me to alert me to its existence and the fact that many in Washington either had it or knew of it. CNN had informed the FBI press office that they were going to run with it as soon as the next day. Whether it was true or not, an important feature of disarming any effort to coerce a public official is to tell the official what the enemy might be doing or saying. The FBI calls that a "defensive briefing."

How on earth could we brief the man about Russian efforts and not tell him about this piece? But it was so salacious and embarrassing that it didn't make sense to tell him in a group, especially not a group led by Obama appointees who were leaving office the moment Trump became president. I was staying on as FBI director, we knew the information, and the man had to be told. It made complete sense for me to do it. The plan was sensible, if the word applies in the context of talking with a new president about prostitutes in Moscow. Still, the plan left me deeply uncomfortable.

There was more to the discomfort: I long ago learned that people tend to assume that you act and think the way they would in a similar situation. They project their worldview onto you, even if you see the world very differently. There was a real chance that Donald Trump, politician and hardball dealmaker, would assume I was dangling the prostitute thing over him to jam him, to gain leverage. He might well assume I was pulling a J. Edgar Hoover, because that's what Hoover would do in my shoes. An eyebrow raise didn't quite do this situation justice; it was really going to suck.

The bit about "pulling a J. Edgar Hoover" made me keen to have some tool in my bag to reassure the new president. I needed to be prepared to say something, if at all possible, that would take the temperature down. After extensive discussion with my team, I decided I could assure the president-elect that the FBI was not currently investigating him. This was literally true. We did not have a counterintelligence case file open on him. We really didn't care if he had cavorted with hookers in Moscow, so long as the Russians weren't trying to coerce him in some way.

The FBI's general counsel, Jim Baker, argued powerfully that such an assurance, although true, could be misleadingly narrow: the president-elect's other conduct was, or surely would be, within the scope of an investigation looking at whether his campaign had coordinated with Russia. There was also the concern that the FBI might then be obligated to tell President Trump if we did open an investigation of him. I saw the logic of this position, but I also saw the bigger danger of the new president, who was known to be impulsive, going to war against the FBI. And I was determined to do all I could, appropriately, to work successfully with the new president. So I rejected Jim Baker's thoughtful advice and headed to Trump Tower with "we are not investigating you" in my back pocket.

Once again, we were in an unprecedented spot.

By the beginning of 2017, after all the controversies over the Clinton case, I had become a relatively identifiable public figure. Even if I wanted to hide from view, my height made that even harder. It was clear that any number of Republicans shared Hillary Clinton's view that I'd affected the election result in Trump's favor. As much as Clinton partisans felt anger — and in some cases even hatred — toward me, in Trump World, I was something of a celebrity. Which made my entrance into Trump Tower really uncomfortable. I didn't want to be seen as anything different from the other intelligence leaders doing their jobs.

We gathered in a small conference room belonging to the Trump Organization. It was blandly decorated and had been outfitted with a temporary heavy gold ceiling-to-floor curtain to block the glass wall that would otherwise show our meeting to the hallway. The president-elect entered the room on time, followed by the vice president–elect and the rest of the designated senior White House team.

This was the first time I'd ever seen Donald Trump face-to-face. He appeared shorter than he seemed on a debate stage with Hillary Clinton. Otherwise, as I looked at the president-elect, I was struck that he looked exactly the same in person as on television, which surprised me because people most often look different in person. His suit jacket was open and his tie too long, as usual. His face appeared slightly orange, with bright white half-moons under his eyes where I assumed he placed small tanning goggles, and impressively coiffed, bright blond hair, which upon close inspection looked to be all his. I remember wondering how long it must take him in the morning to get that done. As he extended his hand, I made a mental note to check its size. It was smaller than mine, but did not seem unusually so.

Trump brought his entire senior team into the small conference room. Vice President–Elect Mike Pence, Chief of Staff Reince Priebus, National Security Adviser Mike Flynn, and Press Secretary Sean Spicer sat at the oval conference table, with Trump and Pence seated at opposite ends. They were quiet and serious. As we shook hands, the vice president–elect held the handshake an extra few seconds and said my first name, drawing it out — "Jiiiimm." It struck me as an odd combination of someone greeting an old friend and consoling that friend. I don't think we had ever met, although I recall our speaking on the phone once fourteen years earlier, in 2003, when I was United States Attorney in Manhattan and we were investigating a guy who registered common misspellings of popular children's websites so that when a child mistyped "Disneyland.com" or "Bobthebuilder.com" they were directed to a pornography website. My reaction was "That should be a crime." When I found it had become a federal crime only months earlier, I asked for the contact information of the member of Congress responsible for the Truth in Domain Names Act so I could thank that person. It turned out to be Indiana congressman Mike Pence, who told me on the phone that he had pushed for the law after one of his own children was redirected in that sick way.

Director Clapper sat closest to the president-elect, with CIA Director John Brennan, NSA Director Mike Rogers, and me to his right. Against the wall behind me sat Trump's future CIA Director Mike Pompeo and designated Homeland Security Adviser Tom Bossert and Deputy National Security Adviser K. T. McFarland. The president-elect's CIA intelligence briefer —

a career employee assigned to deliver regular intelligence briefings to the incoming president — was also in the room to take notes.

By this point, I had worked relatively closely with two presidents, in addition to scores of other leaders in government. I was curious to see how Trump, the classic "fish out of water," would operate in a totally foreign role. Running a private family-held company is, of course, quite different from running a nation — or even running a large public corporation. You have to deal with various constituencies who don't report to you and to live under a web of laws and regulations that don't apply to a typical CEO.

As I'd seen from other leaders, being confident enough to be humble — comfortable in your own skin — is at the heart of effective leadership. That humility makes a whole lot of things possible, none more important than a single, humble question: "What am I missing?" Good leaders constantly worry about their limited ability to see. To rise above those limitations, good leaders exercise judgment, which is a different thing from intelligence. Intelligence is the ability to solve a problem, to decipher a riddle, to master a set of facts. Judgment is the ability to orbit a problem or a set of facts and see it as it might be seen through other eyes, by observers with different biases, motives, and backgrounds. It is also the ability to take a set of facts and move it in place and time — perhaps to a hearing room or a courtroom, months or years in the future — or to the newsroom of a major publication or the boardroom of a competitor. Intelligence is the ability to collect and report what the documents and witnesses say; judgment is the ability to say what those same facts mean and what effect they will have on other audiences.

In my first meeting with Trump, I looked to see how he struck that balance of confidence and humility and whether he showed signs of having sound judgment. I confess I was skeptical going in. My impression from the campaign was that he was a deeply insecure man, which made it impossible for him to demonstrate humility, and that he seemed very unlikely to be confident and humble enough to ask the "What am I missing" question at the heart of sound judgment. But I didn't see enough at Trump Tower that day to see whether that assessment was correct or not. The president-elect was appropriately subdued and serious.

Director Clapper presented the intelligence community assessment, just as he had to President Obama and the Gang of Eight. There were a few questions and comments, most of which came from Tom Bossert in the back row. During the discussion of Russia's involvement in the election, I recall Trump listening without interrupting, and asking only one question, which was really more of a statement: "But you found there was no impact on the result, right?" Clapper replied that we had done no such analysis, which was not our business or expertise. What we could say is that we found no evidence of alteration of the vote count.

What I found telling was what Trump and his team didn't ask. They were about to lead a country that had been attacked by a foreign adversary, yet they had no questions about what the future Russian threat might be. Nor did they ask how the United States might prepare itself to meet that threat. Instead, with the four of us still in our seats — including two outgoing Obama appointees — the president-elect and his team shifted immediately into a strategy session about messaging on Russia. About how they could spin what we'd just told them. Speaking as if we weren't there, Priebus began describing what a press statement about this meeting might look like. The Trump team

— led by Priebus, with Pence, Spicer, and Trump jumping in — debated how to position these findings for maximum political advantage. They were keen to emphasize that there was no impact on the vote, meaning that the Russians hadn't elected Trump. Clapper interjected to remind them of what he had said about sixty seconds earlier: the intelligence community did not analyze American politics, and we had not offered a view on that.

I had been in many intelligence briefings with the two previous presidents and had never seen Presidents Bush or Obama discuss communications and political strategy in front of intelligence community leaders. There had always been a line. The intelligence community does facts; the White House does politics and spin, and does it on its own. The searing lesson of the Iraq war — based on bad intelligence about weapons of mass destruction — was "never mix the two." I tried to tell myself that maybe this was because Trump and his team had little experience on these matters — Trump, of course, had no experience in government whatsoever — but in an instant, the line between intelligence and politics began to fade.

As I was sitting there, the strangest image

filled my mind. I kept pushing it away because it seemed too odd and too dramatic, but it kept coming back: I thought of New York Mafia social clubs, an image from my days as a Manhattan federal prosecutor in the 1980s and 1990s. The Ravenite. The Palma Boys. Café Giardino. I couldn't shake the picture. And looking back, it wasn't as odd and dramatic as I thought it was at the time.

The Italian Mafia, as noted earlier, called itself La Cosa Nostra — "this thing of ours" — and always drew a line between someone who was a "friend of yours," meaning someone outside the family, and someone who was a "friend of ours," meaning an official member of the family. I sat there thinking, Holy crap, they are trying to make each of us an *"amica nostra"* — friend of ours. To draw us in. As crazy as it sounds, I suddenly had the feeling that, in the blink of an eye, the president-elect was trying to make us all part of the same family and that Team Trump had made it a "thing of ours." For my entire career, intelligence was a thing of mine and political spin a thing of yours. Team Trump wanted to change that.

I should have said something right then. After all, I hadn't exactly been shy when it came to asserting myself to leaders in other administrations. I'm not sure it would have made a difference, but maybe I should have told the new team about the norms of behavior, developed over generations, in fits and starts, to try to keep politics out of intelligence, to ensure that the president gets the best facts, whether he likes them or not, and to insulate the intelligence community from charges that its conclusions are politically cooked. Thinking that intelligence leaders would willingly contribute to a conversation about how to do PR in support of any presidential administration was at best a naïve notion, reflecting a misunderstanding of our role. Thinking that members of the outgoing Obama administration would be part of such an effort was just dumb.

But in that moment, I convinced myself that speaking up would be crazy. I didn't know these people and they didn't know me. We had just served up "the Russians tried to get you elected." Should I now give them a lecture about how to behave with us? And when I'm about to have a private session with the president-elect to talk about Russian hookers? Nope. Don't think so. So I said nothing. And nobody else said anything, either. Nobody on the Trump team thought to say, "Hey, maybe this is a conversation for later," or "Perhaps we should move on, Mr. President-Elect."

I actually think it was Trump who ended the communications strategy session by saying they could talk about it at another time. At that point, Reince Priebus asked if there was anything else that we should tell them.

Here we go, I thought.

Clapper said, "Well, yes, there is some additional sensitive material that we thought it made sense for Director Comey to review with you in a smaller group. We will excuse ourselves so he can discuss it privately with you."

"Okay, how small?" the president-elect asked, looking at me.

"It's up to you, sir," I said, "but I was thinking the two of us."

Reince Priebus interjected, "How about me and the vice president–elect?"

"That's fine sir," I answered, turning to the president-elect. "It's entirely up to you. I just didn't want to do it with a larger group."

I don't know if Trump knew what I was about to say, but the president-elect waved his hand at Priebus and then pointed at me. "Just the two of us. Thanks, everybody."

The group shook hands with the visitors and everyone filed out. Jeh Johnson's words banged around my head. "Jim, please be careful. Be very careful."

We waited quietly while the others filed out. When we were alone, the president-elect spoke first, throwing out compliments. "You've had one heck of a year," he said, adding that I handled the email investigation "honorably" and had a "great reputation." This was nice of him to say, and there seemed to be genuine concern and appreciation in his voice. I nodded in gratitude, with a tight smile. He said that the people of the FBI "really like you" and expressed his hope that I would stay on as director.

I replied, "I intend to, sir."

Though it might have been the polite or obvious thing to say to ingratiate myself with the president-elect, I didn't thank him for saying this, because I already had the job, for a stated ten-year term, and didn't want it to appear as if I needed to reapply. In fact, only once in the Bureau's history was an FBI director fired before the end of his term — when Bill Clinton, without controversy, removed William Sessions in 1993 over allegations of serious ethical improprieties. Ironically, the man Clinton replaced him with, Louis Freeh, turned out to be a thorn in the administration's side as he pressed aggressively for investigations of alleged administration misdeeds.

After Trump finished with his opening monologue, which lasted for a minute or so, I explained the nature of the material I was about to discuss and why we thought it important that he know about it. I then began to summarize the allegation in the dossier that he had been with prostitutes in a Moscow hotel in 2013 and that the Russians had filmed the episode. I didn't mention one particular allegation in the dossier — that he was having prostitutes urinate on each other on the very bed President Obama and the First Lady had once slept in as a way of soiling the bed. I figured that single detail was not necessary to put him on notice about the material. This whole thing was weird enough. As I spoke, I felt a strange out-of-body experience, as if I were watching myself speak to the new president about prostitutes in Russia. Before I finished, Trump interrupted sharply, with a dismissive tone. He was eager to protest that the allegations weren't true.

I explained that I wasn't saying the FBI believed the allegations. We simply thought it important that he know they were out there and being widely circulated.

I added that one of the FBI's jobs is to

protect the presidency from any kind of coercion, and, whether or not the allegations were true, it was important that he know Russians might be saying such things. I stressed that we did not want to keep information from him, particularly given that the press was about to report it.

He again strongly denied the allegations, asking — rhetorically, I assumed — whether he seemed like a guy who needed the services of prostitutes.

He then began discussing cases where women had accused him of sexual assault, a subject I had not raised. He mentioned a number of women, and seemed to have memorized their allegations. As he began to grow more defensive and the conversation teetered toward disaster, on instinct, I pulled the tool from my bag: "We are not investigating you, sir." That seemed to quiet him.

My job done, the conversation ended, we shook hands and I left the conference room. The entire private session took about five minutes, and now I was away, retracing my steps to go out the back entrance. The other directors had gone ahead. On the way down the hall I passed two men in winter coats coming the other way. One looked familiar, but I kept walking. When he was past me, he called, "Director Comey?" and I stopped and turned. Jared Kushner introduced himself, we shook hands, and I continued on my way.

I walked out the side door, stepped into the armored car, and headed to the Manhattan FBI office to do what I loved. I walked floor upon floor of FBI offices and cubicles, thanking incredible people for their work. After the uncomfortable conversation I'd just had, it was like taking a shower.

On January 10, four days after my meeting with Trump, the online publication BuzzFeed published in full the thirty-five-page dossier that I had briefed Trump on. The article began:

A dossier making explosive — but unverified — allegations that the Russian government has been "cultivating, supporting and assisting" President-elect Donald Trump for years and gained compromising information about him has been circulating among elected officials, intelligence agents, and journalists for weeks. The dossier, which is a collection of memos written over a period of months, includes specific, unverified, and potentially unverifiable allegations of contact between Trump aides and Russian operatives, and graphic claims of sexual acts documented by the Russians.

In response, the president-elect tweeted: "FAKE NEWS — A TOTAL POLITICAL WITCH HUNT!"

The following day, January 11, I had another conversation with the future president. In three years working under President Obama, I had never spoken to him on the phone and only talked to him alone in person twice. Yet here I was, still in the Obama administration, standing at my FBI headquarters office window, having my second private conversation with Donald Trump in five days. Below me, as I held the phone to my ear, I could see cars moving on a darkened Pennsylvania Avenue. Across the street, the Justice Department was aglow with busy offices. I remember looking up and to my right at the brightly lit Washington Monument. I could see it rising high above the new Trump hotel that had just been opened on Pennsylvania Avenue, walking distance from the White House.

President-Elect Trump was calling from New York. He started the call by again praising me, which now seemed like a conversational device rather than a sincere expression of approval. He added, "I sure hope you are going to stay." I assured him, again, that I was staying at the FBI.

He then moved to the purpose of the call. He said he was very concerned about the "leaking" of the Russian "dossier" and how it happened. I wasn't sure if he was implying that a federal agency had leaked it, so I explained that the dossier was not a government document. It had been compiled by private parties and then given to many people, including in Congress and the press. The FBI hadn't asked that it be created or paid for it to be created. The document was not classified and not a government document, so it wasn't really correct that it had been "leaked."

He then said he had been thinking more about the part I had briefed him about privately at Trump Tower. He had been talking to people who had gone with him on the trip to Moscow for the Miss Universe 2013 pageant. He now recalled that he had not even stayed overnight in Moscow. He claimed he had flown from New York, had only gone to the hotel to change his clothes, and had flown home that same night. And then he surprised me by bringing up the one allegation I had specifically tried not to discuss with him.

"Another reason you know this isn't true:

I'm a germophobe. There's no way I would let people pee on each other around me. No way."

I actually let out an audible laugh. I decided not to tell him that the activity alleged did not seem to require either an overnight stay or even being in close proximity to the participants. In fact, though I didn't know for sure, I imagined the presidential suite of the Ritz-Carlton in Moscow was large enough for a germophobe to be at a safe distance from the activity. I thought all of that and said none of it.

Instead, I stared out at the monuments and wondered what had happened to me and our country that the FBI director was talking about this with our incoming president. Having delivered his defense on a subject I didn't care about, for the second time, the president-elect ended the call. I went to find my chief of staff, Jim Rybicki, to tell him the world had gone crazy and I was caught in the middle of it.

It stayed crazy.

CHAPTER 13
TESTS OF LOYALTY

Friendship, connections, family ties, trust, loyalty, obedience — this was the glue that held us together.
— MAFIA BOSS JOSEPH BONANNO,
IN HIS AUTOBIOGRAPHY,
MAN OF HONOR

Donald J. Trump was inaugurated the forty-fifth president of the United States on January 20, 2017, before a crowd whose number immediately and famously came into dispute. The new president was determined to demonstrate that the number of spectators who turned out for him, which was sizable, surpassed the number of people present for Barack Obama's 2009 inauguration. They did not. No evidence, photographic or otherwise, would move him off his view, which, as far as everyone but his press team seemed to agree, was simply false. This small moment was deeply disconcerting to those of us in the business of trying to find the truth, whether in a criminal investigation or in assessing the plans and intentions of America's adversaries. Much of life is ambiguous and subject to interpretation, but there are things that are objectively, verifiably either true or false. It was simply not true that the biggest crowd in history attended the inauguration, as he asserted, or even that Trump's crowd was bigger than Obama's. To say otherwise was not to offer an opinion, a view, a perspective. It was a lie.

Two days later, on Sunday, January 22, I attended a late-afternoon reception at the White House for the leaders of the various law enforcement agencies who had provided security and support for the inaugural activities. The FBI's counterterrorism, intelligence, and SWAT capabilities had been deployed that day, closely integrated with the Secret Service, as they are for every inauguration. I was told President Trump wanted to thank the agencies for all their hard work. This struck me as a really nice thing for the president to do. Despite that, I didn't love the idea of going personally, for a couple of reasons.

First, I didn't think it would be helpful for the FBI if I were seen in videos or photographs hanging around with the new president. Given that so many people seemed to think I'd helped to elect him, it made little sense to support a false narrative that I, and by inference the Bureau, was somehow close to President Trump. Second, the NFL conference championship games were on TV. The 5:00 P.M. reception would cause me to miss the end of the Packers against the Falcons and the beginning of the Steelers against the Patriots. Was the new president not a football fan?

But my staff argued that it was important for me to go. I was the FBI director. I didn't want to insult the other leaders or the new administration by not showing up. And I told myself my concerns were overblown. This would be a group reception, and that meant no individual press pictures of me with the president. Also, I decided to record the football games on my DVR and avoid any conversation about the scores until I had a chance to watch. So I went to the White House.

Just as I'd hoped, the reception began as a pleasant mingling with the law enforcement leaders from local, state, and federal agencies. There were about thirty of us there, including leaders from the United States Capitol Police, the Washington Metropolitan

Police, and the United States Park Police. These people and their agencies were long-standing partners of the FBI, and many of us knew each other from that work. We gathered in the large oval Blue Room in the Residence of the White House. At the edges of the room, the White House staff had set up small tables with finger foods and nonalcoholic drinks. I moved around the room shaking hands and thanking folks for their work with the FBI.

I was preoccupied about keeping a healthy distance from Trump. So I figured out which way the president would likely enter the room and mingled my way to the opposite end, by the windows looking over the South Lawn toward the Washington Monument. I couldn't get farther away without climbing out of the window, an option that would begin to look more appealing as time went by.

Feeling safe at the far end of the room, I settled next to Joe Clancy, the director of the Secret Service. Clancy, a former head of the Presidential Protective Division, had been called out of retirement by President Obama to lead the troubled agency. His wife remained in Philadelphia, so I inquired after her and their daughter, whom I'd seen sing at a ceremony marking the 150th anniversary of the Secret Service. I often joked that the Secret Service was an older sibling to the FBI, which was only a century old, and its agents had trained our first special agents.

Clancy is a wonderful, warm, down-to-earth person. As he and I were chatting, the double doors opened and White House staffers entered with tall klieg lights, setting them up to illuminate the area farthest from me, by the doors. I had guessed the location of the president's entrance correctly. But I worried that the bright lights meant there would be cameras and reporters, which struck me as unusual for an event to thank low-key law enforcement officials. Moments later, the president and vice president entered. A crush of photographers and TV cameras were ushered in and encircled the two men.

The president began speaking, and his eyes swept the room at the leaders, who were spread around the perimeter. His gaze passed me, mercifully, and instead came to rest on Joe Clancy. He called Joe's name and motioned him across the room to join him and the vice president. Joe never seeks the spotlight, but he dutifully walked into the near-blinding glow of TV lights. The president hugged him, awkwardly, and asked him to stand with him and the vice president, as if on display.

Trump then continued talking, looking to his left and away from me. I couldn't believe my luck. He hadn't seen me! How is that possible? Then it occurred to me. I was standing against a heavy blue curtain. I was wearing a blue suit that didn't match the curtain exactly, but was pretty close. It must be camouflaging me! How great is that? I was thinking, I'm so lucky they held the event in this room, because I didn't have suits that blend in the Green or Red Rooms. Now that it was my salvation, I moved even closer to the curtain, pressing my back against it, desperately trying to erase myself from the president's field of vision. I literally clung to the blue curtain, all in the hope that I could avoid an ill-advised and totally awkward televised hug from the new president of the United States.

My curtain call worked.

Until it didn't.

Still speaking in his usual stream-of-consciousness and free-association cadence, the president moved his eyes again, sweeping from left to right, toward me and my protective curtain. This time, I was not so lucky. The small eyes with the white shadows stopped on me.

"Jim!" Trump exclaimed. The president called me forward. "He's more famous than me." Awesome.

My wife Patrice has known me since I was nineteen. In the endless TV coverage of what felt to me like a thousand-yard walk across the Blue Room, back at our home she was watching TV and pointing at the screen: "That's Jim's 'oh shit' face." Yes, it was. My inner voice was screaming: "How could he think this is a good idea? Isn't he supposed to be the master of television? This is a complete disaster. And there is no fricking way I'm going to hug him."

The FBI and its director are not on anyone's political team. The entire nightmare of the Clinton email investigation had been about protecting the integrity and independence of the FBI and the Department of Justice, about safeguarding the reservoir of trust and credibility. That Trump would appear to publicly thank me on his second day in office was a threat to the reservoir.

Near the end of my thousand-yard walk, I extended my right hand to President Trump. This was going to be a handshake, nothing more. The president gripped my hand. Then he pulled it forward and down. There it was. He was going for the hug on national TV. I tightened the right side of my body, calling on years of side planks and dumbbell rows. He was not going to get a hug without being a whole lot stronger than he looked. He wasn't. I thwarted the hug, but I got something worse in exchange. The president leaned in and put his mouth near my right ear. "I'm really looking forward to working with you," he said. Unfortunately, because of the vantage point of the TV cameras, what many in the world, including my children, thought they saw was a kiss. The whole world "saw" Donald Trump kiss the man who some believed got him elected. Surely this couldn't get any worse.

President Trump made a motion as if to invite me to stand with him and the vice president and Joe Clancy. Backing away, I waved it off with a smile. "I'm not worthy," my expression tried to say. "I'm not suicidal," my inner voice said. Defeated and depressed, I retreated back to the far side of the room.

The press was excused, and the police chiefs and directors started lining up for pictures with the president. They were very quiet. I made like I was getting in the back of the line and slipped out the side door, through the Green Room, into the hall, and down the stairs. On the way, I heard someone say the score from the Packers-Falcons game. Perfect.

It is possible that I was reading too much into the usual Trump theatrics, but the episode left me worried. It was no surprise that President Trump behaved in a manner that was completely different from his predecessors — I couldn't imagine Barack Obama or George W. Bush asking someone to come onstage like a contestant on *The Price Is Right*. What *was* distressing was what Trump symbolically seemed to be asking leaders of the law enforcement and national security agencies to do — to come forward and kiss the great man's ring. To show their deference and loyalty. It was tremendously important that these leaders *not* do that — or be seen to even look like they were doing that. Trump either didn't know that or didn't care, though I'd spend the next several weeks quite memorably, and disastrously, trying to make this point to him and his staff.

On Friday, January 27, 2017 — twenty-one days into my relationship with Donald Trump — I was back at the White House. I had been eating my lunch at my desk, as usual, when my assistant Althea James connected a woman calling from the White

House and telling me to hold for the president. He came on the line to ask if I "wanted to come over for dinner" that night. This was not normal, but I felt like I had no choice. I replied, "Of course, sir." He asked whether six or six thirty would be better. I said, "Whatever works for you, sir." He chose six thirty. I hung up and then called Patrice, to break a Thai food dinner date.

That afternoon I saw the recently retired director of national intelligence, Jim Clapper, at an event at the FBI, where we were awarding him the rare status of Honorary Special Agent. As we stood waiting to walk onstage, I told him about the dinner invitation, explaining that it made me deeply uncomfortable. He assumed it would be a group event, saying he had heard others were being invited to dinner at the White House. That made me relax a bit.

There was no way a president would be dining alone with the FBI director. Someone at the White House had to have told him that it just wasn't done, at least not since the days of Nixon and Hoover. I recalled when President Obama invited me to the White House for a wide-ranging conversation before I was nominated because, as he explained, "Once you are director, we won't be able to talk like this," meaning he would not be able to debate wide-ranging philosophical issues with me. The head of the FBI could not be put into the position of meeting and chatting privately with the president of the United States — especially after an election like 2016. The very notion would compromise the Bureau's hard-won integrity and independence. My fear was that Trump expected exactly that.

I arrived at the White House on West Executive Drive, the small roadway between the basement entrance to the White House and the Old Executive Office Building. The FBI security team stopped the vehicle at the same awning-covered entrance I used to go to the Situation Room. I walked in and told the Secret Service officer on duty that I was here for dinner with the president. He looked slightly confused and asked me to have a seat. Shortly thereafter, a young woman escorted me on the long walk through the West Wing, along the Rose Garden and into the ground floor of the White House Residence. She took me up a staircase I had never seen before, which emptied next to the Green Room on the main floor.

As I waited in the doorway, I chatted with two navy stewards while discreetly looking around for the president's other dinner guests. The stewards were African American men, close to my age, and had been working at the White House for about ten years. They were each well over six feet tall, and yet both had worked on submarines during their active-duty years. Naturally, this led to a conversation about the headroom on subs, and one reported that the bunks were six feet, four inches long, which was precisely his height. Chuckling, we agreed a submarine was no place for me. Standing at the entrance to the Green Room, as we continued waiting and chatting, I saw it — a table unmistakably set for two. One place setting was marked with a calligraphy card reading, "Director Comey." The other spot, presumably, was for the president. I was deeply uncomfortable, and not just because I did not love the idea of a third discussion of Russian hookers.

The president arrived at the appointed time of 6:30 P.M. The compliments soon followed. Seeing me already standing in the doorway, he said, "I like that. I like people who are on time. I think a leader should always be on time."

He was wearing his usual dark blue suit, white shirt, and too-long red tie. He did not speak to the stewards at all. He gestured me to the table, which sat us about four feet apart and was placed directly beneath the ornate chandelier in the center of the rectangular room.

As the name suggests, the walls of the Green Room are covered in silk fabric of that color. I read afterward that John Adams used it as a bedroom and Thomas Jefferson made it a dining room, but presidents since have used it as a sitting room. That evening the furniture had been removed in favor of our small dining table. Over the president's right shoulder, I could see one of two statues that stand on either side of the fireplace, the white marble mantelpiece resting on their heads, which looked really painful.

On my plate, I had found a large cream-colored card describing the entire four-course menu in cursive script. Salad, shrimp scampi, chicken parmesan with pasta, and vanilla ice cream. The president began by admiring his own menu card, which he held up.

"They write these things out one at a time, by hand," he marveled, referring to the White House staff.

"A calligrapher," I replied, nodding.

He looked quizzical. "They write them by hand," he repeated.

At some point early on, maybe by the time the navy stewards brought us the shrimp scampi, Trump asked bluntly, "So what do you want to do?" It was an odd question that I didn't entirely understand at first, but without waiting for an answer, he launched into a monologue that made it crystal clear what he was referring to: whether I wanted to keep my job.

He said lots of people wanted to be director of the FBI, but that he thought very highly of me. He said he had heard great things about me and knew the people of the FBI thought very highly of me as well. He said despite that, he would understand if I wanted to "walk away" given all I had been through, although then he noted that that would be bad for me personally because it would look like I had done something wrong. He finished by saying that he knew he could "make a change at FBI" if he wanted to, but that he wanted to know what I thought.

Now it was pretty clear to me what was happening. The setup of the dinner, both the physical layout of a private meal and Trump's pretense that he had not already asked me to stay on multiple occasions, convinced me this was an effort to establish a patronage relationship. Somebody probably had told him, or maybe it just occurred to him at random, that he'd "given" me the job for "free" and that he needed to get something in return. This only added to the strangeness of the experience. The president of the United States had invited me to dinner and decided my job security was on the menu.

I responded that I agreed he can fire the FBI director any time he wishes, but that I wanted to stay and do a job I loved and thought I was doing well. I said I hadn't expected to return to government but found the job hugely rewarding and wanted to serve out my term. Sensing that he needed more from me, I added that he could count on me as being "reliable" in one way. Not in the way political people sometimes use the term — like a "reliable" vote for one team. I said he could count on me to always tell him the truth.

I didn't do sneaky things, I told him, and I don't leak. But, I said, I am not on anybody's side politically and could not be counted on in the traditional political sense, explaining that that was in the president's best interest. The FBI and the Department of Justice are drawn into the most controversial investigations in the country, investigations that frequently involve prominent members of a presidential administration, as we had been with the investigation of Karl Rove and Scooter Libby during the Bush administration. The FBI is able to do that work credibly because it is not — and is not seen as — a tool of the president. Without that reputation and reality at both Justice and the FBI, a president is left with no way to resolve investigations of his administration, short of appointment of some kind of special prosecutor.

This discourse obviously did not appease him. A short time later, with a serious look on his face, he said, "I need loyalty. I expect loyalty."

During the silence that followed, I didn't move, speak, or change my facial expression in any way. The president of the United States just demanded the FBI director's loyalty. This was surreal. To those inclined to defend Trump, they might consider how it would have looked if President Obama had called the FBI director to a one-on-one dinner during an investigation of senior officials in his administration, then discussed his job security, and then said he expected loyalty. There would undoubtedly be people appearing on Fox News calling for Obama's impeachment in an instant. This, of course, was not something I could ever conceive of

Obama doing, or George W. Bush, for that matter. To my mind, the demand was like Sammy the Bull's Cosa Nostra induction ceremony — with Trump, in the role of the family boss, asking me if I have what it takes to be a "made man." I did not, and would never. I was determined not to give the president any hint of assent to this demand, so I gave silence instead. We looked at each other for what seemed an eternity, but was maybe two seconds or so. I stared again at the soft white pouches under his expressionless blue eyes. I remember thinking in that moment that the president doesn't understand the FBI's role in American life or care about what the people there spent forty years building. Not at all.

In an earlier time in my career and at a younger age, I wouldn't have had the nerve to keep my composure, to not break the icy stare with a nod or some muffled word, signaling agreement. Even at the age of fifty-six, with a fair number of scars, and in my fourth year as director of the FBI, I still had to talk to myself as I sat inches from the president, staring him directly in the face. The voice inside said, "Don't do anything; don't you dare move."

Trump broke the awkward standoff, looking down at his plate and moving to another topic. My cold response didn't seem to faze him much, if at all. Dinner continued, pleasantly enough.

As we continued our encounter — I don't use the word "conversation," because the term doesn't apply when one person speaks nearly the entire time — I tried again to help President Trump understand the value that the separation between the FBI and the White House offers the president. But it was very hard to get a word in. For the rest of the meal, pausing only now and then to eat, he spoke in torrents, gushing words about the size of his inauguration crowd, how much free media coverage he had been able to generate during the election, the viciousness of the campaign. He offered his view of the Clinton email investigation, referring to it in three phases, each of which, in his telling, bore my name. In "Comey One," he said, I "saved her" with my July 5 announcement that there was no prosecutable case against her. Although he added that I was wrong about that conclusion. In what he called "Comey Two," I did what I had to do by informing Congress that we had restarted the investigation. In "Comey Three," which was my final letter to Congress, closing the case for a second time, he said I saved Hillary again, but that she "totally misplayed" that. He sounded like he was reciting the plotline to his favorite TV show.

He talked about the trappings of the White House, saying something to the effect of "This is luxury. And I know luxury." I remember glancing again at the one poor statue I could see over his shoulder with the mantelpiece on its head and thinking that made sense. He went into another explanation — I'd seen many of them on television — about how he hadn't made fun of a disabled reporter. He said he hadn't mistreated a long list of women, reviewing each case in detail, as he had in our earlier conversation. There was no way he groped that lady sitting next to him on the airplane, he insisted. And the idea that he grabbed a porn star and offered her money to come to his room was preposterous. His method of speaking was like an oral jigsaw puzzle contest, with a shot clock. He would, in rapid-fire sequence, pick up a piece, put it down, pick up an unrelated piece, put it down, return to the original piece, on and on. But it was always him picking up the pieces and putting them down. None of this behavior, incidentally, was the way a leader could or should build rapport with a subordinate.

All of us struggle to realize something Patrice spent years telling me, as I took on one position or another: "It's not about you, dear." She often needed to remind me that, whatever people were feeling — happy, sad, frightened, or confused — it was unlikely it had anything to do with me. They had received a gift, or lost a friend, or gotten a medical test result, or couldn't understand why their love wasn't calling them back. It was all about their lives, their troubles, their hopes and dreams. Not mine. The nature of human existence makes it hard for us — or at least for me — to come to that understanding naturally. After all, I can only experience the world through me. That tempts all of us to believe everything we think, everything we hear, everything we see, is all about us. I think we all do this.

But a leader constantly has to train him- or herself to think otherwise. This is an important insight for a leader, in two respects. First, it allows you to relax a bit, secure in the knowledge that you aren't that important. Second, knowing people aren't always focused on you should drive you to try to imagine what they are focused on. I see this as the heart of emotional intelligence, the ability to imagine the feelings and perspective of another "me." Some seem to be born with a larger initial deposit of emotional intelligence, but all of us can develop it with practice. Well, most of us. I got the sense that no one ever taught this to Donald Trump.

The president asked very few questions that might prompt a discussion. Instead he made constant assertions, leaving me wondering whether by my silence I had just agreed with "everyone" that he had the biggest inauguration crowd in history, had given a great inauguration speech, had never mistreated women, and so on. The barrage of words was almost designed to prevent a genuine two-way dialogue from ever happening.

Then there were the baffling, unnecessary lies. At one point, for example, the president told me that Chief of Staff Reince Priebus didn't know we were meeting, which seemed incredible. A chief of staff should know when the president is dining alone with the FBI director. Then, later on in that same dinner, Trump said casually, "Reince knows we're meeting."

Unprompted, and in another zag in the conversation, he brought up what he called the "golden showers thing," repeating much of what he had said to me previously, adding that it bothered him if there was "even a one percent chance" his wife, Melania, thought it was true. That distracted me slightly because I immediately began wondering why his wife would think there was *any* chance, even a small one, that he had been with prostitutes urinating on each other in Moscow. For all my flaws, there is a zero percent chance — literally absolute zero — that Patrice would credit an allegation that I was with hookers peeing on each other in Moscow. She would laugh at the very suggestion. In what kind of marriage, to what kind of man, does a spouse conclude there is only a 99 percent chance her husband didn't do that?

I'm almost certain the president is unfamiliar with the proverb "The wicked flee when no man pursueth," because he just rolled on, unprompted, explaining why it couldn't possibly be true, ending by saying he was thinking of asking me to investigate the allegation to prove it was a lie. I said it was up to him. At the same time, I expressed the concern that such a thing would create a narrative that we were investigating him personally and added that it is also very difficult to prove something never happened. He said I might be right, but repeatedly asked me to think about it, and said he would as well.

One of his few questions, again seemingly out of nowhere, was to ask me how I compared Attorneys General Eric Holder and Loretta Lynch. I explained that Holder was much closer to President Obama, which had its advantages and its perils. I used the opportunity as an excuse to again explain why it was so important that the FBI and the Department of Justice be independent of the White House. I said it was a paradox: Throughout history, some presidents have decided that because "problems" come from Justice, they should try to hold the department close. But blurring those boundaries ultimately makes the problems worse by undermining public trust in the institutions and their work. I got no sense he had any idea about — or interest in — what I was saying.

Something else occurred to me about President Trump at that dinner that I found very instructive. I don't recall seeing him laugh, ever. Not during small talk before meetings. Not in a conversation. Not even here, during an ostensibly relaxed dinner. Months later, the thought of a man whom I had never seen laugh stayed with me. I wondered if maybe others had noticed it or if in thousands of hours of video coverage, he had ever laughed. He had spent literally decades in front of video cameras, between his highly choreographed career as a business mogul and his years as a reality television star. So, out of curiosity, I googled it and looked through YouTube videos. In all of my searching, I found one video of something that could be called Donald Trump exhibiting a laugh, and a mean one at that — in January 2016, when he asked a New Hampshire audience about the origin of a noise in the background that sounded like a dog barking and someone shouted: "It's Hillary." There is a risk that I'm over-interpreting this, and I suppose it's possible that in private he may keep his wife or children or some favorite staff member in stitches or that I have missed a collection of his public laughs, but I don't know of another elected leader who doesn't laugh with some regularity in public. I suspect his apparent inability to do so is rooted in deep insecurity, his inability to be vulnerable or to risk himself by appreciating the humor of others, which, on reflection, is really very sad in a leader, and a little scary in a president.

Near the end of our dinner, he asked another question — the first that was actually an effort to learn something about his guest. He wondered how I ended up as FBI director. In answering, I told him I had been pleasantly surprised that President Obama thought of the job as I did: he wanted competence and independence, and didn't want the FBI involved in policy but wanted to sleep at night knowing the FBI was well run. I recounted our first discussion in the Oval Office together, which, even in that moment, occurred to me as the polar opposite of what was unfolding at this dinner. President Trump replied by saying he was happy I wanted to stay because he had heard such great things about me from so many people, including his picks for secretary of defense and attorney general.

He then returned to the issue of loyalty, saying again, "I need loyalty."

I paused, again. "You will always get honesty from me," I said.

He paused. "That's what I want, honest loyalty," he said. This appeared to satisfy him as some sort of "deal" in which we were both winners.

I paused. "You will get that from me," I said, desperate to end our awkward standoff and telling myself that I had done enough to make clear where I stood.

In that moment, something else occurred to me: The "leader of the free world," the self-described great business tycoon, didn't understand leadership. Ethical leaders never ask for loyalty. Those leading through fear — like a Cosa Nostra boss — require personal loyalty. Ethical leaders care deeply about those they lead, and offer them honesty and decency, commitment and their own sacrifice. They have a confidence that breeds humility. Ethical leaders know their own talent but fear their own limitations — to understand and reason, to see the world as it is and not as they wish it to be. They speak the truth and know that making wise decisions requires people to tell them the truth. And to get that truth, they create an environment of high standards and deep consideration — "love" is not too strong a word — that builds lasting bonds and makes extraordinary achievement possible. It would never occur to an ethical leader to ask for loyalty.

After dessert — two scoops of ice cream, for each of us — I went home and wrote a memo about the dinner, which quickly became my practice with President Trump after occasions when we spoke alone. I had never done something like that before in my conversations with other presidents, and didn't write memos as FBI director about encounters with any other person, but a number of factors made it seem prudent to do so with this president. For one, we were touching on topics that involved the FBI's responsibilities and the president personally, and I was discussing those things with a person whose integrity I had come to seriously doubt after watching him campaign for president and since. I needed to protect the FBI and myself because I couldn't trust this person to tell the truth about our conversations. As was my practice, I printed two copies of the memo. One I shared with the FBI senior leadership team and then had my chief of staff keep in his files. The other I locked up at home, for two reasons: I considered the memo my personal property, like a diary; and I was concerned that having accurate recollections of conversations with this president might be important someday, which, sadly, turned out to be true.

CHAPTER 14
THE CLOUD

> If honor were profitable,
> everybody would be honorable.
> — THOMAS MORE

On February 8, 2017, Chief of Staff Reince Priebus invited me to the White House to meet with him in his office, a large room with a conference table and fireplace that offered a view of the grand Eisenhower Executive Office Building. This was the same room I had been in thirteen years earlier with Vice President Dick Cheney to hear his view that thousands would die if the Justice Department didn't bend its view of lawful electronic surveillance. It was the same room I sat in near midnight later that same week in 2004, after the standoff at John Ashcroft's hospital bed.

I was there now as a follow-up to my dinner with President Trump and because Priebus wanted to understand, and I wanted to explain, the proper relationship between the FBI and the White House. Priebus had never worked in a presidential administration and seemed genuinely interested in getting it right.

By that point, I'd interacted with two other White House chiefs of staff. My most memorable and contentious interaction was the race to the hospital against Andy Card during the Bush administration. As FBI director under President Obama, I had come to know his chief of staff best. Denis McDonough was an extraordinarily decent, thoughtful, and yet tough person. All chiefs of staff differ, as all people do, in their personalities and leadership qualities. But they all share the experience of prolonged sleep deprivation, as they try to manage the effective operation of the White House and bring some order to what could be, at the best of times, a chaotic enterprise. No president in our history, of course, came close to Donald Trump, who brought his own skills and challenges, and a unique brand of chaos.

I did not know Priebus well. He often seemed both confused and irritated, and it was not hard to imagine why. Running the Trump White House would be a difficult job for even an experienced manager, which

Priebus wasn't. Previously chairman of the Republican National Committee and before that a Wisconsin lawyer, Priebus had never served in the federal government. How could someone like that — or anyone, for that matter — manage someone like Donald Trump? I have no idea. But Priebus seemed to be trying.

Our meeting lasted about twenty minutes, was pleasant, and covered a variety of classified topics, as well as how the FBI and the Department of Justice should interact with the White House. As we were winding up, he asked me if I wanted to see the president. Ironically, the request perfectly undercut the entire point of our meeting. I had just finished discussing the importance of the White House working in a disciplined fashion through the Department of Justice if it wished to communicate with the FBI, except about national security emergencies and National Security Council policy discussions — like encryption — in which the FBI was a key participant. The theme of the conversation was that the FBI must be at arm's length. Priebus said he understood, and then he immediately wanted to bring me even closer.

After my last encounters, another visit with the president was not high on my priority list. So I said no — thanks, but no thanks — adding that I was sure the president was too busy. He asked again. I demurred again.

He then said, "Sit. I'm sure he'd love to see you. Let me see if he's in the Oval." He walked down the hall, the short distance to the Oval Office, and returned moments later. With a smile, he said, "He'd love to see you."

Without a smile, I replied, "Great."

When the two of us walked into the Oval Office, the president was talking with White House Press Secretary Sean Spicer, who left shortly after we arrived, leaving Priebus and me with the president alone.

Though this was not the first time I'd seen the new president, it was the first time I had seen him in his new office. He didn't look comfortable. He was sitting, suit jacket on, close against the famous *Resolute* desk, both forearms on the desk. As a result, he was separated from everyone who spoke to him by a large block of wood.

In dozens of meetings in that space with Presidents Bush and Obama, I cannot recall ever seeing them stationed at their desk. They instead sat in an armchair by the fireplace and held meetings in a more open, casual arrangement. That made sense to me.

As hard as it is to get people to relax and open up with a president, the chances are much better in the sitting area, where we can pretend we are friends gathered around a coffee table. There, the president can try to be one of a group, and draw the others out to tell him the truth. But when the president sits on a throne, protected by a large wooden obstacle, as Trump routinely did in my interactions with him, the formality of the Oval Office is magnified and the chances of getting the full truth plummet.

I also noticed President Trump had changed the curtains, which were now a bright gold. I later learned they were Bill Clinton's curtains, which, considering Trump's public views of the former president and his candidate wife, seemed an odd twist. (The press reported that President Trump later replaced the Clinton curtains with his own version of gold.)

As the president greeted me, I sat down in a small wood chair, my knees touching his desk. Priebus tried to steer the conversation to the subject of the so-called Russian dossier that we'd already discussed numerous times. I'm not sure why he did that, but for once the president wasn't interested in discussing that particular topic. Instead, sitting at the desk once used by Presidents

Kennedy and Reagan, he launched into one of his rapid-fire, stream-of-consciousness monologues. This time the focus was on a television interview he had given to Bill O'Reilly on Fox News several days earlier. The interview had run during the Super Bowl pregame show, which I had skipped. But I saw plenty of commentary about it afterward.

During the interview, O'Reilly had pressed President Trump as to whether he "respected" Russian president Vladimir Putin:

"I do respect him," Trump said, "but I respect a lot of people. That doesn't mean I'm going to get along with him."

"But he's a killer," O'Reilly said. "Putin's a killer."

"There are a lot of killers. We've got a lot of killers," Trump replied. "What do you think? Our country's so innocent?"

Trump's answer, seeming to equate Putin's thuggish regime with American democracy, led to a flurry of criticism from all sides. It also played into a narrative that Trump was too close to the Russian government, an odd line for Trump to encourage. I had often wondered why, when given numerous opportunities to condemn the Russian government's invasions of its neighbors and repression — even murder — of its own citizens, Trump refused to just state the plain facts. Maybe it was a contrarian streak or maybe it was something more complicated that explained his constant equivocation and apologies for Vladimir Putin. Still, it struck me as odd. Perhaps there was some sound geopolitical rationale for not publicly condemning bad behavior of a foreign government in its own internal matters. But, four weeks earlier at Trump Tower, the president had seemed untroubled when the leaders of the intelligence community unanimously briefed him that Russia had intervened to damage our democracy and had tried to tip the scales of our election. Even behind closed doors, he didn't recoil about Russian behavior. He didn't wonder what our adversary might do next. We knew that Vladimir Putin had interfered with the U.S. election in an unprecedented fashion, at least in part to help Trump win. Comments like the one to O'Reilly only underscored why Putin wanted him in office.

In his own blustery way, O'Reilly had challenged the president on his apparent affinity for Putin. And again, Trump had doubled down on his unwillingness to criticize the Russian government.

Now, three days later, seemingly stung or

at least preoccupied by the criticism, the president was still fuming and justifying himself.

"What am I going to do?" Trump asked no one in particular. "Say I don't respect the leader of a major country I'm trying to get along with?"

At first, neither Priebus nor I said anything. We couldn't even if we'd wanted to, because, as was his practice, President Trump left no space for others to talk. O'Reilly had posed a hard question, he told us. "So I gave a good answer," he said, looking at us, all but insisting that there was no other rational way to see it. "Really, it was a great answer. I gave a really great answer."

As Trump kept talking, I could see he was convincing himself of this story line and clearly thought he was convincing us, too. Of course, I didn't think O'Reilly's question was hard, or Trump's answer good, but this wasn't about him seeking feedback.

In fact, by this point, I had dealt with the president enough to have something of a read on what Trump was doing. His assertions about what "everyone thinks" and what is "obviously true" wash over you, unchallenged, as they did at our dinner, because he never stops talking. As a result, Trump pulls all those present into a silent circle of assent. With him talking a mile a minute, with no spot for others to jump into the conversation, I could see how easily everyone in the room could become a coconspirator to his preferred set of facts, or delusions. But as Martin Luther once said, "You are not only responsible for what you say, but also for what you do not say."

As I sat there, I watched the president building with his words a cocoon of alternative reality that he was busily wrapping around all of us. I must have agreed that he had the largest inauguration crowd in history, as he asserted in our previous meetings, because I didn't challenge that. I must therefore agree that his interview with O'Reilly was great, his answers brilliant, because I sat there and didn't object. But I'd be damned if I was going to let this trick work on me again. And this time he gave me the opening. Looking at me, he said, "You think it was a great answer, right?" and started to move on.

I jumped on it and did something I might never have done as a younger person — especially to a president of the United States. Something I'd never seen anyone else do around Trump in the limited number of interactions I'd had with him. I can't remember if it was midsentence or in a brief

418

pause before he launched into the next set of assertions to which we were all supposed to agree, but I interrupted his monologue.

"The first part of your answer was fine, Mr. President," I said, as he took a breath and looked at me with a blank expression. "But not the second part. We aren't the kind of killers that Putin is."

At that remark, Trump stopped talking altogether. In that brightly lit room, with its shiny gold curtains, a shadow seemed to cross his face. I could see something change in his eyes. A hardness, or darkness. In a blink, the eyes narrowed and his jaw tightened. He looked like someone who wasn't used to being challenged or corrected by those around him. He was the one who was supposed to be in complete control. With a small comment, I had just poured a cold dose of criticism and reality on his shameful moral equivalence between Putin's thugs and the men and women of our government. And just as quickly as the glower crossed his face, it was gone. It was as if I had not spoken, and had never been born. The meeting was done.

The president thanked me for coming in. Priebus, who had said nothing throughout this exchange, escorted me from the room, and I walked off without further conversation.

I went back to the FBI headquarters and told members of my staff that I had probably ended any personal relationship with the president with that move. I had resisted his request for a pledge of loyalty two weeks earlier, and now I had just cut through the cocoon to criticize the man behind the desk. We weren't going to have a friendly rapport, as I did with Presidents Bush and Obama. That was not necessarily a bad thing. FBI directors shouldn't be too close to a sitting president or his administration — which, of course, was the original reason I was at the White House that day.

Still, the encounter left me shaken. I had never seen anything like it in the Oval Office. As I found myself thrust into the Trump orbit, I once again was having flashbacks to my earlier career as a prosecutor against the Mob. The silent circle of assent. The boss in complete control. The loyalty oaths. The us-versus-them worldview. The lying about all things, large and small, in service to some code of loyalty that put the organization above morality and above the truth.

Less than a week later, I was back at the

scene, my knees again touching the *Resolute* desk.

On February 14, I went to the Oval Office for a scheduled counterterrorism briefing of President Trump. He again held forth from behind the desk, and a group of us sat in a semicircle of about six chairs facing him on the other side. I was seated in that semicircle with Vice President Pence, the deputy director of the CIA, the director of the National Counterterrorism Center, the secretary of Homeland Security, and my new boss, Attorney General Jeff Sessions. The new attorney general had been in office less than a week at that point. My first impressions of him were that he was eerily similar to Alberto Gonzales — both overwhelmed and overmatched by the job — but Sessions lacked the kindness Gonzales radiated.

The president seemed oddly uninterested and distracted during the classified briefing. I had some concerning and important things to say about the current terrorism threat inside the United States, but they drew no reaction. At the end of the low-energy session, he signaled that the briefing was over. "Thanks, everybody," he said in a loud voice. Then, pointing at me, he added, "I just want to talk to Jim. Thanks, everybody."

Here we go again.

I didn't know what he wanted to talk about, but this request was so unusual that I suspected another memo lay in my immediate future. As such, I knew I needed to try to remember every word he spoke, exactly as he said them.

Having no choice in the matter, I stayed in my chair, as the participants started to leave the Oval Office. The attorney general, however, lingered by my chair. As my boss at the Justice Department, he undoubtedly and rightly thought he should be present for this conversation. "Thanks, Jeff," the president said in a dismissive manner, "but I want to talk to Jim."

Then it was Jared Kushner's turn. Kushner had been sitting behind me, with other White House aides, on the couches and chairs by the coffee table. He likely knew his father-in-law better than anyone else in the room and seemed to be attempting a similar sort of intervention. By engaging me in a conversation while the others were clearing out — Jared talked about the Clinton email investigation and how hard it must have been — perhaps he thought Trump would forget that he'd asked everyone out, including him. No dice.

"Okay, Jared, thank you," Trump said. His

son-in-law seemed as reluctant as Sessions, but he too made his exit.

When the door by the grandfather clock closed and we were alone, the president set his eyes on me.

"I want to talk about Mike Flynn," he said. Flynn, his national security adviser, had been forced to resign the previous day. I didn't know Flynn well, but had testified alongside him in 2014 when he served as director of the Defense Intelligence Agency. I found him likable.

Flynn, who was a retired U.S. Army general, had spoken to the Russian ambassador to the United States multiple times during December 2016, to seek the Russians' help in derailing a United Nations resolution — which the Obama administration was not going to veto — condemning Israel for the expansion of its settlements in occupied territory, and also to urge the Russians not to escalate their response to Obama administration sanctions imposed as a result of Russian interference in the 2016 election. The conversations about sanctions had become the subject of intense public interest after they were reported in the media in early January and Vice Presi- dent–Elect Pence went on television to deny Flynn had talked about sanctions with the

Russians. Pence said he knew this because he had talked to Flynn. On January 24, as part of our continuing investigation of Russian influence efforts, I dispatched two agents to the White House to interview Flynn about his conversations with the Russians. He lied to the agents, denying that he had discussed the very topics he had talked about in detail with the Russian ambassador.

The president began by saying General Flynn hadn't done anything wrong in speaking with the Russians, but he had to let him go because he had misled the vice president. He added that he had other concerns about Flynn, which he did not then specify.

The president then made a long series of comments about the problem with leaks of classified information — a concern I shared. Like all presidents before him, he was frustrated that people with access to classified information were out there talking to reporters about it. I explained that this was a long-standing problem that had plagued his predecessors and that the cases were hard to make because they required us to sometimes have investigative contact with members of the media (for example, by subpoenaing phone records). But I also told him that if we could make a case — if we could nail a leaker of classified information to the wall — it would serve as an important deterrence signal. Although I had made no reference or suggestion about going after members of the media, the president said something about how we once put reporters in jail and that made them talk. This was a reference to the Scooter Libby investigation, when *New York Times* reporter Judith Miller spent nearly three months in jail in 2005 for contempt of court in refusing to comply with a court order for information about her conversations with Libby. He then urged me to talk to Attorney General Sessions about ways to be more aggressive in making cases against leakers of classified information. I told him I would convey that message.

After the president had spoken for a few minutes about leaks, Reince Priebus leaned in through the door by the grandfather clock. I could see a group of people, including the vice president, waiting behind him. The president waved at him to close the door, saying he would be done shortly. The door closed.

The president then returned to the topic of Mike Flynn, saying, "He is a good guy and has been through a lot." He repeated that General Flynn hadn't done anything wrong on his calls with the Russians, but had misled the vice president.

He then said, "I hope you can see your way clear to letting this go, to letting Flynn go. He is a good guy. I hope you can let this go."

At the time, I had understood the president to be requesting that we drop any investigation of Flynn in connection with false statements about his conversations with the Russian ambassador in December. I did not understand the president to be talking about the broader investigation into Russia or possible links to his campaign. Regardless, it was very concerning, given the FBI's role as an independent investigative agency. Imagine the reaction if a President Hillary Clinton had asked to speak to the FBI director alone and urged him to back off the investigation of her national security advisor.

I did not interrupt the president to protest that what he was asking was inappropriate, as I probably should have. But if he didn't know what he was doing was inappropriate, why had he just ejected everyone, including my boss and the vice president, from the room so he could speak with me alone?

Instead, I only agreed that "he is a good guy," or seemed to be from what I knew of him. I did not say I would "let this go."

The president showed no reaction to my reply and returned briefly to the problem of leaks. The conversation ended and I got up and left through the door by the grandfather clock, making my way through the large group of people waiting there, including Priebus, the vice president, and the new secretary of health and human services, Tom Price. No one spoke to me.

In the car, I emailed my staff that the counterterrorism briefing they had spent so much time preparing me for had gone well, but "now I have to write another memo." What I meant was that I had another conversation with the president that I needed to document. I prepared an unclassified memo of the conversation about Flynn and discussed the matter with FBI senior leadership, including Deputy Director McCabe; my chief of staff, Jim Rybicki; and the FBI's general counsel, Jim Baker. In a little over a month, I had now written multiple memos about encounters with Donald Trump. I knew I would need to remember these conversations both because of their content and because I knew I was dealing with a chief executive who might well lie about them. To protect the FBI, and myself, I needed a contemporaneous record.

The other FBI leaders agreed that it was important not to infect the investigative team looking at Flynn — and more broadly at alleged Russian coordination with the Trump campaign during the 2016 election — with the president's request, which we did not intend to follow. We also concluded that, given that it was a one-on-one conversation, there was no way to corroborate my account. We decided it made little sense to report it to Attorney General Sessions, who we expected would likely recuse himself from involvement in Russia-related investigations. (He did so two weeks later.) The deputy attorney general's role was then filled in an acting capacity by a United States Attorney who would not be staying in the job. We resolved to figure out down the road what to do with the president's request and its implications as our investigation progressed.

After the February 14 meeting with the president, I directed Jim Rybicki to arrange for me to speak to the attorney general at the completion of our regular Wednesday threat briefing the next morning. At the close of the regular meeting, everyone left the room, except the attorney general, me, and our chiefs of staff. Sessions was sitting across the table from me in the secure conference room at the Department of Justice. He was in the same place, and likely the same chair, where Loretta Lynch had been sitting when she told me to call the Clinton email investigation "a matter."

When the room was clear, I did what I had promised the president and passed along his concerns about leaks and his expectation that we would be aggressive in pursuing them. Under the optimistic assumption that the attorney general had any control over President Trump, I then took the opportunity to implore him to prevent any future one-on-one communications between the president and me. "That can't happen," I said. "You are my boss. You can't be kicked out of the room so he can talk to me alone. You have to be between me and the president." He didn't ask me whether anything happened that troubled me, and I didn't say, for reasons discussed above. Instead, in a move that would become familiar to me, Sessions cast his eyes down at the table, and they darted quickly back and forth, side to side. To my memory, he said nothing. After a brief moment of eye darting, he put both hands on the table and stood, thanking me for coming. I read in his posture and face a message that he would not be able to help me. Rybicki and I left. I was so thrown by the silent eye darting that I had Rybicki follow up with a call to Sessions's chief of staff to make sure he understood my concern and the importance of the attorney general's shielding me from the president. His chief of staff said they got it.

But they didn't. Or couldn't.

I would struggle with President Trump for three more months. On March 1, I was about to get on a helicopter to fly to an opioid summit in Richmond when my assistant, Althea James, called me on my cell phone to say the president wanted to speak with me. I had no idea what the subject was, but assumed it must be important, so I waited in the FBI Suburban on the helipad. The Drug Enforcement Administration's leader, my old friend Chuck Rosenberg, waited for me on the helicopter.

After several minutes, my cell phone rang and a White House operator announced the president. He came on the line to say he was calling "just to see how you're doing." I replied that I was doing fine and had a lot going on. To make conversation, I told him the attorney general seemed to have hit the ground running with a good speech about violent crime. He replied, "That's his thing." The awkward conversation, which lasted less than a minute, struck me as yet another effort to bring me close, to ensure I was an *amica nostra,* a friend of ours. Why else would the president of the United States, who presumably had a million things to do, call the FBI director just to "see how you're doing"? I got out of the car and joined the DEA leader, apologizing that the delay was because the president just wanted to say "wassup."

On March 30, Trump called me at the FBI to describe the Russia investigation as "a cloud" that was impairing his ability to act on behalf of the country. He said he had nothing to do with Russia, had not been involved with hookers in Russia, and had always assumed he was being recorded when in Russia. For about the fourth time, he argued that the "golden showers thing" wasn't true, asking yet again, "Can you imagine me, hookers?" In an apparent play for my sympathy, he added that he has a beautiful wife and the whole thing has been very painful to her.

He asked what we could do to "lift the cloud." I responded that we were investigating the matter as quickly as we could, and that there would be great benefit, if we didn't find anything, to our having done the work well. He agreed, but then reemphasized the problems this was causing him.

Then the president asked why there had been a congressional hearing about Russia the previous week — at which I had, as the Department of Justice directed, confirmed the FBI investigation into possible coordination between Russia and the Trump campaign. I explained the demands from the leadership of both parties in Congress for more information, and that the chairman of the Senate Judiciary Committee, Iowa senator Charles Grassley, had even held up the confirmation of the deputy attorney general until we briefed him in detail on the investigation. I also explained that we had briefed the leadership of Congress on exactly which individuals we were investigating and that we had told those congressional leaders that we were not personally investigating President Trump. He repeatedly told me, "We need to get that fact out." I did not tell the president, mostly because I knew he wouldn't want to hear it, that the FBI and the Department of Justice had been reluctant to make public statements that we did not have an open case on President Trump for a number of reasons, most important that it would create a duty to correct that statement should that status change.

The president went on to say that if there were some "satellite" associates of his who did something wrong, it would be good to find that out. He repeated that he hadn't done anything wrong and he hoped I would find a way to get it out that we weren't investigating him.

In an abrupt shift, he turned the conversation to FBI Deputy Director Andrew McCabe. He said he hadn't brought up "the McCabe thing" because I had said McCabe was honorable, although Virginia's Democratic governor, Terry McAuliffe, was close to the Clintons and had given him (I think he meant McCabe's wife) campaign money. I knew what he was referring to. McCabe's wife, Jill, a physician in northern Virginia, had run for the Virginia state legislature and lost in 2015, when McCabe was in charge of the FBI's Washington, D.C., field office. She had been recruited to run by Governor McAuliffe, and her campaign was funded in large part by money from political action committees the governor controlled. Trump had repeatedly accused the FBI during the presidential campaign of going soft on Hillary Clinton because Andy's wife was connected to the Virginia governor, an old friend of the Clintons. As a presidential candidate, Trump also had claimed, incorrectly, that Hillary Clinton herself had given money to McCabe's wife.

In any event, the assertion was nonsense, for a bunch of reasons — including that the FBI was not exactly a secret cabal of Clinton lovers. Although special agents are trained to check their politics at the door, they tend to lean to the right side of the political spectrum — and McCabe had long considered himself a Republican. And the FBI spent years investigating various Clinton-related cases, including during the Bill Clinton presidency, when FBI Director Louis Freeh, a former special agent, famously surrendered his White House pass because he considered Clinton a criminal investigative subject. But Trump had twice asked me early in his tenure whether "Mc-Cabe has a problem with me, because I was pretty tough on his wife." I had answered that Andy was a true professional and put all that stuff to the side.

I didn't understand why the president was bringing this up on the phone now — it might well have been his attempt at trading favors, or a threat that he would start attacking the deputy director. I repeated that McCabe was an honorable person, not motivated by politics.

President Trump finished by stressing "the cloud" that was interfering with his ability to make deals for the country and said he hoped I could find a way to get out that he wasn't being investigated. I told him I would see what we could do, and that we would do our investigative work well and as quickly as we could.

Immediately after that conversation, I called Acting Deputy Attorney General Dana Boente (because Sessions had recused himself on Russia-related matters and there was no confirmed deputy attorney general) to report the president's request to lift the cloud of the Russia investigation, and said I would await his guidance. I did not hear back from him before Trump called me again two weeks later.

On the morning of April 11, the president called to ask what I had done about his request that I "get out" that he is not personally under investigation. In contrast to most of our other interactions, there were no compliments thrown, no cheery check-ins just to see what I was up to. He seemed irritated with me.

I replied that I had passed his request to the acting deputy attorney general, but I had not heard back. He replied that "the cloud" was getting in the way of his ability to do his job. He said that perhaps he would have his people reach out to the acting deputy attorney general. I said that was the way his request should be handled. The White House counsel should contact the leadership of DOJ to make the request, which was the traditional channel.

He said he would do that. Then he added, "Because I have been very loyal to you, very loyal. We had that thing, you know."

I did not reply or ask him what he meant by "that thing," but it seemed an attempt to invoke a mutual pledge of loyalty, one he struggled to deliver as he recalled I had actually resisted pledging loyalty. At "the thing" we had, a private dinner in the Green Room, he was promised only "honest loyalty." Regardless, I responded to his odd effort to invoke loyalty by saying only that the way to handle it was to have the White House counsel call the acting deputy attorney general. He said that was what he would do, and the call ended.

That was the last time I spoke with President Trump. We reported the call to the acting deputy attorney general. He had apparently done nothing since March 30, replying, "Oh, God, I was hoping that would just go away."

It wouldn't go away.

Fittingly, it all finally ended in a blizzard of awful behavior. I was in Los Angeles on May 9, 2017, to attend a Diversity Agent Recruiting event. This was an effort we had previously mounted in Washington and Houston, where we invited talented young lawyers, engineers, and business school graduates of color to come listen to why they should take cuts in pay and become FBI special agents. I loved these events — which were in keeping with our quest to attract more minority agents — and the two so far had been hugely successful. Diversifying the Bureau was the key to our sustained effectiveness. As noted earlier, the major obstacle was that so many young people, especially high-potential black and Latino men and women, thought of the FBI as "The Man." Who would want to work for "The Man"? I loved these events because it gave me and other FBI leaders the chance to show these talented people a bit more about what "The Man," and the woman, of the FBI were really like.

These young people were hungry to make a difference, and we could show them what lives of service, sacrifice, and making an extraordinary difference for good looked like. Almost nobody leaves the FBI once they taste the life of a special agent. My mission was to dare these great young people to try to join that life. The yield from events in Washington and Houston had been surprisingly high. I was coming to L.A. to speak to more than five hundred potential new agents. I knew that audience held many future special agents. I couldn't wait to connect with them.

Although the recruiting event was in the evening, I went early enough to have time to visit the FBI's Los Angeles field office. I was committed to walking around FBI offices everywhere, floor by floor and cubicle by cubicle, meeting every employee and shaking every hand. It was worth the effort because I could tell it meant a lot to our people to have the director thank them personally. In a big organization like the FBI, with offices around the country and the world, it helps to remind people that you appreciate the hard work they do. That you care about them, not just professionally, but about them — and their families. Every time I traveled, I carved out hours to visit the field offices to meet the amazing people that staffed them.

I met dozens of L.A. employees standing

at their desks. The L.A. office leadership had also done something thoughtful and assembled those who didn't have desks — the cleaning staff and those working in the communications room. They were all sitting at tables in a large command center room. I began addressing them at about 2 P.M. Los Angeles time, 5 P.M. in Washington. I explained that we had rewritten the FBI's mission statement in 2015 to make it shorter and to better express the importance of our responsibility. Our newly defined mission was to "protect the American people and uphold the Constitution of the United States." I said I wanted it shorter so everyone would know it, connect to it, and share it with neighbors and especially young people. I expected everyone to realize . . .

And then I stopped in midsentence.

On the TV screens along the back wall I could see COMEY RESIGNS in large letters. The screens were behind my audience, but they noticed my distraction and started turning in their seats. I laughed and said, "That's pretty funny. Somebody put a lot of work into that one." I continued my thought. "There are no support employees in the FBI. I expect . . ."

The message on the screens now changed. Across three screens, displaying three different news stations, I now saw the same words: COMEY FIRED. I wasn't laughing any longer. There was a buzz in the room. I told the audience, "Look, I'm going to go figure out what's happening, but whether that's true or not, my message won't change, so let me finish it and then shake your hands." I said, "Every one of you is personally responsible for protecting the American people and upholding the Constitution of the United States. We all have different roles, but the same mission. Thank you for doing it well." I then moved among the employees, shaking every hand, and walked to a private office to find out what was happening.

The FBI director travels with a communications team so he can be reached by the Justice Department or White House in seconds, any time of day or night. But nobody called. Not the attorney general. Not the deputy attorney general. Nobody. I actually had seen the attorney general the day before. Days earlier, I had met alone with the newly confirmed deputy attorney general at his request so he could ask my advice on how to do his job — which I held from 2003 to 2005. In late October, shortly before the election, the now-DAG had been serving as the United States Attorney in

Baltimore, and he invited me to speak to his entire staff about leadership and why I made the decisions I did in July about the Clinton email case. He praised me then as an inspirational leader. Now, he not only didn't call me, he had authored a memo to justify my firing, describing my conduct during 2016 as awful and unacceptable. That made absolutely no sense to me in light of our recent contacts.

All I knew was what was being reported in the media. After much scrambling, we learned that a White House employee was down on Pennsylvania Avenue in Washington, trying to deliver a letter to me from the president. I took a call from my wife, who said she and the kids had seen the news. I replied that I didn't know whether it was true and we were trying to find out what was going on. Pat Fitzgerald called and I told him the same thing.

I took an emotional call from General John Kelly, then the secretary of Homeland Security. He said he was sick about my firing and that he intended to quit in protest. He said he didn't want to work for dishonorable people who would treat someone like me in such a manner. I urged Kelly not to do that, arguing that the country needed principled people around this president.

Especially this president.

My amazing assistant, Althea James, got the letter from the White House guy at the front door down on Pennsylvania Avenue. She scanned it and emailed it to me. I was fired, effective immediately, by the president who had repeatedly praised me and asked me to stay, based on a recommendation from the deputy attorney general, who had praised me as a great leader, a recommendation accepted by the attorney general, who was both recused from all Russia-related matters and who, according to President Trump at our dinner, thought I was great. The reasons for that firing were lies, but the letter was real. I felt sick to my stomach and slightly dazed.

I stepped out of the office, and a large group of L.A. FBI employees had gathered. Many were tearful. I spoke to them briefly, telling them that the FBI's values were bigger and stronger than any one of us. It broke my heart to leave them, I said, but they should know it was their quality as people — honest, competent, and independent — that made this so painful. I hated to leave *them.* I went to the office of the Los Angeles FBI leader, Deirdre Fike. I had chosen her for that job and trusted her judgment. My first instinct, and hers, was that I should attend the diversity event anyway, as a private citizen. This was something I cared deeply about, and I could still urge these talented men and women to join this life, even if I would no longer be part of it. Eventually, though, we decided I would be a distraction because a media circus would crash the event. I could do more harm than good. I decided to go home.

Which raised the question: How would I get home? I left that decision to the man who minutes earlier had become the acting director of the FBI, my deputy, Andrew McCabe. The news had been just as big a surprise to him as it had been to me. Now he was in command. He and his team had to figure out what was lawful and appropriate. In the shock of the moment, I gave some thought to renting a convertible and driving the twenty-seven hundred miles back alone. But then I realized I was neither single nor crazy. The acting director decided that, given the FBI's continuing responsibility for my safety, the best course was to take me back on the plane I came on, with a security detail and a flight crew who had to return to Washington anyway. We got in the vehicle to head for the airport.

News helicopters tracked our journey from the L.A. FBI office to the airport. As we rolled slowly in L.A. traffic, I looked to my right. In the car next to us, a man was driving while watching an aerial news feed of us on his mobile device. He turned, smiled at me through his open window, and gave me a thumbs-up. I'm not sure how he was holding the wheel.

As we always did, we pulled onto the airport tarmac with a police escort and stopped at the stairs of the FBI plane. My usual practice was to go thank the officers who had escorted us, but I was so numb and distracted that I almost forgot to do it. My special assistant, Josh Campbell, as he often did, saw what I couldn't. He nudged me and told me to go thank the cops. I did, shaking each hand, and then bounded up the airplane stairs. I couldn't look at the pilots or my security team for fear that I might get emotional. They were quiet. The helicopters then broadcast our plane's taxi and takeoff. Those images were all over the news.

President Trump, who apparently watches quite a bit of TV at the White House, saw those images of me thanking the cops and flying away. They infuriated him. Early the next morning, he called McCabe and told him he wanted an investigation into how I had been allowed to use the FBI plane to return from California.

McCabe replied that he could look into how I had been allowed to fly back to Washington, but that he didn't need to. *He* had authorized it, McCabe told the president. The plane had to come back, the security detail had to come back, and the FBI was obligated to return me safely.

The president exploded. He ordered that I was not to be allowed back on FBI property again, ever. My former staff boxed up my belongings as if I had died and delivered them to my home. The order kept me from seeing and offering some measure of closure to the people of the FBI, with whom I had become very close.

Trump had done a lot of yelling during the campaign about McCabe and his former candidate wife. He had been fixated on it ever since.

Still in a fury at McCabe, Trump then asked him, "Your wife lost her election in Virginia, didn't she?"

"Yes, she did," Andy replied.

The president of the United States then said to the acting director of the FBI, "Ask her how it feels to be a loser" and hung up the phone.

I sat by myself on the flight home, trying to

gather my thoughts and committing what would have been a rules violation if I were still an FBI employee. I reached into my suitcase and retrieved a bottle of pinot noir I was bringing home from California. I drank red wine from a paper coffee cup and stared out the window at the lights of the country I love so much. As we approached Washington, I asked the pilots if I could sit up front with them to experience the landing at Reagan Airport in a way I never had, despite hundreds of flights on FBI planes. I sat in the jump seat just behind them, headphones on, and watched two talented special agent–pilots land the plane, for the last time with me as a passenger. They had taken me all over the country and the world and now squeezed my hand an extra beat as we said good-bye, with tears in our eyes.

As I flew home from California that night, sipping red wine, I was left with my thoughts about what might come next. I wasn't planning to do anything except take some time to figure out what to do with my life. In the days that followed, on their own initiative, friends shared with the media things I had told them about my struggle to establish appropriate boundaries between the FBI and the Trump White House and my effort to resist pledging loyalty to President Trump at our dinner, but there were dark stories about my experience with the president that were not yet in the media.

It may sound strange, but throughout my five months working under Donald Trump, I wanted him to succeed as president. That's not a political bias. Had Hillary Clinton been elected, I would have wanted her to succeed as president. I think that's what it means to love your country. We need our presidents to succeed. My encounters with President Trump left me sad, not angry. I don't know him or his life well, but he seems not to have benefited from watching people like Harry Howell demonstrate what tough and kind leadership looks like, or worked under someone who was confident enough to be humble, like Helen Fahey, and felt the difference that makes. Although I am sure he has seen human suffering and encountered personal loss, I never saw any evidence that it shaped him the way it did Patrice and me in losing our son Collin, or the millions of others who suffer loss and then channel their pain into empathy and care for others. I learned searing lessons from being a bully and from lying about my own basketball career and seeing how "easy lies" can become a habit. I see no evidence that a lie ever caused Trump pain, or that he ever recoiled from causing another person pain, which is sad and frightening. Without all those things — without kindness to leaven toughness, without a balance of confidence and humility, without empathy, and without respect for truth — there is little chance President Trump can attract and keep the kind of people around him that every president needs to make wise decisions. That makes me sad for him, but it makes me worry for our country.

On Friday, May 12, President Trump tweeted a warning to me and his thirty-nine million followers: "James Comey better hope there are no 'tapes' of our conversations before he starts leaking to the press." This struck me as bizarre. Was he threatening me? I had no plans to talk to the press or leak classified information. All I wanted was to get Donald Trump out of my head, so I didn't spend time thinking about what it meant. Instead, I stayed inside my house, sleeping, exercising, and avoiding the media crowd gathered at the end of my driveway.

On Tuesday, May 16, Patrice and I were planning to sneak past the press and get out of town for a few days. I woke up at about 2:00 A.M. that morning, jolted awake by a thought: the president's tweet changes my perspective on how to address our February

14, 2017, meeting, when he expressed his "hope" that I would drop an investigation of his former national security adviser, Mike Flynn. Though I had written an unclassified memo about the conversation, the FBI leadership and I had gotten stuck there because it would be my word against the president's. We hadn't given up on pursuing it, but instead had decided to hold it — and keep it away from the investigative team so they wouldn't be influenced by the president. We could think about it more once the Department of Justice decided how they would supervise the investigations related to the Trump administration and Russia after the attorney general was recused. But this tweet about tapes changed everything, I thought, lying there in the dark. If there are tapes of my conversations with President Trump, there will be corroboration of the fact that he said he wanted me to drop the Flynn investigation. It will no longer be my word against his. If there is a tape, the president of the United States will be heard in the Oval Office telling me, "I hope you can let it go."

I lay in bed thinking through this delayed revelation. I could leave it alone, and hope the FBI leadership team saw what I saw in Trump's tweet about tapes and that they would start pushing the Department of Justice to go get the tapes. Maybe the FBI would even urge Justice to appoint an independent prosecutor to pursue this. Maybe I could trust that the system would work. But I had trusted the system years earlier on the question of torture. Then, I had trusted the attorney general to carry our department's concerns about torture policy to the White House, to a meeting I was excluded from, but nothing happened. No, I wasn't going to make that mistake again. This time I could and would do something because, ironically, thanks to Donald Trump, I was a private citizen now.

I trusted the FBI, but I didn't trust the Department of Justice leadership under the current attorney general and deputy attorney general to do the right thing. Something was needed that might force them to do the right thing. Now that I was a private citizen, I could do something. I decided I would prompt a media story by revealing the president's February 14 direction that I drop the Flynn investigation. That might force the Department of Justice to appoint a special prosecutor, who could then go get the tapes that Trump had tweeted about. And, although I was banned from FBI property, I had a copy of my unclassified memo about his request stored securely at home.

Tuesday morning, after dawn, I contacted my good friend Dan Richman, a former prosecutor and now a professor at Columbia Law School. Dan had been giving me legal advice since my firing. I told him I was going to send him one unclassified memo and I wanted him to share the substance of the memo — but not the memo itself — with a reporter. If I do it myself, I thought, it will create a media frenzy — at my driveway, no less — and I will be hard-pressed to refuse follow-up comments. I would, of course, tell the truth if asked whether I played a part in it. I did. I had to. To be clear, this was not a "leak" of classified information no matter how many times politicians, political pundits, or the president call it that. A private citizen may legally share unclassified details of a conversation with the president with the press, or include that information in a book. I believe in the power of the press and know Thomas Jefferson was right when he wrote: "Our liberty depends on the freedom of the press, and that cannot be limited without being lost."

I don't know whether the media storm that followed my disclosure of the February 14 "let it go" conversation prompted the

Department of Justice leadership to appoint a special counsel. The FBI may already have been pushing for the appointment of a special counsel after seeing the Trump tweet about tapes. I just know that the Department of Justice did so shortly thereafter, giving Robert Mueller the authority to investigate any coordination between the Russian government and the Trump campaign and any related matters.

I also don't know whether the special counsel will find criminal wrongdoing by the president or others who have not been charged as of this writing. One of the pivotal questions I presume that Bob Mueller's team is investigating is whether or not in urging me to back the FBI off our investigation of his national security advisor and in firing me, President Trump was attempting to obstruct justice, which is a federal crime. It's certainly possible. There is at least circumstantial evidence in that regard, and there may be more that the Mueller team will assemble. I've prosecuted and overseen many cases involving obstruction of justice, but in this case, I am not the prosecutor. I am a witness. I have one perspective on the behavior I saw, which while disturbing and violating basic norms of ethical leadership, may fall short of being illegal. Central to the question of obstruction, for example, is a showing of President Trump's intent. Is there sufficient proof that he intended to take those actions and others to derail a criminal investigation, with corrupt intent? Because I don't know all the evidence, I can't answer that question with any certainty. I do know that, as of this writing, Special Counsel Mueller and his team are hard at work and the American people can have confidence that, unless their investigation is blocked in some fashion, they will get to the truth, whatever that is.

On June 8, 2017, I testified publicly before the Senate Select Committee on Intelligence, which wanted to hear about my interactions with President Trump. For whatever reason, the president had only increased people's interest in my perspectives. I decided to write an account of some of my dealings with him and submit it in advance to the committee, so that I wouldn't need to speak for a long time at the start of my testimony, and to give the senators a chance to digest what I wrote and ask follow-up questions.

I wanted to use my brief opening statement to accomplish one thing — to say good-bye to the people of the FBI, something President Trump did not have the grace or charity of spirit to allow me to do. It also allowed me to deny, on their behalf and mine, the lies the administration had told about the FBI being in disarray. I knew they would be watching and I could speak directly to them.

I practiced what I wanted to say in front of Patrice and one of our daughters. They were shocked that I intended to speak without notes, but I told them it had to come from the heart and that, if I brought a text, I would end up staring at it. As nerve-racking as it was to speak without notes in front of millions of people, that was the way it would mean the most to the people of the FBI. Patrice was also concerned that in my nervousness, I would smile like a fool or frown as if somebody had died. I had to find a place between those two.

I questioned my decision to go without notes as I stood in a conference room waiting to walk into the Senate hearing room. What if I freeze? What if I get all tangled up in my words? I don't normally get nervous in public, but this was nuts. But it was too late. I walked with the leaders of the committee down the long private hall behind the dais, turned left, and stepped into something surreal. I have seen lots of cameras in my day and heard my share of shutter clicks. Nothing compared to this scene.

As I sat at the witness table in the eye of the storm, I kept hearing Patrice's voice in my head: "Think about the people of the FBI; that will bring light to your eyes." And so I did. I stumbled a bit, and nearly lost control of my emotions at the end when speaking about the people of the FBI, but I spoke from the heart:

When I was appointed FBI Director in 2013, I understood that I served at the pleasure of the President. Even though I was appointed to a 10-year term, which Congress created in order to underscore the importance of the FBI being outside of politics and independent, I understood that I could be fired by a President for any reason or for no reason at all.

And on May the 9th, when I learned that I had been fired, for that reason I immediately came home as a private citizen. But then the explanations, the shifting explanations, confused me and increasingly concerned me. They confused me because the President and I had had multiple conversations about my job, both before and after he took office, and he had repeatedly told me I was doing a great job and he hoped I would stay. And I had repeatedly assured him that I did intend to stay and serve out the remaining six years of my term.

He told me repeatedly that he had talked to lots of people about me, including our current attorney general, and had learned that I was doing a great job and that I was extremely well liked by the FBI workforce.

So it confused me when I saw on television the President saying that he actually fired me because of the Russia investigation and learned, again from the media, that he was telling privately other parties that my firing had relieved great pressure on the Russia investigation.

I was also confused by the initial explanation that was offered publicly, that I was fired because of the decisions I had made during the election year. That didn't make sense to me for a whole bunch of reasons, including the time and all the water that had gone under the bridge since those hard decisions that had to be made. That didn't make any sense to me.

And although the law required no reason at all to fire an FBI Director, the administration then chose to defame me and, more importantly, the FBI by saying that the organization was in disarray, that it was poorly led, that the workforce had lost confidence in its leader.

were lies, plain and simple, and I am
 that the FBI workforce had to hear
 and I'm so sorry that the American
 le were told them. I worked every day at
the FBI to help make that great organization
better. And I say "help" because I did nothing
alone at the FBI. There are no indispensable
people at the FBI. The organization's great
strength is that its values and abilities run
deep and wide. The FBI will be fine without
me. The FBI's mission will be relentlessly
pursued by its people, and that mission is to
protect the American people and uphold the
Constitution of the United States.

I will deeply miss being part of that mission,
but this organization and its mission will go on
long beyond me and long beyond any particular administration.

I have a message before I close for my
former colleagues at the FBI. But first I want
the American people to know this truth: The
FBI is honest. The FBI is strong. And the FBI
is and always will be independent.

And now, to my former colleagues, if I may.
I am so sorry that I didn't get the chance to
say good-bye to you properly. It was the honor
of my life to serve beside you, to be part of
the FBI family. And I will miss it for the rest of
my life. Thank you for standing watch. Thank
you for doing so much good for this country.

Do that good as long as ever you can.

And, Senators, I look forward to your questions.

EPILOGUE

I am writing in a time of great anxiety in my country. I understand the anxiety, but also believe America is going to be fine. I choose to see opportunity as well as danger.

Donald Trump's presidency threatens much of what is good in this nation. We all bear responsibility for the deeply flawed choices put before voters during the 2016 election, and our country is paying a high price: this president is unethical, and untethered to truth and institutional values. His leadership is transactional, ego driven, and about personal loyalty. We are fortunate some ethical leaders have chosen to serve and to stay at senior levels of government, but they cannot prevent all of the damage from the forest fire that is the Trump presidency. Their task is to try to contain it.

I see many so-called conservative commentators, including some faith leaders, focusing on favorable policy initiatives or court appointments to justify their acceptance of this damage, while deemphasizing the impact of this president on basic norms and ethics. That strikes me as both hypocritical and morally wrong. The hypocrisy is evident if you simply switch the names and imagine that a President Hillary Clinton had conducted herself in a similar fashion in office. I've said this earlier but it's worth repeating: close your eyes and imagine these same voices if President Hillary Clinton had told the FBI director, "I hope you will let it go," about the investigation of a senior aide, or told casual, easily disprovable lies nearly every day and then demanded we believe them. The hypocrisy is so thick as to almost be darkly funny. I say this as someone who has worked in law enforcement for most of my life, and served presidents of both parties. What is happening now is not normal. It is not fake news. It is not okay.

Whatever your politics, it is wrong to dismiss the damage to the norms and traditions that have guided the presidency and our public life for decades or, in many cases, since the republic was founded. It is also wrong to stand idly by, or worse, to stay silent when you know better, while a president brazenly seeks to undermine public confidence in law enforcement institutions that were established to keep our leaders in check. Every organization has its flaws, but the career prosecutors and agents at the Justice Department and the FBI are there for a reason — to rise above partisanship and do what's right for the country, regardless of their own political views. Without these checks on our leaders, without those institutions vigorously standing against abuses of power, our country cannot sustain itself as a functioning democracy. I know there are men and women of good conscience in the United States Congress on both sides of the aisle who understand this. But not enough of them are speaking out. They must ask themselves to what, or to whom, they hold a higher loyalty: to partisan interests or to the pillars of democracy? Their silence is complicity — it is a choice — and somewhere deep down they must know that.

Policies come and go. Supreme Court justices come and go. But the core of our nation is our commitment to a set of shared values that began with George Washington — to restraint and integrity and balance and transparency and truth. If that slides away from us, only a fool would be consoled by a tax cut or a different immigration policy.

But I choose to be optimistic. Yes, the current president will do significant damage in the short term. Important norms and traditions will be damaged by the flames. But forest fires, as painful as they can be, bring growth. They spur growth that was impossible before the fire, when old trees crowded out new plants on the forest floor. In the midst of this fire, I already see new life — young people engaged as never before, and the media, the courts, academics, nonprofits, and all other parts of civil society finding reason to bloom.

This fire also offers an opportunity to rebalance power among the three branches of our government, closer to the model the founders intended. There is reason to believe this fire will leave the presidency weaker and Congress and the courts stronger, just as the forest fire of Watergate did. There is a lot of good in that.

Thoughtful people are staring at the vicious partisanship that has grown all around us. Far from creating a new norm where lying is widely accepted, the Trump presidency has ignited a focus on truth and ethics. Parents are talking to their children about truth-telling, about respect for all people, about rejecting prejudice and hate. Schools and religious institutions are talking about values-driven leadership.

The next president, no matter the party, will surely emphasize values — truth, integrity, respect, and tolerance — in ways an American leader hasn't needed to for more than forty years. The fire will make something good grow.

I wrote this book because I hope it will be useful to people living among the flames who are thinking about what comes next. I also hope it will be useful to readers long after the flames are doused, by inspiring them to choose a higher loyalty, to find truth among lies, and to pursue ethical leadership.

ACKNOWLEDGMENTS

Because a group of people cared enough to tell me the truth, I think this book will be useful.

My beloved family made this book, and me, better.

Keith Urbahn and Matt Latimer at Javelin guided me through the process and taught me so much, including how to write a book.

Flatiron Books and my editor, Amy Einhorn, pushed me, in a great way, through multiple drafts.

And, finally, I'm grateful to those who taught me, worked beside me, and laughed with me all these years. You know who you are. Thank you for the joy and the journey, which isn't over yet.

ABOUT THE AUTHOR

A Yonkers, New York native, **James Comey** attended the College of William and Mary and the University of Chicago Law School. After law school, Comey returned to New York and joined the U.S. Attorney's Office for the Southern District of New York as an Assistant U.S. Attorney. There, he took on numerous crimes, most notably Organized Crime in the case of the *United States v. John Gambino, et al.* Afterwards, Comey became an Assistant U.S. Attorney in the Eastern District of Virginia, where he prosecuted the high-profile case that followed the 1996 terrorist attack on the U.S. military's Khobar Towers in Khobar, Saudi Arabia. Jim Comey returned to New York after 9/11 to become the U.S. Attorney for the Southern District of New York. At the end of 2003, he was tapped to be the Deputy Attorney General at the Department of Justice (DOJ) under then-U.S. Attorney General John Ashcroft and moved to the Washington, D.C. area. Comey left DOJ in 2005 to serve as General Counsel and Senior Vice President at Defense contractor Lockheed Martin. Five years later, he joined Bridgewater Associates, a Connecticut-based investment fund, as its General Counsel. In early 2013, Comey became a Lecturer in Law, a Senior Research Scholar, and Hertog Fellow in National Security Law at Columbia Law School. On September 4, 2013, James Comey was sworn in as the seventh Director of the FBI.